Saturday Night Live & American TV

SATURDAY NIGHT LIVE
& AMERICAN TV

EDITED BY NICK MARX,
MATT SIENKIEWICZ,
AND RON BECKER

INDIANA UNIVERSITY PRESS

Bloomington and Indianapolis

This book is a publication of

Indiana University Press
Office of Scholarly Publishing
Herman B Wells Library 350
1320 E. 10th Street
Bloomington, Indiana 47405 USA

iupress.indiana.edu

Telephone orders 800-842-6796
Fax orders 812-855-7931

⊖ The paper used in this publication
meets the minimum requirements of
the American National Standard for
Information Sciences—Permanence
of Paper for Printed Library Materials,
ANSI Z39.48-1992.

*Manufactured in the United States of
America*

Library of Congress Cataloging-in-
Publication Data

Saturday night live and American TV /
edited by Nick Marx, Matt Sienkiewicz,
and Ron Becker.
    pages cm
  Includes bibliographical references and
index.
  ISBN 978-0-253-01077-3 (cl : alk.
paper) — ISBN 978-0-253-01082-7 (pb :
alk. paper) — ISBN 978-0-253-01090-2
(eb) 1. Saturday night live (Television
program) 2. Television programs—Social
aspects—United States. I. Marx, Nick. II.
Sienkiewicz, Matt. III. Becker, Ron.
  PN1992.77.S273S22 2013
  791.45'72—dc23
                                    2013022243

1 2 3 4 5   18 17 16 15 14 13

CONTENTS

Part III. Social Politics and Comedic Representation

Part IV. Beyond Saturday Night, Beyond Television

ACKNOWLEDGMENTS

The editors wish to thank the following for their participation at important stages in the process of assembling this collection: Victoria Johnson, Christine Becker, and Jonathan Gray for their guidance and feedback; our graphic designer, Thomas Sullivan; Jane Kupersmith, Raina Polivka, and Nancy Lightfoot at Indiana University Press; and Jill Jarvis Marx, Marc Loy, Denise McCoskey, and Carrie Benedon for their love and moral support.

Saturday Night Live & American TV

Introduction: Situating *Saturday Night Live* in American Television Culture

NICK MARX, MATT SIENKIEWICZ,

AND RON BECKER

As *Saturday Night Live* opened its thirty-eighth season in the fall of 2012, the program faced yet another in a long history of transitional moments. In one sense, it was a time of enormous promise. With the presidential election taking center stage in popular discourse, *SNL* was primed once again to play a lead role in helping the American public understand and enjoy the spectacle of democracy. Just as impersonations of Gerald Ford, Bill Clinton, two George Bushes, Sarah Palin, and a host of other political figures had provided a quadrennial boost to *SNL's* public profile, there was little doubt that an autumn's worth of fun at the expense of Barack Obama, Mitt Romney, Joe Biden, and Paul Ryan would bring new energy to NBC's Saturday night. At the same time, however, the 2012 season brought with it tremendous uncertainty. As had happened so often in the show's history, it would be forced to reinvent itself while simultaneously maintaining decades of tradition.

Gone were two of *SNL's* brightest lights, Kristen Wiig and Andy Samberg. These departures marked more than a loss of star power for Lorne Michaels's crew. They also put into question the show's very identity. Over the previous decade *SNL* had rebuilt its brand around two key pillars: an exceptionally strong cast of female comedians and a dynamic engagement with short-form digital comedy. Wiig, the last prominent connection to the days of Tina Fey, represented the former. Samberg, the star of digital shorts such as "Lazy Sunday," "Dick in a Box," "Mother-lover," and dozens of other *SNL* videos gone viral, embodied the latter. *SNL* successfully negotiated this transition, just as it had weathered the losses of Chevy Chase, John Belushi, Eddie Murphy, Will Ferrell, Amy Poehler, and every other star the program had helped create. For decades *SNL* had always adapted, transforming its youthful comedic energy into a sense of continuity and a source of profitability. In other words, *SNL*, with some help from Mitt Romney's stiff personality and Joe Biden's loose tongue, did what it had always done best: it changed by staying the same. New characters took the stage, new stars emerged, and new catchphrases took hold. But it all still happened from Studio 8H, featuring an opening monologue, a mix of live and taped sketches, two songs, "Weekend Update," and, of course, the program's opening tagline, "Live from New York, it's Saturday night!"

There is no single media institution that embodies every element of the cultural, technological, political, and aesthetic evolutions embedded in the history of television. However, *Saturday Night Live* comes as close as any program does. Debuting in October 1975 as *NBC's Saturday Night* and continuing without interruption for almost forty seasons, *SNL* offers a unique opportunity for the student, scholar, fan, or viewer to consider one of the great paradoxes of the American broadcasting industry. Television, as much as any business, needs to refresh itself constantly, often by indulging even the most fleeting and idiosyncratic elements of a given moment's popular culture. Yet, despite decades of necessarily short-term thinking, a handful of companies have steadfastly remained at the center of American television. Certainly, government regulation and the conservative proclivities of corporate strategy help enable this consistency. Nonetheless, the story of American television centers on the industry's need to balance flexibility and stability—to put forth apparently fresh ideas every season and adapt to new technologies yet keep the basic structure of the business as predictable as possible. A key premise of this volume is that one productive way to study American television culture is to look closely at a program that embodies this negotiation as much if not more than any other.

SNL was born in the heart of the classic network era, a time during which powerhouses NBC, CBS, and ABC fought to win a bigger piece of what was essentially a three-slice pie. Today, *SNL* competes with scores of demographically attuned cable channels, the contents of digital video recorders, countless gaming options, Netflix's streaming catalog, and a seemingly endless supply of online video content. And yet, *SNL* has remained a constant feature in NBC's 11:30 PM Eastern time slot. *SNL* has certainly changed to accommodate this radically new media environment, incorporating new modes of performance, cultural attitudes, and comedic strategies. Yet in crucial ways, the program has remained the same. Perhaps most obvious is the show's striking structural consistency. Each episode starts with a cold open and faithfully progresses through a series of live sketches, recorded pieces, and musical performances, before ending in that strangely sentimental moment when the cast smiles through the rolling credits, waving goodbye to both the studio audience and the home viewer. But the continuity goes beyond these surface-level consistencies. Despite changing its cast, writing staff, visual style, and comedic sensibility, *SNL* has always aimed to position itself as an alternative to "mainstream" comedy and as a timely commentator on contemporary events. As such, the program offers a fantastic opportunity to engage with some of the most significant questions faced by scholars and students of television and American culture. Because it has held onto both its format and its self-constructed, alternative identity, *SNL*'s nearly forty years of programming provide a lens through which the critic can focus on television's evolving construction of what is new, normative, and noteworthy in American culture.

It must be said that *SNL* is not the only program to beat the long industrial odds and survive for decades. Most notably, soap operas such as *General Hospital* (1963–present), *Guiding Light* (1952–2009), and *Days of Our Lives* (1965–present) have put together broadcast runs exceeding even that of *SNL*. Network news programs also provide examples of long-standing shows with consistent time slots and formats. These examples afford scholars many advantages that *SNL* cannot as a control for research into the changing elements of American culture. However, the flexibility of *SNL*'s live sketch format gives it an additional virtue as an object of study. Engaging creatively with dozens of ideas in every episode, *SNL* provides snapshots of American television culture taken with such frequency that they create a map of a wide variety of cultural discourses. Whereas a soap opera like *General Hospital* deals with crucial

Figure 0.1. *SNL*'s original cast says goodnight as the credits roll on the 1975 Christmas episode.

changes in culture through incremental adjustments in story and character development, *SNL* has consistently and intentionally debated the politics, pop culture, and social norms of American life in five different decades. It is due to this variability that the program serves as an ideal venue through which to contemplate the intersections of television studies and disciplines such as critical race studies, gender studies, performance studies, political science, and literary criticism. The chapters in this volume explore the myriad avenues of analyses afforded by *SNL*'s textual complexity.

Surprisingly, despite *SNL*'s long-running success and popularity, it has been the subject of few book-length studies. The most common focus of academic attention has been the careers of cast members after they have left the program. For example, Jim Whalley's *Saturday Night Live, Hollywood Comedy, and American Culture* traces the relationship between generational shifts and the types of star personas that succeed in transitioning from television to the big screen. The program also appears prominently in studies regarding the political impact of comedy, most notably in Jonathan Gray, Jeffrey P. Jones, and Ethan Thompson's *Satire TV: Politics and Comedy in the Post-Network Era* and in Jody Baumgartner and Jonathan S. Morris's *Laughing Matters: Humor and American Politics in the Media Age.* Each of these volumes includes discussion of *SNL*'s "Weekend Update" segment and its political parody sketches. A variety of other works, such as Bambi Haggins's *Laughing Mad: The Black Comic Persona in Post-Soul America* and Jeffrey S. Miller's *Something Completely Different: British Television and American Culture,* incorporate useful discussion of the program into broader explorations of mediated humor. However, there has never been an extended academic study of the program itself, taking it on its own terms and aiming to distill its relationship to the broader world of American television and culture.

The most commonly cited resources on the show (you will see them referred to often throughout this volume) are popular works such as Doug Hill and Jeff Weingrad's *Saturday Night: A Backstage History of Saturday Night Live;* former writer Tom Davis's *Thirty-Nine Years of Short-Term Memory Loss;* and, most notably, Tom Shales and James Andrew Miller's sprawling 2002 work, *Live from New York.* An oral history spanning the show's run from its 1975 inception to the late 1990s, *Live from New York* is undoubtedly a valuable resource. However, the book has a variety of limitations, not the least of which is its tendency toward hagiography in the service of telling a good story. Many of the authors in the present volume draw upon Shales and Miller's research, while adding to it a critical edge that brings *SNL* into dialogue with the field of television studies. Furthermore, there has been no book-length work incorporating the past ten years of *SNL.* Not only does this situation omit a large portion of the program, but it also means that little has been written on the fascinating ways in which *SNL* has grappled with the accelerated changes in American broadcasting and digital media culture of the first decade of the twenty-first century.

In tracing *SNL*'s history from its very first broadcast to the end of its thirty-seventh season, *Saturday Night Live and American TV* strives to fill these gaps. We have organized the volume into four parts that frame *SNL* from distinct perspectives and place the program in dialogue with a number of cultural, industrial, and social discourses. Moving through these four parts affords the scholar both a broad view of the history of *SNL* and different avenues of inquiry into specific aspects of television studies. The chapters in part I, for example, take us back to *SNL*'s origins by examining the program as a product of 1970s American television culture and raise important questions about the role of authorship, cultural geography, and genre in the early history of the program. Part II examines *SNL*'s approaches to politics, comedic taste, music, and branding, all of which evolved over time as the program worked to remain relevant across decades of industrial and cultural change. The contributions in part III approach *SNL* as a site for the contested articulation of race, gender, and ethnicity by analyzing the political context of its production and reception. Finally, the chapters in part IV examine how *SNL* has extended its industrial and cultural footprint far beyond the boundaries of its weekly airing on viewers' television sets.

PART I: LIVE FROM NEW YORK ON NBC

In the popular imagination, the 1970s marks the Golden Age of *SNL*. It is the era of the original Not Ready for Prime Time Players, whose memorable characterizations onscreen and wild antics offscreen have been mythologized in popular literature and selectively chronicled in best-of DVDs and television specials. *SNL* in the 1970s is also commonly understood as a story about Lorne Michaels's singular vision for revolutionizing American comedy in the face of the television industry's notorious aversion to risk. This version of the program's history makes for a compelling narrative and certainly contains seeds of truth. Michaels has, in fact, been an important source of televisual innovation and, early on, it was not clear how *SNL* would build the foundation of a comedy empire from its late-night time slot. However, overly romanticized views obscure important historical elements of the show and the context out of which it initially emerged.

When *NBC's Saturday Night* premiered in the fall of 1975, the American television industry was largely controlled by an oligopoly composed of the Big Three broadcast networks. ABC, CBS, and NBC drew the vast majority of audiences each night and continued to retain 90 percent of American television viewers in prime time through the end of the decade.[1] For much of the 1960s and '70s, then, broadcasters competed with one another for bigger and bigger audience shares with programming that often appealed to as large an audience as possible. But toward the end of the network era, industry attitudes toward its audience began to shift. *SNL*, for example, was not an instant ratings success. Its initial ratings, in fact, were no higher than the reruns of Johnny Carson's *Tonight Show* (1962–1992) that NBC had been airing in that time slot. As Jeffrey S. Miller argues, however, demographic breakdowns revealed that the show was drawing a higher share of the increasingly desirable youth audience than any program on television at the time.[2] In this regard, *SNL* was aligned with NBC's emerging commercial imperatives. Thus, a closer look at the history of *SNL* reveals a far more complex story than the underdog tale that often circulates in popular memories of the show.

In "The Evolution of Saturday Night," Michele Hilmes locates the origins of *SNL* within the industrial context of the classic network era, detailing the program's innovations as well as its debt to comedic predecessors like vaudeville. As Hilmes's discussion makes clear, NBC's interest in developing a series for Saturday's late-night fringe period was part of the broadcast network's efforts to extend its control over programming beyond prime time—an ambition representative of the oligopolistic structure of U.S. broadcasting in the 1970s. Hilmes's central goal is to situate *SNL* within the history of live comedy-variety programming that started in the earliest days of broadcast radio in the 1920s and peaked in the 1950s with popular TV series like *Your Show of Shows* (1950–1954). Hilmes demonstrates how *SNL* combined important features of that long tradition with newer comic sensibilities and aesthetic styles drawn from youth-oriented programs like *Rowan & Martin's Laugh-In* (1967–1973), the recent British import *Monty Python's Flying Circus* (1969–1974), and the rise of comedy club circuits. For all of *SNL*'s groundbreaking elements, Hilmes helps us see how it was also tied to a proven cultural format with a long history in broadcasting.

Susan Murray's chapter, "Live from New York!" continues the mapping of *SNL*'s early years by historicizing the program's close identification with New York City—a relationship most obviously signaled through its iconic tagline and opening credit sequence. Popular discourse on the program often characterizes New York City as a place where *SNL* could easily access new talent or as a playground for notorious nighthawks like John Belushi. Both may have been true, but Murray also analyzes the relationship in connection to NBC's and New York City's efforts in the 1970s to rebrand themselves at a time when the reputation of both needed help.

Murray reminds us that the decision to broadcast the program live and to do so from New York would have evoked for many people the city's still-recent history as the source of live television production during the 1950s. According to Murray, *SNL's* liveness, as well as its repeated invocation of a New York "sensibility," were a welcome alternative for many TV critics who lamented what they considered to be the stale aesthetics and banality of most network-era programming. In this way, *SNL* and NBC used New York's edginess and the aura surrounding "Golden Age" live broadcasts as a source of distinction. *SNL's* weekly construction of the city as hip, exciting, and alive was, in turn, valuable to New York as it struggled to recover from a financial crisis and a reputation as the dirtiest and most dangerous city in the nation. The program's present incarnation, particularly its opening montage of cast members enjoying a sanitized vision of New York's night life, obscures the dynamic, messy relationship between *SNL* and America's largest city that existed at the program's birth.

Similarly, a lack of nuanced historical memory has contributed to a reductive understanding of *SNL's* authorship by fostering the iconic status of its longtime executive producer, Lorne Michaels. NBC tapped the former *Laugh-In* writer in 1974 to produce what would become *Saturday Night Live*. Michaels remained executive producer until 1980 before handing control over to Jean Doumanian (1980–1981) and Dick Ebersol (1981–1985), whose reigns are often viewed as blights on the otherwise proud *SNL* legacy. Shales and Miller, for example, playfully suggest of that era, "*Saturday Night Live* was competing against the memory of itself. And losing."[3] In 1985, Michaels returned as executive producer, a position he has held ever since. His steady presence stands in stark contrast with the comparatively short tenure of the program's high-profile comedic stars, and, in fact, Michaels has become a character within the show itself, frequently appearing in front of the camera in the role of the program's all-powerful executive figure. As a result, Michaels has arguably become the individual most strongly associated with the program's success and unique comedic sensibility.

In an intervention into this mythology, Evan Elkins's chapter, "Michael O'Donoghue, Experimental Television Comedy, and *Saturday Night Live's* Authorship," examines oft-overlooked sketches and monologues from other creative voices during the earliest seasons. He argues that the

Michaels-as-auteur narrative obscures the fact that *SNL* has always been the product of various authorial voices and that this reductive understanding works to erase the wide range of comedic styles *SNL* has showcased. One of these voices was Michael O'Donoghue, a member of *SNL*'s early writing team who worked in the "anti-comedy" and "sick comedy" traditions and penned sketches that had a decidedly more violent and mordant tone than those commonly associated with Michaels. Elkins's contribution encourages us to reconsider the show's early aesthetic as the result of complex creative processes, not of one producer's single-minded vision.

PART II: STAYING ALIVE ON SATURDAY NIGHT

Lorne Michaels's return to *SNL* as executive producer in 1985 coincided with a number of important changes in the American television industry after the network era—changes that would shift the program's business and aesthetic strategies. The decline of the network era was hastened by "expanded choice and control"; cable, direct broadcast satellite, remote control technologies, and home video recording offered audiences viewing options well beyond those traditionally controlled by broadcast networks.[4] By 1990, cable was in well over half of American homes,[5] and the broadcast networks won just 60 percent of the prime-time television audience share that year.[6] Broadcasters became targets for takeover by multimedia conglomerates that placed networks under the same corporate infrastructure as magazines, film studios, record labels, publishers, and theme parks. Over the course of the 1980s and 1990s, buzzwords like "synergy" drove networks to consider more carefully how a program could and should exist profitably beyond its initial moment of broadcast and across other entertainment platforms. Unlike during the classic network period, in the multichannel era *SNL* would increasingly deploy its dexterity in comedic innovation in the service of broader industrial strategies.

Aided by FCC mandates fostering the growth of independent production, in 1979 Michaels had created his own production and distribution company, Broadway Video, to assist in post-production duties for *SNL*. By the late 1980s Broadway Video had moved into the syndication and home video markets as well. In addition to releasing numerous best-of collections for cast members like Chevy Chase, John Belushi, Gilda Radner, Dan Aykroyd, and Chris Farley, Broadway Video retained many of the lucrative distribution rights for *SNL*. The company prospered when *SNL* started to be rerun on cable outlets and internationally. As Derek Kompare argues, reruns are vital to American commercial television.[7] In the case of *SNL*, they served to reinforce the program's already-robust (self-)mythology of envelope-pushing comedy, solidifying its legacy in the minds of viewers and driving those viewers back to the live broadcasts.

Amid the demands of the emerging multichannel environment, Michaels turned *SNL* into a brand that could be flexibly leveraged beyond broadcast. The program's sketch variety format provided an ideal source for exploitable content. Cast members like Phil Hartman, Mike Myers, and Dana Carvey, for example, could try out new material every week with relatively little risk; if a character bombed, they could experiment with a new one the following week. Characters that struck a chord became regular fixtures on the show and bankable commodities. *SNL* began to condition audiences to think of the program not only as a once-weekly live broadcast, but also as a repository for recurring characters and catchphrases. As cast member David Spade notes, "It's never been the case, in any sketch that's worked in history, to leave it at one. It's usually 'leave it at thirty.'"[8] Shales and Miller suggest that Michaels was under direct pressure from NBC to develop recurring characters that could be spun off into sitcoms for the network, and the program responded with the likes of Jon Lovitz's Pathological Liar and Dana Carvey's Church Lady. While many television projects for various *SNL* characters fizzled, the *SNL* brand has led to TV projects featuring former cast members (e.g., Tina Fey on *30 Rock* [2006–2013] and Maya Rudolph on *Up All Night* [2011–2012]).

Michaels extended the *SNL* brand most aggressively into movies, producing several films based on characters from the show (*The Blues Brothers* [1980], *Coneheads* [1993], and *A Night at the Roxbury* [1998], among others). Michaels's greatest financial success came with the 1992 film spin-off of Myers and Carvey's popular "Wayne's World" sketches; the film has earned well over $180 million worldwide. In contrast, *It's Pat* (1994) and *Stuart Saves His Family* (1995) flopped. Despite *SNL*'s ability to repurpose material and thus meet new industry mandates to expand television content across platforms, its middling record of synergistic success serves as a useful reminder of the imprecise nature of the culture industries. A perfect business plan for moving content across media still requires a certain serendipity in order to transform late-night laughs into mainstream revenue.

SNL's growing cultural footprint in the multichannel era came with the perception that the program was increasingly straying from its original, innovative aesthetics. A widely discussed 1995 *New York* magazine piece entitled "Comedy Isn't Funny: *Saturday Night Live* at Twenty— How the Show That Transformed TV Became a Grim Joke," for instance, describes the *SNL* workplace as "obsessed with maintaining its internal pecking order" and compares the viewing experience of that season to "watching late-period Elvis—embarrassing and poignant."[9] To be sure, the article—like many others that have invoked the now-familiar "Saturday Night Dead" trope—wistfully yearns for the edginess of the original Not Ready for Prime Time Players. But the article also highlights how the discursive construction of *SNL*'s edginess needed to be more carefully managed in the multichannel era. *SNL* could no longer presume its status as the leading proprietor of boundary-pushing comedy in the face of growing competition from more demographically attuned outlets on cable, such as HBO and Comedy Central.

SNL has become increasingly adept at managing the perception of its content's originality, refreshing the program's place in the television industry, and maintaining a fundamental position of stability. During the multichannel era and into the contemporary moment, the audience members most coveted by television advertisers have experienced a dizzying array of entertainment options, making it all the more important for *SNL* to foster a sense of cultural relevance in order to hold its place in the collective consciousness. Furthermore, the program has strived to remain relevant in the world of comedy, where keeping up with fickle taste preferences is a notoriously daunting task. While the program's success with audiences and critics has clearly been uneven, it has nonetheless survived each down period to find new successes and to reclaim a place in mainstream American television culture.

The contributions in part II outline the relationship between *SNL*'s strong sense of institutional stability and its need to make one of television's longest-running formats feel innovative to successive generations of viewers. A particularly successful means of achieving this goal has been through its engagement with politics, a realm in which the main players are always in flux, but the overarching structure rarely changes. In "Politics and the Brand: *Saturday Night Live*'s Campaign Season Humor," Jeffrey P. Jones argues that *SNL* has long relied on political satire, especially the impersonation of political figures during national campaigns, as a means of maintaining its cultural relevance and, by extension, its ratings. Impersonation-based sketches that successfully link cast members to specific political figures (e.g., Will Ferrell as George W. Bush, Tina Fey as Sarah Palin), for example, can help establish standout stars and serve as sources for recurring content, making production easier and promoting repeat viewing. Jones analyzes the unique dynamics that continue to make *SNL*'s brand of political satire distinct from others, and he explores how *SNL*'s satiric sketches have informed U.S. politics more broadly. *SNL*'s long history of satiric political humor makes it an important precursor to the contemporary moment, when political, satiric television flourishes across the media landscape.

Viewers have long turned to *SNL* for political commentary unavailable via conventional news and have spread the program's political satire in both personal and remediated interactions. In order for a topical show like *SNL* to last for nearly forty seasons, it must successfully respond to the continually changing cultural context upon which it is so dependent. In "Speaking Too Soon: *SNL*, 9/11, and the Remaking of American Irony," Matt Sienkiewicz considers the impact of the events of September 11, 2001, on *SNL*'s comedic strategies. Engaging with popular discourse on the "end of irony" in the wake of the national tragedy, he outlines changes in the program's approaches to humor, irony, and political engagement before and after the 9/11 attacks. Via close analysis of specific sketches, Sienkiewicz traces a transition from a nihilistic, apolitical irony to a short-lived effort at sincerity to an eventual new ironic mode of address—one that he argues has been more socially and politically committed.

Responding to politics and current affairs has long played into *SNL*'s live sketches. Even more consistent has been the show's reliance on musical guests. Integrating the vagaries of live musical performances and connecting them to the *SNL* brand, however, has proven difficult at times. In "*Live* Music: Mediating Musical Performance and Discord on *Saturday*

Night Live," Alyxandra Vesey explores the show's ambivalent relationship with music. Although booking hip musical performers has allowed *SNL* to appear fresh, Vesey suggests that television's commercial mandates often lead the show to undercut the very edginess it wants to exploit. Musical performance thus fits uncomfortably within *SNL's* attempts to position itself industrially and culturally.

Just as *SNL* has aimed to control and develop its brand through music, it has also attempted to enhance its imprint by moving away from Saturday night whenever possible. Most obviously this has taken place in the form of midweek prime-time specials and tributes on NBC that frame the show's history and work to expand its audience. However, during the 2006–2007 season, this expansion took on a new direction, as NBC's prime-time lineup included not one, but two different series that took viewers behind the scenes of *SNL*-like sketch comedy shows: *30 Rock* and *Studio 60 on the Sunset Strip*. In "Going Backstage: Network Heritage, Industrial Identities, and Reiterated Mediation of *Saturday Night Live's* Work Worlds," Derek Johnson analyzes NBC's curious programming decision in relation to the dynamics of media franchising in the post-network era. He traces the sometimes converging, sometimes conflicting goals of NBC executives, *SNL's* Lorne Michaels, and the producers behind both *30 Rock* and *Studio 60* as each tried to exploit the legacy of *SNL* in their efforts to differentiate their programs and assert their authorial credibility. Although *SNL's* cultural relevance seemed uncertain at the time (i.e., it faced declining ratings and critics who claimed it was being passed by cable and online competitors), Johnson helps us see the various ways the *SNL* brand continued to influence the formation of the industrial identities of myriad creative personnel affiliated with the two programs.

PART III: SOCIAL POLITICS AND COMEDIC REPRESENTATION

For all of the challenges posed by shifting demographics and network business structures throughout *SNL's* history, these changes represent only a fraction of the obstacles the program has confronted in its efforts to maintain relevance. *SNL's* sketch format and desire to remain on the cutting edge of contemporary comedy has pushed the show to confront hot-button political and social issues. As a result, *SNL*'s identity is very much connected to changing norms in the representation and comedic mediation of race, religion, gender, and sexuality. Audiences have come to expect jokes and characters built around these sensitive subjects, requiring *SNL* to push boundaries enough to garner laughs and reinforce its countercultural reputation while nonetheless remaining within the realm of what is acceptable for network broadcast. Though far from radical in its approach to the politics of identity, *SNL* has often preceded its television comedy peers in key areas of humor and representation. As David Zurawik argues, *SNL* embraced Jewish-centric comedy at a time when most networks feared exposing middle America to the coastal, often Semitic, origins of TV content creators.[10] Eddie Murphy's much-celebrated run on *SNL* anticipated the targeting of African American audiences that formed so much of Fox's early network identity with programs such as *In Living Color* (1990–1994), *Martin* (1992–1997), and *Living Single* (1993–1998). And Julia Sweeney's androgynous character, Pat, and Al Franken's seemingly closeted self-help host, Stuart Smalley, predated the mainstreaming of LGBTQ characters found on *Will and Grace* (1998–2006) and beyond.

While *SNL* may have been anxious to exploit comedy's ability to engage with highly charged cultural discourses about race, ethnicity, religion, gender, and sexuality, it has always done so within the constraints of commercial broadcasting and its own workplace ideologies. Thus, *SNL* provides fertile terrain for an examination of America's evolving social politics and television's role as a site where those political changes are negotiated in uneven ways. Despite the show's self-perpetuated reputation for urban edginess, for example, there have been only two openly gay or lesbian cast members in the program's history, and women have consistently played a secondary role to strong, alpha-male comedic personalities. Such absences and hierarchies have long been associated with *SNL*'s workplace culture. Janeane Garofalo, for instance, described her only season on the show as "the year of fag-bashing and using the words 'bitch' and 'whore' in a sketch."[11]

The chapters in part III of this collection interrogate *SNL*'s relationship to identity, politics, and representation. They emphasize the constantly changing nature of tastes and taboos, detailing the ways in which one moment's controversy becomes another's comedy. The pieces consider how intermittently progressive approaches to race, gender, and sexuality have coexisted alongside Eurocentric, heterosexist, and patriarchal norms, and they analyze how *SNL* has both challenged and reinforced dominant cultural discourses.

SNL has not been an accommodating place for racial minority performers. African Americans have been consistently underrepresented as cast members, and the program has repeatedly been accused of tokenism with regard to minority performers. Given this history, Eddie Murphy's enormously successful run on the show during the early 1980s presents a unique opportunity to investigate the program's racial politics. In "Bringing the Black: Eddie Murphy and African American Humor on *Saturday Night Live*," Racquel Gates challenges the long-held assumption that Murphy's comedy only found success on a mainstream series like *SNL* because it eschewed the kind of pointed social critique of edgier comics like Richard Pryor. Analyzing a number of Murphy's most memorable sketches, Gates places his work on *SNL* within a long tradition of African American performative strategies that have enabled black comics to criticize racist practices from within mainstream institutions. *SNL*'s discriminatory workplace culture (including its pattern of treating black comics as racial tokens), Gates argues, even helped provide an opening for Murphy's often-subversive satire of U.S. race relations during the politically conservative 1980s.

In "'Is this the Era of the Woman?': *SNL*'s Gender Politics in the New Millennium," Caryn Murphy takes on the program's fluid and uneasy history with feminism, arguing that popular press coverage of the "Tina Fey era" overstates the extent to which gender equity has been achieved at *SNL*. While the most egregious forms of sexist behavior that occurred in the 1970s, '80s, and '90s may have abated, Murphy convincingly analyzes the ways male-dominated bias continues to structure *SNL*'s production culture.

Nearly three decades after Eddie Murphy's tenure on the show, *SNL* still confronts many of the same issues of race and identity articulation. In "*SNL*'s 'Fauxbama' Debate: Facing Off over Millennial (Mixed-)Racial Impersonation," Mary Beltrán examines the program's representational strategies via analyses of satiric sketches about Barack Obama (first as a candidate, then as president) that aired in 2008 and 2009. Her analysis, however, is not focused on what the sketches say about Obama's political policies or his character. Instead, Beltrán examines the range of opinions on the appropriateness of casting Fred Armisen as Obama. Were the sketches just harmless examples of an *SNL* staple—parodic impersonations of public figures—or were they tantamount to blackface minstrelsy? Beltrán provides a nuanced analysis that situates the debate over the politics of this cross-racial impersonation in relationship to a variety of factors: the confusion over Armisen's mixed racial heritage, shifting cultural memories of blackface performances, and uneven investments in the idea that the United States has entered a "post-racial" era. Beltrán's chapter foregrounds the potential political pitfalls facing a comedy-variety show like *SNL*—one that relies on impersonations of public figures for comedic fodder, but that also consistently employs few actors of color.

PART IV: BEYOND SATURDAY NIGHT, BEYOND TELEVISION

With television increasingly integrated with other media technologies and experiences, *SNL*'s comedy is now situated among and competes with myriad other cultural referents. In the present day, memorable moments on *SNL*—whether political, musical, or pop cultural—become hyper-mediated discourses that circulate beyond the control that Lorne Michaels (as executive producer) and NBC (as distributor) have so carefully cultivated. Although the show's format has hardly changed over the past four decades, the way it is consumed has been revolutionized through the advent of video-sharing platforms, social media websites, and time-shifting devices.

The spread of *SNL* not only onto other media platforms, but also into other discursive realms, highlights how the trends of the multichannel era have accelerated in the contemporary television industry. Content and outlet choices continue to multiply, as have the devices and services through which viewers can access and engage with television. One key in this acceleration is the digital format of television, which facilitates the rapid and widespread distribution and consumption of content. The quick remediation of television content has also created a number of new venues in which viewers engage with programs, often synthesizing disparate discourses through commenting and cross-posting. Comedy's malleability makes it especially appealing for such audience activity as well as for producers hoping to target desirable, tech-savvy consumers. In the still-young digital era, *SNL* has provided key moments of contention between industry and audience, as well as paved the way for how those interactions will happen in the future.

Contemporary *SNL* thus represents a unique site for considering the overlaps between "old" and "new" media and their respective cultural and industrial protocols. The program persists in presenting audiences with the same familiar cold open, followed by the "Live from New York!" tagline and an array of live sketches in front of a studio audience. Yet it has also appropriated elements of emerging media aesthetics to rejuvenate its own comedic sensibilities, all while providing indications of how network television content will fit into the uncertain industrial landscape of television's not-so-distant future. The program's "Lazy Sunday" digital short, for instance, became one of YouTube's earliest hits in 2005–2006, and it was at the center of a number of converging legal, cultural, industrial, and popular discourses debating how consumers and media conglomerates could or could not share copyrighted content. Most popular histories of *SNL,* though, end their accounts of the program prior to the rise of Internet culture. As a result, the pieces in part IV focus their analyses on *SNL*'s integration among industrial and cultural discourses in which television is just a small part. In doing so, the chapters provide a clearer picture of the role of comedy in driving transmedial mobility and of the ongoing redefinition of television culture.

Traditionally, the aesthetic influence of *SNL* has spread beyond television through films based on specific *SNL* characters or ones starring former cast members whose performances clearly invoke the program's sketch sensibilities. In "Skits Strung Together: Performance, Narrative, and the Sketch Comedy Aesthetic in *SNL* Films," Nick Marx examines such films in order to help us better understand the transmedial nature of comedy, particularly the ways in which humor can be rooted in viewers' engagement with the cross-media-constructed persona of a comedic star like Will Ferrell or Tina Fey just as much as it can be generated through the narrative structure of a specific text. Recurring complaints about *SNL*-influenced films (i.e., that a specific *SNL* sketch or the sketch-based mode of comedy is ill suited to the feature film genre), Marx argues, fail to acknowledge how comedy has always operated beyond textual boundaries, a dynamic historically present among the films of many studio-era comedians and becoming more common in our increasingly transmedial landscape today.

In "Andy Samberg's Digital Success Story and Other Myths of the Internet Comedy Club," Ethan Thompson and Ethan Tussey look more closely at the transmedial landscape and how *SNL* has responded. Thompson and Tussey challenge the idea that Andy Samberg's rise from online obscurity to *SNL* stardom is evidence of a new, more democratic era for comedy—one in which anyone can make a funny video, post it online, and end up with a TV deal. The myth, Thompson and Tussey argue, obscures the fact that *SNL* and the television industry in general have been taming digital comedy venues, transforming them into their own talent filtration system in ways that actually help them maintain their hegemony. By hiring Samberg and Lonely Island and incorporating the lo-fi aesthetics of their "Digital Shorts" series, *SNL* has adapted to the new modes of comedy developing online and has partially neutralized the threat from the Internet's decentralized modes of distribution.

SNL's embrace of the digital has not simply impacted the program at the level of production and exhibition. It has also had a profound impact on *SNL*'s consumption. In "Sketches Gone Viral: From Watercooler Talk to Participatory Comedy," David Gurney examines audience engagement with *SNL* in the digital era, such as the posting of previously aired *SNL* clips alongside user-generated remixes of and homages to favorite sketches. Although *SNL* fans have long reiterated character catchphrases and impersonations in interpersonal contexts, online video and social networking communities have made these fan activities much more widespread and complex. Despite a dip in *SNL*'s ratings, Gurney argues that *SNL*'s vibrant second life online attests to its continued cultural relevance; as evidence he provides in-depth analyses of several of the most active *SNL*-related memes, including amateur videos inspired by "Lazy Sunday" and the "Laser Cats" digital shorts.

CONCLUSION

There is an experiential difficulty that often plagues both the student and researcher of American television. Though television has had a long evolution, beginning with pre–World War II experiments and leading to the digital, cross-platform medium we experience today, there is nonetheless a strong pull to consider it in the present tense. The television industry, despite its deep-down penchant for conservatism, works tirelessly to foster a sense that each offering is something new and that to watch this season's programs is to engage with the latest in American culture. Furthermore, television is so much a part of the daily lives of so many Americans, including those who aim to approach it from a scholarly perspective, that it can be rather tempting to see it as a kind of eternally renewed present as opposed to the product of a multifaceted historical process.

Teachers of television confront this problem on a daily basis. In a contemporary classroom, terms such as "VHF," "superstation," and sometimes even "broadcast television" can confuse students. Though crucial to television's current place in the world, these concepts can nonetheless seem so removed from the contemporary experience of the medium that they may feel entirely unrelated. Researchers, though well versed in these connections, can face a related difficulty. It is one thing to know the landmark moments that have shaped television's history and even their relationships to major events and movements in U.S. politics and society. It is another truly to see television as a continuum, constantly evolving and interacting with the countless forgotten but impactful fads, political shifts, and momentary cultural obsessions of the recent, perhaps not yet documented, past.

The contributions in Saturday Night Live *and American TV* are put forth as a small effort to aid in overcoming these challenges. By critically examining *SNL,* the collection works to illuminate the balance of continuity and change inherent in the medium, providing the scholar and student an opportunity to understand television on both the diachronic and synchronic axes. The book not only engages with many of the key areas in contemporary television studies, but also highlights television's ability to adapt as an industry and art form—all while maintaining its corporate-friendly sense of stability. This collection is thus meant to provide a valuable supplement to a more broadly focused study on the history of the medium. Most people who watched *SNL*'s debut episode did so via a picture-tube TV equipped with a rabbit ear antenna. Since then, cable boxes, satellite dishes, computers, plasma screens, fiber optics, and smartphones have transformed the medium's distribution, and changes no less revolutionary have taken place at the level of production and consumption. Yet, for all these changes, *SNL* will premier once again in the fall, putting forth an effort very different, and yet somehow fundamentally similar, to what it offered in October 1975. To understand that dynamic is, we suggest, a key to unlocking the nature of American television culture.

Notes

1. Hindman and Wiegand, "The Big Three's Prime-Time Decline," 126.
2. Miller, "What Closes on Saturday Night," 202.
3. Shales and Miller, *Live from New York,* 192.
4. Lotz, *The Television Will Be Revolutionized,* 13.
5. Mullen, *The Rise of Cable Programming in the United States,* 129.
6. Hindman and Wiegand, "The Big Three's Prime-Time Decline," 126.
7. Kompare, *Rerun Nation,* xi–xv.
8. Qtd. in Shales and Miller, *Live from New York,* 379.
9. Smith, "Comedy Isn't Funny."
10. Zurawik, *The Jews of Prime Time.*
11. Qtd. in Smith, "Comedy Isn't Funny."

Works Cited

Baumgartner, Jody, and Jonathan S. Morris. *Laughing Matters: Humor and American Politics in the Media Age.* New York: Routledge, 2008.

Davis, Tom. *Thirty-Nine Years of Short-Term Memory Loss.* New York: Grove, 2009.

Gray, Jonathan, Jeffrey Jones, and Ethan Thompson, eds. *Satire TV: Politics and Comedy in the Post-Network Era.* New York: New York University Press, 2009.

Haggins, Bambi. *Laughing Mad: The Black Comic Persona in Post-Soul America.* New Brunswick, NJ: Rutgers University Press, 2007.

Hill, Doug, and Jeff Weingrad. *Saturday Night: A Backstage History of Saturday Night Live.* New York: Beech Tree, 1986.

Hindman, Douglas Blanks, and Kenneth Wiegand. "The Big Three's Prime-Time Decline: A Technological and Social Context." *Journal of Broadcasting and Electronic Media* 52(1) (2008):119–135.

Kompare, Derek. *Rerun Nation: How Repeats Invented American Television.* New York: Routledge, 2005.

Lotz, Amanda. *The Television Will Be Revolutionized.* New York: New York University Press, 2007.

Miller, Jeffrey S. *Something Completely Different: British Television and American Culture.* Minneapolis: University of Minnesota Press, 2000.

———. "What Closes on Saturday Night: NBC and Satire." In *NBC: America's Network,* edited by Michele Hilmes. Berkeley: University of California Press, 2007.

Mullen, Megan. *The Rise of Cable Programming in the United States.* Austin: University of Texas Press, 2003.

Shales, Tom, and James Andrew Miller. *Live from New York: An Uncensored History of Saturday Night Live*. Boston: Little, Brown, 2002.

Smith, Chris. "Comedy Isn't Funny: *Saturday Night Live* at Twenty—How the Show That Transformed TV Became a Grim Joke." *New York,* March 13, 1995, http://nymag.com/arts/tv/features/47548/ (accessed February 1, 2012).

Whalley, Jim. *Saturday Night Live, Hollywood Comedy, and American Culture*. London: Palgrave Macmillan, 2010.

Zurawik, David. *The Jews of Prime Time*. Lebanon, NH: Brandeis University Press, 2003.

PART ONE

Live from New York on NBC

The Evolution of Saturday Night

MICHELE HILMES

What happened to transform the small hours of Saturday night from the low-rent haunt of old movies, reruns, dusty talk shows, and strange preachers to a must-see event for three generations of youthful viewers? The answer can be found by looking at changes in the American broadcasting industry, the rise of the youth audience, and the new prominence of sketch comedy, powered by transatlantic currents of popular culture flowing across the airwaves. *Saturday Night Live* drew on all these factors to create a new type of serialized sketch comedy format with one foot in vaudeville and the other in television's future, but few would have guessed that it would continue to serve as an incubator and showcase of film, television, and musical talent across more than three decades. It also began a return to high-profile, live television production, after two decades of increased reliance on filmed series, and marked the death throes of the prime-time variety show, a staple of broadcasting since the 1920s.

In many ways *Saturday Night Live,* when it debuted at 11:30 PM Eastern time on October 11, 1975, simply represented the latest manifestation of a broadcast form that had dominated U.S. radio and television schedules from the beginning: the comedy-variety show. Drawing directly on the vaudeville tradition of combining musical performances, comedy sketches, humorous emcee-hosts, and a wide variety of other materials ranging from tap dancing to poetry readings, such programs proliferated on local radio stations around the nation, although we will never know about many of them since records, if kept, have long since disappeared. Networks, when they emerged in the late 1920s, took up the form immediately, and for the next thirty years, comedy-variety was never missing from their lineups (though not typically on Saturday nights; Sunday was by far the more popular). The comedy-variety format carried over to early television, often directly, as in the migration of the long-successful *Texaco Star Theater* from radio to TV in 1948 complete with its host, Milton Berle.

In other ways, however, *SNL* represented a significant break with that tradition as it had developed by the 1970s, revolutionizing the form and creating a new kind of audience for comedy, yet remaining a singular exception—an innovation network TV could not repeat, leaving it to stand alone until cable TV and new, targeted networks of the 1990s managed to replicate some of the unique conditions that it had created. Though other shows, such as Fox's *MADtv* (1995–2009) and *In Living Color* (1990–1994), clearly owe much of their format to *Saturday Night Live,* they reproduced neither its conditions of truly live production (being filmed before live studio audiences and broadcast later) nor the wide reach of NBC in its prime. This chapter examines the history of the comedy-variety format, from its roots in radio to its early television manifestations, in order to set up an analysis of what has made *SNL* unique and what it has contributed to the ongoing development of television forms and practices. In today's media arena of fragmented platforms and segmented audiences, it is easy to lose sight of the conditions under which innovation occurred in the earlier network period, conditions that tie *SNL* to its roots in pre-TV radio and early live television as much as to current programs. Yet these are precisely the factors that contributed to its success and that mark its truly original trajectory.

RADIO ROOTS

Two of the most influential early comedy-variety programs on radio were *The Capitol Theater Gang,* hosted by Samuel "Roxy" Rothafel, manager of New York City's Capitol Theater (later, *Roxy and His Gang*), and *The Eveready Hour,* hosted by xylophonist-turned-ukelele-player Wendell Hall. Both debuted on WEAF, the first experimental network in the United

States, operated by AT&T, in 1922 and 1923, respectively, becoming early radio's first big hit shows. We know about them because they were WEAF programs and AT&T promoted and publicized them; no doubt there were many others on local stations that remain lost to the historical record. Roxy's program was a direct carry-over from the vaudeville shows put on in the Capitol Theater before film screenings, a common custom in the 1920s. *The Eveready Hour* may represent the first comedy-variety program created specifically for commercial network radio, since it was originated by its sponsor, the National Carbon Company, to promote its Eveready batteries, much used in early radio sets. Both continued the vaudeville tradition of presenting a wide variety of disparate acts linked together by a host or emcee.

But the serializing structure of radio, with new shows presented to a consistent audience every week (unlike vaudeville's fixed show with changing audiences), meant that a new combination of continuity and innovation was necessary. Each week's show had to be different from the week before, yet similar enough from one to the next to create a brand presence and attract listeners back week after week. Thus the radio variety format was born, adapting vaudeville's content to radio's technological, aesthetic, and economic needs for stability and predictability, as well as its "intimate" presence in the home. A genial host served as the main anchor and trademark of the program, at the center of a comedic and musical "family" of regular performers and personalities punctuated by guest appearances, keeping to a general theme or fictional setting while introducing controlled variations for each weekly installment.

Early listings refer to several different types of variety show on network schedules: general variety, like *The Eveready Hour,* with a broad combination of acts; musical variety, by far the most common, whose host might crack a few mild jokes but mainly served to introduce a mix of musical performances; and comedy-variety.[1] For the first decade of radio, the comedy-variety form was closely linked to the minstrel/blackface format, such as the Majestic Theater Hour's *Two Black Crows,* starting in 1928; the *Henry George Program,* billed as "negro comedy," in 1929; and much of the early humor of Eddie Cantor, who debuted on radio in 1931. Not until 1932 did the comedy-variety form begin to proliferate, with twelve shows on the air that year, up from only two the year before. No doubt this had something to do with radio's stabilizing economic situation, as networks extended their reach across the country and sponsors began to regard radio as a profitable advertising medium. As advertising agencies embraced showmanship and began to take over prime-time program production from the networks, well-known comedians began to rival famous bandleaders as star attractions. Most of 1932–1933's astonishing crop of comedy-variety hosts had started out in vaudeville, many went on to long careers on radio and in film, and a few eventually turned up on early television: Al Jolson, George Burns and Gracie Allen, Ed Wynn, Fred Allen, Jack Benny, the Marx Brothers.

Interestingly, the only night *not* featuring a comedy-variety program during the early 1930s, as the format found its footing, was Saturday. Sundays through Fridays were good nights for comedy-variety, it seems, but Saturday network schedules remained dominated by musical variety programs, many of them broadcast live from hotel ballrooms and clubs. If you couldn't go out on Saturday night, listening at home to a popular orchestra playing from the Plaza ballroom in New York was an excellent substitute. Here we see the meaning of "live" begin to make a shift from the dominant form of early radio—preexisting entertainments transmitted live on location—to the production of specialized radio programs transmitted live from a broadcast studio, the direction in which radio innovation would grow.

Comedy-variety hit its peak on radio in the mid-1940s, with nearly twenty programs aired in prime-time hours. They earned some of the top ratings in radio, especially for staples like *Bob Hope, Burns and Allen, Charlie McCarthy, Fibber McGee and Molly, Fred Allen, Jack Benny, Judy Canova,* and *Red Skelton.* Typically, such programs combined both stand-up and sketch comedy routines, along with music and guest-star turns.[2] But over the course of two decades, as the list above suggests, sketch comedy had become the dominant mode, so thoroughly integrated within the format that it had become serialized along with the rest of the show. By the mid-1940s most of the long-running comedy-variety programs on radio had developed a central sketch situation—often a self-referential one, such as Jack Benny's "group of performers trying to put on a radio show" or Judy Canova's "country girl star in Hollywood" persona—from which each week's episodes were spun. Such recurring sketches employed ongoing storylines and character development that were looser than the emergent format of the situation comedy—well under way by 1947—but certainly different from the intermittent, loosely connected sketches of earlier years.

TRANSITION TO TV

This well-established format changed again when television entered the scene. By now, the genre referred to as situation comedy had emerged to move broadcast humor in a new direction. Radio sitcoms had grown out of sketches developed in the comedy-variety matrix, and many of them, or their stars, made a smooth transition to television. This was the case with *The Burns and Allen Show.* Starting as comedy-variety, it gradually took on most of the characteristics of a sitcom: a half-hour divided into two fifteen-minute extended sketches with a continuing storyline, with a brief musical performance in between. This is the format its veteran stars carried over to TV in 1950. Joan Davis, who debuted doing sketch comedy as a summer replacement host on *The Rudy Vallee Show,* quickly built it into a radio sitcom, *The Joan Davis Show,* then brought it to television in *I Married Joan* (NBC, 1952–1955).[3] This kind of extended sketch, often with a domestic setting, provided far more favorable conditions for female comedians than the comedy-variety format, with its emphasis on suggestive one-liners and gags.[4] The radio and early television situation comedy was built by women like Davis, Lucille Ball, Marie Wilson, Fanny Brice, Eve Arden, Ann Sothern, and Hattie McDaniel. By the 1960s it would be television comedy's most popular form.

However, in the early 1950s, the live variety format dominated early television. More than forty variety shows aired weekly, from fifteen-minute musical variety shorts that still might feature big stars—Perry Como, Dinah Shore—to high-profile hour-long showcases, available nearly every night of the week and hosted by names made famous in radio and in Hollywood: Kate Smith, Ed Sullivan, Arthur Godfrey, Dinah Shore, Faye Emerson.[5] In contrast to radio, Saturday nights were the prime time for television comedy, anchored by NBC's ninety-minute behemoth, *Your Show of Shows* (1950–1954). Hosted by veteran comedians Sid Caesar and Imogene Coca, it featured radio's mix of sketch comedy and stand-up, along with television's retrieval of slapstick comedy from vaudeville's repertoire. Musical productions now could feature not only singing but dancing as well, and television allowed orchestras some

Figure 1.1. *The George Burns and Gracie Allen Show* integrated elements from sitcoms and variety shows. The resulting hybrid is evident in this shot: Burns, standing next to the proscenium arch, addresses the studio and TV audience while Allen is visible in the sitcom set behind him.

literal and figurative visibility. Over its four-year run, *Your Show of Shows* displayed the talents of an astonishing variety of later-famous writers, including Mel Tolkin, Mel Brooks, Larry Gelbart, Neil Simon, and Woody Allen. Caesar and Coca created a number of recurring characters whose stories continued sporadically from show to show, most notably the dysfunctional couple Charlie and Doris Hickenlooper. Other classic live comedy-variety shows from this early period include *The Texaco Star Theater* (1948–1956) with Milton Berle and the *The Colgate Comedy Hour* (1950–1955), whose varied hosts included Dean Martin and Jerry Lewis most prominently.

As the 1950s segued into the '60s, filmed series grew in number while live shows of all kinds declined on the prime-time airwaves. Variety was one of the last to go, though by 1965 most variety shows had shifted to being filmed in front of a live studio audience. That year only three variety shows remained in prime time—*The Red Skelton Hour* (1951–1971),

The Bob Hope Show (1952–1975), and *The Jackie Gleason Show* (1952–1970) (all comedy-variety); in 1975, the year that *SNL* debuted, the number was the same—*Tony Orlando and Dawn* (1974–1976), the long-running *Carol Burnett Show* (1967–1978), and *Cher* (1975–1976) as all that (briefly) remained of the old *Sonny and Cher Comedy Hour* (1971–1974). However, this broad leap through the decades obscures several important developments in the late '60s and early '70s that led in a wandering, indirect, yet still important line to *SNL*.

THE ROOTS OF SNL

In the late 1960s the networks awoke to the notion that a new youth audience existed out there. Baby boomers, many of whom were in their teen spending years, would require some variation on the types of programs that had been entertaining their parents on radio and television for the last thirty years. Youthful characters were written into crime dramas and soap operas, and a new focus on "relevance" introduced a more political note into sitcoms, all attempting to attract the baby boomer crowd while not alienating the rest of the audience. The impact of this strategy could be seen in the comedy-variety format with two of the most notable variations on the themes that led to *SNL: The Smothers Brothers Comedy Hour* (1967–1969) and *Rowan & Martin's Laugh-In* (1968–1973).

The travails of the Smothers Brothers have been well traced: beginning as a fairly traditional comedy-variety show with the two brothers as hosts and combining comedy skits and musical performances complete with an orchestra and a dancing troupe, the Smothers guest list became increasingly political and the network increasingly censorious.[6] Musical performances by left-leaning guests like Pete Seeger, Joan Baez, and Harry Belafonte were summarily cut; comedians like David Steinberg and routines by the brothers themselves were rejected. Finally the show, despite growing ratings, received a mid-season cancellation notice in March 1969, effective immediately. This seemed to mark a limit of what networks deemed permissible in terms of incorporating the more political elements of 1960s youth culture into network television during the prime-time hours.

A more successful though less politically edgy attempt to capture something of the '60s ethos in television comedy was *Rowan & Martin's*

Laugh-In. Henry Jenkins pithily sums up the show's significance: "If *The Smothers Brothers Comedy Hour* captured the political earnestness of the 1960s counterculture, *Laugh-In* snared the decade's flamboyance, its anarchic energy, and its pop aesthetic, combining the blackout comedy of the vaudeville tradition with a 1960s-style 'happening.'"[7]

Influenced by a short-lived adaptation of a more edgy British news satire show, *That Was the Week That Was,* which aired on NBC in 1964–1965, *Laugh-In* returned to the tradition of gag comedy, with very short sketches and one-liners performed by a cast of recurring characters, eschewing the guest-star convention. Its style was zany and frenetic, its pace furious: most sketches lasted for less than a minute before another completely unrelated gag bumped them off the screen. Gyrating women in bikinis and lots of pop dancing rounded out its audience appeal. *Laugh-In*'s comedy ensemble included Lily Tomlin, Goldie Hawn, Arte Johnson, Ruth Buzzi, Henry Gibson, Pigmeat Markham, and Jo Anne Worley, and many of them were elevated out of obscurity to stardom overnight. Though its topicality and '60s-specific pop breeziness meant a fast fade from cultural memory, Jenkins concludes, "Not until *Saturday Night Live* would another television variety show ensemble leave such a firm imprint on the evolution of American comedy." Among *Laugh-In*'s writers was a young Lorne Michaels.

Outside of prime time, another spot on the network TV schedule was providing some of the other elements that *SNL* would eventually combine with its comedy-variety predecessors. This was the late-night talk show, and NBC led the way. Launched in 1954, NBC's *Tonight* aired five nights a week, Monday through Friday, at 11:30 PM Eastern time, featuring a mix of comedy monologue and improvisation, interviews with famous guests, musical performances, and the occasional sketch comedy routine. This was a lot like the prime-time variety show, along the lines of *The Ed Sullivan Show* (1948–1971), but its late-night slot and its focus on conversation differentiated it. Steve Allen was the first host, from 1954 to 1957. He was succeeded by Jack Paar, who held the post until 1962. During Paar's tenure, production shifted from live to being recorded on videotape earlier in the day. Paar gave way to the show's longtime host and defining persona, Johnny Carson, who held the slot for the next thirty years. In 1965 NBC began airing reruns of the show on Saturday and Sunday nights as well.

The late-night talk show, NBC's singular franchise, contained many of the elements that would later go into making *SNL*, notably an emphasis on comedy combined with musical performances, but it also varied considerably. Its strong focus on a central host, its five-day-a-week schedule, its emphasis on unscripted discussion, and its inclusion of "serious" guests and topics among the more humorous offerings combined to give it a style related just as closely to the venerable talk show format as to comedy-variety. Above all, very little sketch comedy found a space on *Tonight*. Carson's audience, too, skewed older; typically the age of *Tonight*'s average viewer has hovered in the low fifties.

Other networks attempted to populate the late-night hours in the '60s and '70s. ABC tried out *Nightlife* (1965), then *The Joey Bishop Show* (1967–1969), which was succeeded by *Dick Cavett* (1969–1975). Briefly, three late-night entries competed, when CBS's *Merv Griffin Show* aired from 1969 to 1972. But by 1973 Carson's rivals admitted defeat, and though various other formats were tried, NBC retained its hold on the late-night slot, Mondays through Fridays. Aside from *Tonight* repeats, though, Saturday and Sunday late-night fringe hours—after 11 PM—remained the property of local stations, where old movies, syndicated reruns, home shopping, and strange rants ruled supreme.

ON THE FRINGE

In the meantime, on another edge of the television universe, a burst of innovation from Britain had begun providing some of the elements that network prime time lacked. *Monty Python's Flying Circus,* which had originated on the BBC in 1969, began to seep into the consciousness of American viewers, particularly younger ones, as early as 1970 when the Canadian Broadcasting Corporation aired it to enthusiastic audiences. Lorne Michaels, born and raised in Toronto, was among this group. Americans who lived near the Canadian border could also view the program, and a film composed of segments from the show, *And Now for Something Completely Different,* was released in 1971 and expanded its U.S. impact. The Pythons made a tour of the United States in 1973, and even performed on *Tonight,* to muted response. However, the event may have prompted NBC programmers to consider how this BBC version of a late-night program might round out their schedule on Saturday nights.

But it was the struggling public broadcasting sector that really launched the Pythons in the United States. Though it is frequently thought of as a PBS offering, in fact the public network turned *Flying Circus* down when the BBC's U.S. distributor, Time Life Films, offered it for syndication in 1975. It was not the national network but individual stations in Texas, New York, and Iowa that moved first to buy it, no doubt prompted in part by the success of the second Python film, *Monty Python and the Holy Grail,* released early that year. "While public television and PBS get the credit, it was really the stations that introduced *Monty Python* to America," a PBS executive admitted later.[8] The show became one of public television's greatest hits, surpassing more typical fare like *Masterpiece Theatre* (1971–present) and *The Ascent of Man* (1973). Furthermore, it attracted "the youngest audiences of any of its prime-time programs" with greatest popularity in the fifteen-to-twenty-four-year-old demographic. This revolution in public television viewership patterns helped to spread the show's reach across the country.[9]

Monty Python's Flying Circus, drawing on British comedic traditions going back to *The Goon Show* (1951–1972), presented a new kind of sketch comedy to American viewers, one that preserved the spontaneity and improvisational qualities of live performance while taking full advantage of the innovations that recording could bring. The show was shot on videotape, permitting greater elaboration in sets, costumes, makeup, and staging, as well as bringing the lone U.S. member of the troupe, Terry Gilliam, into the mix with his now-iconic animations, which punctuated the sketches. The Pythons were also astute at reworking their routines in other recorded media; besides film, they released several LPs in the 1970s based on the television sketches that circulated particularly well among youthful audiences. In this they joined the growing number of comedians who had turned to the medium of recorded sound to find new audiences in the 1960s and '70s.[10]

The contributions made by *Monty Python's Flying Circus* to the concept of *Saturday Night Live* have been remarked upon by numerous observers. Jeffrey Miller argues that the debut of the Pythons in Canada was a "defining influence" and quotes Lorne Michaels: "It was miraculous to me, a revelation. It seemed that once again the winds of change were blowing from England." Though Michaels used clips from the show to define his vision of comedy, "even going so far as to put a phony *Monty*

Figure 1.2. American viewers watched Britain's innovative sketch comedy series *Monty Python's Flying Circus* on PBS stations in the mid-1970s.

Python writing credit on his résumé," in Miller's view *SNL* might have been inspired by the Pythons but could not adopt many elements of its style due to the other defining aspect of the show: its liveness. "The fact that *Saturday Night* was truly live . . . meant that the televisual production elements so central to the Python attack on the medium could not be used."[11] Yet it was this final factor—the "live" in *Saturday Night Live*—that may arguably have provided the secret sauce of the show's initial and ongoing success.

THE MEANING OF LIVE

By the mid-1970s, little of network prime-time television remained live. The vast majority of shows were shot on film, produced for network broadcast by an increasingly concentrated group of Hollywood studios, which retained rights after an initial airing or two so that a successful show could be released into syndication, where the real money was. Under the newly adopted Financial Interest and Syndication Rules (fin/syn), networks continued to produce a subset of the programs they broadcast, most notably news, talk, and public affairs programs aired outside prime-time hours. *The Tonight Show* was a longtime NBC property, as was *Today* in the early morning slot. *SNL* followed in this tradition, but the idea of returning to a truly live broadcast, especially of a show predicated on the idea of bringing new talent with a countercultural flavor to the airwaves without the safety valve of tape or film, must have caused executives at the network to lose some sleep. And asleep or otherwise engaged is what anxious network executives must have hoped the more easily offended mainstream adult audience would be: *SNL*'s late-night fringe spot on the weekend schedule seemed the only imaginable environment for such an edgy, risk-taking program in that pre-cable era.

What did liveness add to the *Saturday Night* aesthetic? It returned sketch comedy to its roots in live stage and broadcast performance, removing the somewhat calcifying effects that the demands of producing highly syndicatable filmed series for a mainstream audience—call it "sitcomization"—had produced since the 1940s.[12] From the beginning, *SNL* employed many elements of the old, live radio comedy-variety format—structuring features like "Weekend Update," recurring characters, and stable routines, such as the satirizing of political figures—that had helped live programming survive the rigors of serialized production since the 1930s. But it resisted or varied others. Its elimination of a central host in favor of a shifting roster of guest hosts, and its strong roots in ensemble comedy, similar to *Laugh-In* and *Monty Python,* mark differences from the central-personality-driven formats of the past. Likewise its exclusive emphasis on youth-oriented popular music differentiated it from older live performance venues like *The Ed Sullivan Show,* where the Rolling Stones might rub shoulders with Burl Ives. *SNL* became the place on television where the bands and artists the contemporary music audience heard on the radio (and, later, on MTV) could be seen and heard live, with a chance to see them not only perform but clown around a bit with the cast.

Not only does the fact of live performance bring back a "sense of theater missing from prerecorded programming," as Geoffrey Hammill argues, it adds an "element of adventure with each program."[13] This contributes to a sense of the show as an "event" in and of itself, even as it has waxed and waned in popularity over the years. It also remains an unrepeated rarity on network schedules. Few other programs have attempted to replicate the *SNL* formula despite its cultural buzz and critical success. ABC did try to win over declining *SNL* audiences in 1980 with its late-night *Fridays* sketch program (1980–1982), perhaps best remembered today for two of its cast members, Larry David and Michael Richards. When *Nightline* expanded in 1981 and *Fridays* was moved to a later slot, it lost the momentum it had built and was canceled. With the arrival of David Letterman at *Late Night* in 1982—with its strong lead-in from *Tonight*—the late-night talk show field heated up. A variety of would-be competitors cycled through late fringe slots on ABC and CBS in the 1980s and early '90s, including Dick Cavett, Arsenio Hall, Joan Rivers, and Pat Sajak, only to meet with defeat at the hands of NBC's *Tonight/ Late Night* juggernaut.[14] Yet until the end of the classic network period in the 1980s, SNL marked more of a dead end than a revitalized tradition: the last of the long line of live comedy-variety shows. No other broadcast network of the time picked up the gauntlet. The talk show seemed the only kind of late-night program that the other networks dared risk, at least until the advent of competition from cable and new youth-targeted networks in the 1990s.

THE AFTERLIFE OF SNL

It was cable television that finally provided a friendly venue for comedy of all types, beginning with comedy specials on HBO in the 1980s and quickly expanding to basic cable channels like A&E and MTV, and eventually to the dedicated Comedy Channel spun off in 1986. This chapter has focused on *SNL* within the context of broadcasting, treating it in the continuity of radio and television forms. But obviously *SNL* drew on the rise of comedy in many other venues in the 1970s, '80s, and '90s, just as the broadcast comedy-variety format drew on vaudeville. The vaudevillian tradition may have died out in the 1930s, but nightclubs and comedy clubs sprang up in the 1950s and '60s to fill the void. Unlike vaudeville, which was a mainstream venue serving all segments of the audience, the club environment in many ways resembled the late-night fringe hours on television: dark, private, unruly, populated mostly by young adult audiences with a high tolerance for the edgy and outrageous and a low level of interest in the anodyne. By the 1980s, the comedy scene was experiencing a boom, with stand-up comedy at its core. *SNL* both drew from and contributed to this scene. The sketch-derived situation comedy organized around a single comedian flourished as it hadn't since the 1950s—

The Cosby Show (1984–1992), *Roseanne* (1988–1997), *Home Improvement* (1991–1999), *Seinfeld* (1989–1998), to name a few—and the movie business capitalized on the comedy boom as well, with comedian-driven hits like *Caddyshack* (1980), *Ghostbusters* (1984), and the *Airplane* series (1980, 1982). Comedy became a cross-platform enterprise in the 1990s and 2000s, adding online sites like *Funny or Die* in the last decade.

For the comedy-variety genre on network television, however, *SNL* remains unique for its longevity, its format, and above all its live status. The Fox network attempted to revive the comedy-variety format in 1995 with *MADtv*, which combined sketch comedy with musical performances, and arguably with *In Living Color* in 1990, though it excised much of the musical element. Fox even essayed a rare attempt at a live comedy program, the second season of *Roc* in 1992. Yet *Saturday Night Live* lives on in its original form, a television institution. From the arid desert of 1970s late-night schedules to the dense jungle of today's TV offerings at any time of day or night, competing equally with recorded and streamed digital programming, it persists, offering one of the oldest forms of entertainment, always completely new—and live—each week.

Notes

1. These categories are taken from Summers, *A Thirty-Year History of Programs Carried on National Radio Networks.* They are highly provisional in their particulars, but do give a good picture of overall trends.

2. For more on this type of radio comedy, see Wertheim, *Radio Comedy,* and the chapter on comedy in MacDonald, *Don't Touch That Dial!* Sketch comedy is defined as the creation of a humorous setting in which characters interact with each other, as opposed to stand-up comedy, which usually consists of short jokes directed at an audience.

3. See Hilmes, "Femmes Boff Program Toppers." A breezy contemporary account of this transition appeared in Reznik, "A Quick Look into a Gag Factory," X7.

4. This factor is especially apparent in the career of Fanny Brice; see Hilmes, "Fanny Brice and the 'Schnooks' Strategy."

5. Christine Becker discusses the film-to-TV trajectory during this period in *It's The Screen That Got Small,* as does Susan Murray in *Hitch Your Antenna to the Stars.*

6. See Bodroghkozy, "*The Smothers Brothers Comedy Hour* and the 1960s Youth Rebellion"; Carr, "On the Edge of Tastelessness."

7. Jenkins, "Rowan and Martin's Laugh-In."

8. Fischer, "Return of the Pythons."

9. Brown, "B.B.C.'s *Monty Python* Surprise Hit on Public TV," 55.

10. For a succinct overview of this phenomenon, see "Comic LPs" on the PBS companion site to the 2008 documentary series *Make 'Em Laugh: The Funny Business of America,* http://www.pbs.org/wnet/makeemlaugh/episodes/history/comedy-lps/38.

11. Miller, *Something Completely Different*, 162. Miller's book remains definitive for tracing the considerable influence of British programs on American culture. His discussion of the Monty Python phenomenon is particularly insightful.

12. While network prime-time comedy-variety shows could achieve great popularity—most often cited is *The Carol Burnett Show,* which ran on CBS from 1967 to 1978—their decline in the age of cable may result from the "disintermediation" effects of niche programming, so that the constituent parts of the variety format are parceled out to different channels.

13. Hammill, "Saturday Night Live," 14.

14. NBC's long-running dominance in late night may have been due simply to having gotten in first in this fringe period. The number of late-night viewers available at the time was not large enough to sustain more than one national network program, but could be a fairly good source of income for local stations running inexpensive material.

Works Cited

Becker, Christine. *It's the Screen That Got Small: Hollywood Film Stars on 1950s Television.* Middletown, CT: Wesleyan University Press, 2008.

Bodroghkozy, Aniko. "*The Smothers Brothers Comedy Hour* and the 1960s Youth Rebellion." In *The Revolution Wasn't Televised: Sixties Television and Social Conflict,* edited by Lynn Spigel and Michael Curtin. New York: Routledge, 1997.

Brown, Les. "B.B.C.'s *Monty Python* Surprise Hit on Public TV." *New York Times,* March 15, 1975.

Carr, Stephen. "On the Edge of Tastelessness: CBS, the Smothers Brothers, and the Struggle for Control." *Cinema Journal* 31 (Summer 1992):3–24.

Fischer, Theodore. "Return of the Pythons: Their PBS Premiere." *Current,* December 19, 2005, http://www.current.org/prog/prog0523python.shtml.

Hammill, Geoffrey. "Saturday Night Live." In *The Encyclopedia of Television,* edited by Horace Newcomb, 2008–2014. New York: Fitzroy Dearborn, 2004.

Hilmes, Michele. "Fanny Brice and the 'Schnooks' Strategy: Negotiating a Feminine Comic Persona on the Air." *Spectator* 25 (June 2005):11–25.

———. "'Femmes Boff Program Toppers': Women Break into Prime Time, 1943–1948." In *Transmitting the Past: Historical and Cultural Perspectives on Broadcasting,* edited by Emmett Winn and Susan L. Brinson. Tuscaloosa: University of Alabama Press, 2005.

Jenkins, Henry. "Rowan and Martin's Laugh-In." In *The Encyclopedia of Television,* edited by Horace Newcomb, 1967–1969. New York: Fitzroy Dearborn, 2004.

MacDonald, J. Fred. *Don't Touch That Dial!: Radio Programming in American Life, 1920–1960.* Chicago: Nelson Hall, 1979.

Miller, Jeffrey. *Something Completely Different: British Television and American Culture.* Minneapolis: University of Minnesota Press, 2000.

Murray, Susan. *Hitch Your Antenna to the Stars: Early Television and Broadcast Stardom.* New York: Routledge, 2005.

Reznik, Sidney. "A Quick Look into a Gag Factory." *New York Times,* May 9, 1943.

Summers, Harrison B. *A Thirty-Year History of Programs Carried on National Radio Networks in the United States, 1926–1956.* Salem, NH: Ayer, 1993.

Wertheim, Arthur Frank. *Radio Comedy.* New York: Oxford University Press, 1979.

"Live from New York!"

SUSAN MURRAY

"Live from New York . . . it's Saturday night!" is the shouted phrase that has transitioned *Saturday Night Live* viewers from opening sketch to title sequence for more than thirty-five years. It signals the end of a closed fictional moment and initiates direct address, reflexivity, and the spontaneity of liveness, while also highlighting the show's connection to New York City, which is underscored by images of the city's street life at night (diners, taxis, shops, newsstands, bridges, parks, bars, etc.) that run during the title sequence.

But these moments are not *SNL*'s only references to the city, of course. In everything from the setting of sketches, the abundance of New York–centric jokes and references, and the casting of the hosts (Mayors Ed Koch and Rudy Giuliani both hosted the show while in office), the city has always loomed large. And yet, one of the most intriguing references to New York is both intertextual and historical: New York's former position as the center of television production in the 1940s and '50s and, more specifically, the live variety and sketch comedy shows produced there during that period. This chapter will explore the ways that *SNL* refers to and constructs a sense of New York and urban night life through textual references, casting, and setting as well as through its historical relationship to the city and live performance (variety shows, night club comedy, vaudeville, legitimate theater, and radio and television production pre-1960) and the impact that those references had on the program's reception during its first years on the air. By focusing largely on the mid-1970s, a time when both the city and NBC were struggling, we can see how *SNL*'s New York backdrop and sensibility were deployed to create a space where New York, television comedy, and NBC were all subtly (and sometimes not so subtly) rebranded, pleasing critics and city officials alike.

The year 1975, when *SNL* premiered, was a time of crisis for both NBC and the city of New York. After decades of maintaining its position as America's premier network, NBC found itself floundering in the early to mid-1970s, battling for second place in the ratings and lacking a clear brand identity. ABC, which eventually surpassed NBC in the ratings in the latter half of the decade, was being lambasted by critics for mixing sexuality with lowbrow sitcoms and violent dramas and was often pointed to as the worst example of a network sacrificing quality to pander to the masses. However, NBC was criticized too, particularly for its failed attempts to attract younger viewers to its network with programming that lacked the quality that many critics found in successful CBS programs such as *All in the Family* (1971–1979) and *The Mary Tyler Moore Show* (1970–1977). At the start of the 1975 season, NBC had rolled out nine new prime-time programs, and not one survived to see a second season. The network's only solid night was Friday, which featured four of its most watched series: *Sanford and Son* (1972–1977), *Chico and the Man* (1974–1978), *The Rockford Files* (1974–1980), and *Police Woman* (1974–1978).[1]

The title of John Leonard's *New York Times* review of the 1975 fall season, "The Worst Television Season, Ever, Ever, Ever," encapsulated the prevailing sentiment of critics about what they were seeing on the networks, especially ABC and NBC, that year:

> Every year about this time somebody climbs into the pulpit, fixes a baleful eye on the congregation, and sermonizes: this is the worst new TV season in the memory of vertebrates. I've been hearing this autumnal dirge, and occasionally singing it myself for at least a decade. And now at last it's true, and we've used up all our adjectives, and sitting down to this assignment is like sitting down to a plate of congealed moose brains.[2]

Harboring similarly strong feelings of disgust and frustration, Gary Deeb of the *Chicago Tribune* wrote, "The 1975–76 season is barely 10 weeks old, and yet even a casual observer can plainly see that the roof has caved in on the networks."[3] While it was often noted that there was quality to be found on CBS, particularly with the Norman Lear and MTM sit-coms, certain critics found much of the programming on network tele-vision to be too dumbed down, flat, sleazy, sexy, violent, or exploitative. Certainly the emphasis that ABC put on "kid vid" programming (which sought to simultaneously capture a very young audience and the adult mass audience) was part of the problem as was the apparently vacuous nature of what was often referred to as "jiggle TV."[4] To critics, the net-works (especially NBC) appeared desperate as they failed to capture the audience share they needed in order to please advertisers and sustain their programming schedules. Leonard wanted to believe that audiences were fed up with the low quality of programming as well, and that is why, he claimed, they were turning off their sets in droves: "Perhaps the American public is to be congratulated. Perhaps a certain healthy surli-ness is reasserting itself, a therapeutic disinclination to be cutesied into numbdom." Leonard was correct that older viewers—who had formed the base of NBC's audience, at least—were turning off their sets, or at least turning the channel. However, contrary to what Leonard and other critics seemed to want to believe, Fred Silverman's infamous program-ming strategies at ABC did eventually (after a disastrous 1974 season and start of the 1975 season) work to attract younger viewers in droves, and by the spring of 1976, ABC had overtaken CBS for the number one position in the ratings.[5] Nevertheless, in October 1975 Leonard ended his scath-ing review/call to arms by saying, "the new TV season, as entertainment, falls somewhere between reading [an] analysis of New York City's fiscal crisis and reruns of *The Monkees*."[6]

As Leonard's topical analogy hinted, New York City was in even worse shape than NBC in the mid-1970s. The 1975 fiscal crisis there was historically bad in terms of its breadth and depth. The city had borrowed for many years and had used questionable accounting practices to hide some of its debts. It was revealed in the spring of 1975 that those debts had grown to $14 billion; New York was simply out of money and was now in serious danger of default. In order to meet payroll, the city was actually taking out short-term loans (sometimes of only three days' length) from banks and its own pension funds. It was obviously an untenable situa-tion, yet Mayor Abe Beame and his administration continued to deny the seriousness of the problem until the New York State Assembly was forced in September to put the city under the receivership of the newly created Emergency Financial Control Board. In the end, the federal government had to step in with large loans to the city in order to stave off bankruptcy. New York was, in the parlance of 2008–2009, too big to fail, and somebody had to intervene to save it and to prevent any further damage it might do to the larger U.S. financial system.

The fiscal crisis meant that schools, hospitals, public transportation, and other city-run organizations were barely able to function. Crime and unemployment rates were higher than the rest of the country's and the city appeared to many as scarier, dirtier, and more ruinous than at any other point in its history. As Miriam Greenberg points out in her engaging book on the branding of New York during this period, the city was suffering from a major "image crisis" that was "exacerbating the city's wider economic decline."[7] Tourism was down as were real estate prices and investor confidence. As Greenberg argues, it wasn't until the city turned to marketing and media to rebrand itself that New York began its recovery a few years later.

It was in this context of a city in crisis and a network searching for a way to brand itself that *SNL* first aired. After the program's cold open and the "Live from New York!" cry, *SNL*'s title sequence showcased still photos of NYC at night: hot dog carts, newsstands, taxis, restaurants, night clubs, Coney Island, smiling New Yorkers, subway entrances, cigar shops, police officers posing for the camera, and finally the neon lights of Radio City. In the opening, the city at night seemed alive and exciting, rather than appearing to be the dangerous and decaying place of many tourists' fears—an image that had been reinforced by news reports, popular films, and television of the period. A number of films released in the early to mid-1970s used New York City as a dark, nefarious, often nightmarish backdrop to explore crime, poverty, vigilantism, gang warfare, and other issues. *Mean Streets* (1973), *Death Wish* (1974), *The Taking of Pelham One Two Three* (1974), *Dog Day Afternoon* (1975), and *Taxi Driver* (1976) were just a few of the dramatic films to use New York in this way, but even movies like Neil Simon's black comedy *The Prisoner of Second Avenue* (1975) played off New York's reputation as a city on the verge. On television, the city had become the butt of many jokes that referenced muggings, graffiti, and other aspects of New York's decline and dysfunction, and the Association for a Better New York (which had established its "Big Apple" branding campaign in 1971) had been meeting

Figures 2.1–2.2. *SNL*'s opening credits worked hard to locate the program in New York City.

with station and network heads around that time in an attempt to put a halt to such jokes.[8] While *SNL* didn't always present the city in a positive light, it did offer a reminder of the excitement that the city and its artists and performers had to offer—especially in regard to live performance. The show's gritty (but not scary) New York setting also provided a backdrop that was distinct from the majority of the period's prime-time network fare and marked *SNL* as belonging to a separate, late-night space in which raunchy, transgressive, or risky material was more fitting.

Of course, the impressions of New York that audiences and critics had during the 1970s were not limited to those of urban decay and crisis. The glamorous New York of the postwar era was also an active component of cultural ideas and memories about the city and were often mobilized to highlight its relatively recent (and seemingly rapid) decline. For critics especially, the production of live television in New York was connected to memories of early variety shows; Golden Age live anthology dramas;[9] former NBC president Pat Weaver's emphasis on bringing together liveness, sophistication, and education; and the production of an intellectual, liberal, urban, "New York sensibility." These ideas were often put in stark contrast to beliefs about the tastes and culture of middle America—and middle American audiences specifically—that were held by critics and network executives alike.[10] In fact, much of the dismay expressed by critics during this time may be related to the belief that the networks—ABC and NBC in particular—had long ago moved their focus away from urbane tastes and interests and were now only engaged in producing shows that could attract the masses. Networks had also lost interest in live prime-time programming, and the majority of their programming during this period was recorded on videotape. In its liveness and New Yorkness alone (not to mention its young cast and fresh version of sketch comedy) *SNL* was an anomaly in 1970s television.

There was another live variety show that premiered in the fall of 1975, and it bore a strikingly similar title to *SNL*. *Saturday Night Live with Howard Cosell*, which was produced by Roone Arledge, the creator of *Monday Night Football* and many other sports programs, was slaughtered by the critics right out of the gate. There seemed to be a multitude of problems with the show, but what stood out to critics was its lack of understanding of the qualities both of live television and of the variety genre. Sander Vanocur, writing for the *Washington Post,* commented,

"The show is bad. It has been bad live and it has been bad taped. It comes to us from the Ed Sullivan Theater in New York. That is the only resemblance it bears to what was for 20 years television's best variety show."[11] Comparatively, NBC's *Saturday Night* (renamed *Saturday Night Live* after Cosell's show was canceled in early 1976), seemed to tap into the historical features of live variety and New York night life that had worked so well for television during its early days. Tom Shales of the *Washington Post* wrote of the show in 1977: "Partly it may be that the excitement of rediscovering real television is as energizing for them as it is for viewers. *Saturday Night* has considerably broadened the scope and sharpened the bite of TV humor (and is widely if feebly imitated), but its real contribution could be in taking TV back to its live, real-time, you-are-there origins."[12]

In this review, Shales could be referring to television's "origins" as either the period from the late 1940s until the early 1950s when almost all programming was live from New York; more specifically the popularity of variety shows during that time; or what some consider to be the pinnacle of quality television, the live anthology dramas of the 1950s. Two years later, Shales directly referred to the anthology dramas in an *SNL* review with his reference to the "Golden Era": "The program not only brought new audiences to television, it also has been a source of invention and rejuvenation for the medium: a throwback in the most productive sense. It begins with words that carried great weight in TV's Golden Era—'Live, from New York'—and it has remained true to its goals and reluctant to pander even to its fans. It is a reminder that Television Done Right can be as splendid as anything."[13]

I would argue that such praise could reflect certain critics' distaste for the relatively recent adoption of videotape for prime-time productions. In the early years of commercial television in the United States (mid-1940s until the early 1950s), most programs were broadcast live both out of necessity and as a result of long-standing beliefs about the connections between live production and quality in broadcasting, which had carried over from radio.[14] (Kinescope recordings were used primarily to distribute live events to different time zones and to keep for posterity.) By the early to mid-1950s, the introduction of telefilm established a new measure of quality to the TV image—one that was more cinematic, highly standardized, and easily reproducible. By the 1970s, videotape became a popular option for television producers and had surpassed telefilm as the go-to technology for recording. Telefilm was still used for programs that were considered to be high quality in other ways, and live television broadcasts were primarily for news and sports programming. Video, a less expensive production method than film, was considered by some to be more aesthetically flat and less visually engaging than film or live broadcasting. During the mid-1970s there was discussion among some television and cultural critics about the relationship between the use of videotape and the decline of quality in programming.[15] Compared to live broadcasts, and even telefilm, video could sometimes appear quite "dead"—flat or false. In a 1978 interview with *Rolling Stone,* Lorne Michaels said, "Tape? No way! Live laughter from an audience is real, it's theater. With tape you've got to fake it, postsync it, it sounds dead, canned, like laugh tracks. . . . Look, what's occurring here already is a fucking technological miracle—that we have not slipped back into being 'television.'"[16]

In the context of this growing use of video, performing live from New York was, to many, a welcome return to older styles of performance—specifically to the late 1940s, early 1950s variety genre—and to the heyday of live television production. Liveness carries distinct connections to the genres of variety and anthology drama, and both are related to New York's performance history and style and its location for production. During the postwar era, New York–produced variety was a format that seemed to make the most out of liveness—allowing for the pleasures and excitement of spontaneity while activating nostalgia for live vaudeville. Many variety programs also offered audiences an urban, east coast sensibility that was often a bit "blue" and riddled with New York–centric jokes and references as well as an overt New York sensibility. This was partly due to the fact that New York City was, at the time, the home of broadcasting production and business as well as the center of live theater. It was also likely a consequence of the 1948–1952 freeze on licenses that stalled the expansion of stations and left the audience largely concentrated in urban areas, primarily on the east coast. That would change after the freeze was lifted, the use of telefilm became popular, and the production of television programming moved to Hollywood. By the mid-1950s, live entertainment programming was almost exclusively associated with quality through the critical reception of the live anthology programs—many of which were broadcast from New York—that were considered to be a grand meeting between Broadway and the best qualities of the medium of television.[17]

While some television programming was produced in New York during the 1960s and '70s (e.g., network evening news, soap operas, a few prime-time comedies and dramas), the majority of prime-time programming had moved to Hollywood because New York's real estate, cramped studios, and urban landscape were not as flexible, cost effective, or expansive as those old Hollywood back lots put to use by independent television production companies.[18] As *Rolling Stone* noted in 1979, Lorne Michaels insisted on doing *SNL* from New York (in NBC's Studio 8H) even though "the show costs much more to do in New York than in L.A., there aren't the big sound stages here, and sets have to be built in Brooklyn and transported."[19] Herbert Schlosser, VP of programming at NBC at the time, who had an idea for a late-night, New York–based variety show even before Michaels was on board, explained, "I wanted to do the show live if possible, and I wanted to do it in New York City, because New York had lost all of its entertainment shows. Everything had moved to Burbank. Even Carson."[20] New York was a return, not just to a location, but to a production and performance style deeply entwined with New York's historical role in the development of broadcast entertainment.

SNL referenced the New York–produced live variety shows in an era in which variety programs were still on prime-time television, but were considered to be in danger of dying off. *SNL* is most often considered a sketch comedy show since its primary focus is on a series of (often recurring) sketches and part of its origins can be traced to the Chicago-based Second City tradition. However, the structure of the program has the typical characteristics of classic variety—mixing musical numbers with comedy acts, sketches, and a host who opens with a monologue on a proscenium stage in front of a live audience and then performs from that position throughout the program. For example, in the first episode on October 11, 1975, George Carlin as host opened the program with his stand-up monologue and then continued his routine in between the musical acts, commercial parodies, filmed bits, and sketches. While his comedy was exceptionally modern in comparison to that of 1950s variety hosts such as Milton Berle, Carlin's comedy employed classic double entendres and toned-down night club material.

The performances of early *SNL* players also often harked back to early traditions of television variety comedy. Chevy Chase is perhaps the most obvious example, as he became famous for performing classic vaudeville-inspired physical comedy and pratfalls. Gilda Radner, who became an audience favorite for her impersonations of such celebrities as Barbara Walters and for her creation of original characters such as Rose-anne Roseannadanna, was a gifted physical comedian who could also engage in complicated verbal play and broad humor simultaneously. Again, these performers' comedy had a modern flair and interpretation, while also relying on traditional vaudeville tropes and styles.

The cast of *SNL* was obviously too young to have had experience on the vaudeville circuit, which had largely died out thirty to forty years prior, but many of them trained with well-known comedy or improv groups like Second City. And yet, another link they had to vaudeville-type performance and postwar variety performance was the freedom that late night afforded in terms of the content of their comedy. Bawdy, dark, sometimes violent jokes and sketches were aired in *SNL*'s early days; while garnering attention from critics and audiences, they did not attract much more than a raised eyebrow and some expressed caution from in-house censors.[21] Variety comedians in the postwar era, who were on the air during prime time, often used double entendres and the live visuality of television to get around censors' concerns. But beyond the wink-and-a-nudge routine, these early comedians were also understood to be performing to an audience familiar with and appreciative of a more urban sensibility, including a taste for a range of humor from vaudeville, night clubs, and burlesque houses. When television began to spread deeper into middle America and the coastal suburbs in the mid-1950s, the networks and sponsors became more concerned about not offending non-urban sensibilities, and some of the more burlesque aspects of television comedy began to die out.

The 1970s was a far more permissive era than the 1950s, and standards for prime-time content had already been pushed to include some swearing, more sex, and the exploration of potentially controversial political and social subjects. However, the majority of programming in the mid-1970s was playing it relatively safe. In an article about the often risqué and innovative humor of *SNL*, Tom Shales wrote, "Bad taste? Some viewers might think so. But the show's audacity is refreshing in a medium obsessed with the fear of offending anybody."[22] A few years later, he also noted: "People who tune in to *Saturday Night Live* know that there is at least a chance that something wild and exhilarating and daring will happen. People tuning in to prime time know it is virtually hopeless. In addition, the program's late berth seems to provide a natural defense against the network censors, who allow material that wouldn't possibly get on between 8 and 11 PM, when Mr. and Mrs. American and their 2.3 kiddies are watching."[23]

Spontaneity, liveness, and a late-night/night club environment combined to imbue *SNL* with strong connections to the history of television and performance in New York City while the show also appeared fresh, as something new for a time in which the networks were struggling to reach the youth audience. At the same time, NBC was also attempting to maintain its audience base, which was for the most part understood to be "Mr. and Mrs. American"—those square family folks with bland tastes and delicate sensibilities living in middle America far from the sophisticated east coast intellectual crowd. *SNL*'s fringe time slot enabled the network to create an "adult" space where the program could touch on mature themes and language without the risk of alienating more traditional viewers.

Throughout the rest of the 1970s as New York City slowly recovered from its financial crisis, *SNL* continued to participate in the city's rebranding. For example, Miriam Greenberg notes that some of the program's stars, such as Gilda Radner, were recruited to participate in the I ♥ NY campaign, which began in 1977.[24] And, during the first episode of the 1978 season, Mayor Ed Koch spoke directly to the nation about the fiscal crisis and about the city's "renaissance":

> How'm I doin'?! [pause for cheers and applause] I'm delighted to be here to, uh, welcome *Saturday Night Live* back to New York. This is the fourth season and we want them to know how grateful we are that they're here in this great city. [applause] I'm on this for, really, two reasons. One is to speak to the nation. We here in New York want to tell those of you in other states how much we appreciate what you did for it when we were down and out and needed your help—and you came through! We want to say to all of those of you out there: Thanks for the loan—you won't be sorry! [applause] New York City is a great place in which to live. We're very lucky those of us who are here, but this city belongs to everybody and we are going through a great renaissance. *Saturday Night* is one reason

for this renaissance—an insignificant reason, but a reason nevertheless. The people on this show, they could have chosen to go elsewhere but they came here, to New York City instead of Pittsburgh, Denver, Newark.... Some could probably even get work in Hollywood.[25]

Mayor Koch then continued with a bit where he honored John Belushi with a New York City Certificate of Merit, but Belushi acted disappointed, since he was hoping for keys to the city.

Koch's 1978 appearance was doing similar work to the I ♥ NY campaign, while also directly addressing the city's problems and the issue of a national loan. Koch appeared on *SNL* again in 1984 in a commercial parody entitled "Mayor Koch's Neighborhood" that played off of NYC's increasingly outdated image and Koch's role in resolving its fiscal and public relations crises.

It's clear that through its overt references to the city and its intertextual references to the history of live performance and to New York as television's production center during the medium's Golden Age, *SNL* played a central role in the rebranding of New York City and NBC during the 1970s. As the program grew to become one of NBC's most successful and long-lasting programming staples over the years, New York continued to play a large role in *SNL*'s production and reception.

CONCLUSION

As the city and its image changed over the decades, so too did *SNL*'s references to it. One place that this occurred was in the changing images in and references made by the title sequences. By the 1980s, much of the grit and graffiti were replaced by images of a cleaned-up Reagan-era New York. In the opening sequence for the 1984 season, for example, the cast members stood in the midst of a model version of the city, moving the subway cars around, using the top of the Chrysler building as a lighter, and so on. The following year, the city was seen from the view of a limousine as it traveled from the airport, past the Plaza hotel, through Times Square, and arrived at Rockefeller Center. This last example is especially significant because it depicted the gaze of a tourist or guest performer on the show, rather than being from the point of view of a New Yorker or street photographer capturing the everyday people of the city. The tourist who had been too afraid to come to New York City in the 1970s would have a very different impression as she traveled in style and comfort through a rebranded and cleaned-up New York. This short video clip was representative of the ultimate goal of the I ♥ NY campaign, which was "used in a new model of economic recovery that emphasized short-term strategies like city branding and incentives for business over and above long-term investments in public infrastructure, collective consumption, and the support of a mixed economic base."[26]

Like Koch, a number of other New York City mayors have used *SNL* directly as a public relations and city branding tool via their appearances on the show, as either hosts or guests. Their appearances on the program have served to remind viewers of *SNL*'s connection to the economics and culture of the city and to mobilize that connection for specific political ends. For example, Rudolph Giuliani took full advantage of *SNL*'s location, hosting the show multiple times in the late 1990s and then appearing again in October 2001 on the first episode that aired after the events of 9/11. Standing on stage alongside police, fire, and rescue workers and Fire Commissioner Thomas Von Essen and Police Commissioner Bernard Kerik, Mayor Giuliani started by stating simply, "Well, these are the heroes." After addressing the accomplishments of the fire and police departments, Giuliani placed *Saturday Night Live* into the "back to business or the terrorists win" discourse of the moment, stating, "New Yorkers are unified. We will not yield to terrorism. We will not let our decisions be made out of fear. We choose to live our lives in freedom." And then there was the following exchange between him and Lorne Michaels:

> Giuliani: *Saturday Night Live* is one of our great New York City institutions, so that's why it's important for you to do your show tonight.
> Michaels: Can we be funny?
> Giuliani: Why start now? [pause] Live from New York, it's Saturday night![27]

In the immediate weeks after the attack on the World Trade Center, the television industry found it difficult to simply return to its flow and routines. Comedy felt especially awkward, since many wondered if it was appropriate or even possible to laugh after the nation had undergone such terrible trauma. In the above opening, *SNL* was both attaching itself to the images of the heroes and of a heroic New York City, and asking permission from the mayor to proceed with comedy.

The city's current mayor, Mike Bloomberg, has not been on the show, but he was mocked when he was played by Fred Armisen in a skit about his (rather inept) handling of the blizzard of January 2011. New York governor David Paterson had also been made fun of in a series of skits by Armisen on "Weekend Update" and eventually appeared on the show sitting next to Armisen (in his Paterson makeup) at the "Weekend Update" desk.

These appearances by New York officials are occasions in which overt references are made to the city and its connection to *SNL,* which serves as a reminder of the ties between the mayor's office and the use of New York City for television and film production and, once again, highlights the historical origination of the weekly live broadcast. Few programs have been able to so successfully combine the use of live New York production with the variety/sketch format and survive for so long. After over thirty-five years on the air, *Saturday Night Live* and New York City have become so intertwined in the minds of contemporary audiences that it is impossible for almost anyone to imagine separating the program from the city. "Live from New York . . ." hardly needs to be used to open the show any longer, except that it is a tradition that reminds us both of postwar television history and of the dearth of live entertainment currently on air.

Notes

1. See "1975 NBC Fall Line-up Promo Special," http://www.archive.org/details/1975NBC.

2. Leonard, "The Worst Television Season, Ever, Ever, Ever," 131.

3. Deeb, "NBC Puts New Wine in Old Bottles," B13.

4. For more on this, see Levine, *Wallowing in Sex.*

5. See "Television: Struggling to Leave the Cellar"; "Television: The Hot Network."

6. Leonard, "The Worst Television Season, Ever, Ever, Ever."

7. Greenberg, *Branding New York,* 9.

8. Ibid., 120.

9. A 1950s television genre often praised for offering viewers theater-quality programming via live broadcasts of highbrow teleplays.

10. For more on this, see Johnson, *Heartland TV.*

11. Vanocur, "A Live Show, a Deadly Bore," 1.

12. Shales, "*Saturday Night:* A Show the Peacock Can Crow About," B1.

13. Shales, "*Saturday Night:* Finally Ready for Prime Time," D6.

14. I cannot go into more of this historical discussion here, but this belief can, at the very least, be located materially in the distinctions between classes of license, which

privileged live broadcasts as a marker of quality programming for radio stations as early as the 1920s.

15. For an interesting take on this issue, see Leonard, "Vidcult," 83.

16. Partridge, *Rolling Stone Visits Saturday Night Live*, 33.

17. For more on this, see Murray, *Hitch Your Antenna to the Stars*.

18. "TV a Medium in Need of Space." New York City was struggling to attract more film and television productions in the 1970s. As Greenberg points out (*Branding New York*, 150), Mayor John Lindsay's creation of the Mayor's Office of Television, Broadcasting and Film in 1966 (which streamlined the permit process thereby making shooting in the city easier and cheaper) helped revive New York City–based productions, especially films. Greenberg argues that the fact that forty-six films were shot in the city in 1975 speaks not only to its success in attracting film producers, but also to the idea that New York provided the ideal backdrop for films about urban crisis and gritty street life—exactly the types of films which were, ironically, damaging to the city's image and to its tourism industry.

19. Partridge, *Rolling Stone Visits Saturday Night Live*, 33.

20. Qtd. in Shales and Miller, *Live from New York*, 24–25.

21. Although, soon after the first show aired, the network did decide to put the program on a six-second delay in case anything too inappropriate slipped out spontaneously.

22. Shales, "Zingers on Saturday Night: Hidden World," A19.

23. Shales, "Don't Get Outta Here, Bill Murray," B1.

24. Greenberg, *Branding New York*, 210.

25. *Saturday Night Live*, season 4, ep. 1, orig. airdate: October 7, 1978.

26. Greenberg, *Branding New York*, 224.

27. *Saturday Night Live*, season 27, ep. 1, orig. airdate: September 29, 2001.

Works Cited

Deeb, Gary. "NBC Puts New Wine in Old Bottles." *Chicago Tribune*, November 20, 1975.

Greenberg, Miriam. *Branding New York: How a City in Crisis Was Sold to the World*. New York: Routledge, 2008.

Johnson, Victoria E. *Heartland TV: Prime Time Television and the Struggle for U.S. Identity*. New York: New York University Press, 2008.

Leonard, John. "Vidcult—When Video Becomes Our Culture." *New York Times*, August 15, 1976.

———. "The Worst Television Season, Ever, Ever, Ever." *New York Times*, October 26, 1975.

Levine, Elana. *Wallowing in Sex: The Sexual Culture of 1970s American Television*. Durham, NC: Duke University Press, 2007.

Murray, Susan. *Hitch Your Antenna to the Stars: Early Television and Broadcast Stardom*. New York: Routledge, 2005.

Partridge, Marianne, ed. *Rolling Stone Visits Saturday Night Live*. New York: Dolphin, 1979.

Shales, Tom. "Don't Get Outta Here, Bill Murray: The Saturday Night Whackos, Waiting for Freddie, with Noogies." *Washington Post*, May 31, 1978.

————. *Saturday Night:* A Show the Peacock Can Crow About." *Washington Post,* September 28, 1977.

————. *Saturday Night:* Finally Ready for Prime Time." *Washington Post,* January 10, 1979.

————. "Zingers on Saturday Night: Hidden World." *Washington Post,* November 8, 1975.

Shales, Tom, and Andrew Miller. *Live from New York: An Uncensored History of Saturday Night Live.* Boston: Little, Brown, 2002.

"Television: Struggling to Leave the Cellar." *Time,* May 14, 1979.

"Television: The Hot Network." *Time,* March 15, 1976.

"TV a Medium in Need of Space." *New York Times,* March 26, 1978.

Vanocur, Sander. "A Live Show, a Deadly Bore." *Washington Post,* November 23, 1975.

Michael O'Donoghue, Experimental Television Comedy, and *Saturday Night Live*'s Authorship

EVAN ELKINS

One hour into the November 8, 1975, episode of *NBC's Saturday Night,* the new late-night variety show that would later become *Saturday Night Live,* head writer and featured player Michael O'Donoghue walked into the frame and picked up a pay phone. On the other end of the phone, cast member Laraine Newman was playing an airline customer-service operator. O'Donoghue said to her:

> Do you know what I'd like to do to you, lady? I'd like to stick tacks in your neck. Then I'd like to take a chain saw and run it down your spine. Then I'd like to throw garbage at your face. Then I'd like to rent a truck, fill it full of scrap metal and park it on your kneecaps. Then I'd like to hit you in the lungs with a shovel, throw more garbage at your face, and then I'd like to lop off your thumbs with a grapefruit knife. Good-bye.

Newman replied meekly, "Thank you for calling Trans-American Airlines," and hung up the phone, ending the sketch. The studio audience, which generally laughed audibly at least once per sketch, sounded uncomfortable during O'Donoghue's rant. Considering *SNL's*[1] current role as a relatively predictable television comedy institution, such violent and distinctly unfunny material seems contrary to what we might expect from the program even as tales of its early, experimental phase continue to circulate.

This chapter uses O'Donoghue and *SNL*'s early experimental humor as means to interrogate publicly circulated ideas surrounding the program's authorship. O'Donoghue's work as the show's head writer during 1975–1978 and again during 1980–1981 was a high-profile mainstreaming of experimental comedy on American television and serves as a window through which we can begin to analyze the practical and discursive roles of the comedy writer in what has often been considered a producer's medium (with "the comedy writer" here referring to O'Donoghue specifically as well as to television comedy writers more generally). In addition to presenting subversive comedic content, O'Donoghue's aesthetically and politically disruptive sketches and onscreen appearances articulate moments of contested authorship that undermine the idea that show creator and executive producer Lorne Michaels is the show's singular or primary author. In reassessing the performative and aesthetic practices of a period in *SNL*'s history that has been increasingly treated as a historical artifact, I highlight the ways the show's stylistic and authorial variability, exemplified here by O'Donoghue's work, has been subsumed under a vision of *SNL* as Michaels's property.

AUTHORING *SATURDAY NIGHT LIVE*

Publicly expressed authorship often presents a paratextual frame for comic entertainment, and comedy fans have long expressed interest in the creative practices of humor writing and the idealized persona of the comedy writer. Today, a fascination with comic craft is apparent in online comedy fan communities like aspecialthing.com, the proliferation of comedy podcasts such as *Comedy Bang! Bang!* and Marc Maron's *WTF*, and the publication of Mike Sacks's *And Here's the Kicker: Conversations with 21 Top Humor Writers on Their Craft*, which contains interviews with well-known humorists and "quick and painless advice" for aspiring comedy writers. This interest in the comedian/comedy writer has long made good fodder for television, exemplified by *The Dick Van Dyke Show* (1961–1966), *Seinfeld* (1989–1998), *The Larry Sanders Show* (1992–1998), the ascension of Conan O'Brien from writer for *SNL* and *The Simpsons* to late-night celebrity, and the 2006 premieres of *30 Rock* (2006–2013) and *Studio 60 on the Sunset Strip* (2006–2007). Regarding *SNL* in particular, writer-performers Jay Mohr and Tom Davis have each released memoirs detailing their time at the program,[2] and subsequent *SNL* writers like Robert Smigel, Bob Odenkirk, Tina Fey, Jim Downey, and Al Franken have achieved notoriety ranging from cult followings to bona fide stardom.

Although motivated in part by a demand for backstage gossip, continued interest in the comedy writer's work also speaks to a desire to unmask some of the vagaries of comedy production, thereby accessing a more complex view of entertainment's creative processes. Such representations feed a long-standing proclivity among comedy fans to celebrate and fetishize the role of the comedy writer and the space of the writers room.[3] Many of these writers maintain publicly circulated images as cerebral, rebellious, and distinctly creative figures in the mass media industries. Tales of *SNL*'s week-to-week creation promote a comedy production culture evocative of John Thornton Caldwell's description of the "bad-boy" producer-showrunner as "locked in a bunker surrounded by male teenage memorabilia, rock-and-roll pretense, and an impressively odd intellectual pedigree formed by combinations of high culture, low culture, prestige, and kitsch."[4] The comedy writer has long been constructed as a distinctly volatile and idiosyncratic character, and the writers room is often revealed as a hostile environment. From *SNL* and *The Daily Show with Jon Stewart* (1999–present) to *Your Show of Shows* (1950–1954) and *Friends* (1994–2004), accounts of the television comedy writers room characterize the space as a raucous, misogynist boys club that creates an atmosphere of harassment and discomfort.[5]

Regarding O'Donoghue, histories of *SNL* and *National Lampoon* (the satirical magazine for which he wrote before arriving at *SNL*) often detail his violent temper and theatrical outbursts. In one particularly notable tale, he is said to have spray-painted the word "danger" onto a Rockefeller Center wall during a writers meeting, pointing out that this is what the show lacked at the time.[6] Renouncing the cult appeal long held by bad-boy comedy writers, *Entertainment Weekly* critic Ken Tucker suggests that O'Donoghue began one of *SNL*'s "worst legacies . . . the myth of the writer as taboo breaker. What he really was was a smug potty mouth."[7] While such tales perhaps maintain appeal for those invested in the image of network television as a stifling, anti-creative bureaucracy, they also cultivate a cultural representation of the out-of-control writer in need of discipline and restraint.

Stories of destruction, fighting, collaboration, and cocaine-fueled all-night writing sessions abound in the program's lurid backstage histories, which have well documented the struggles accompanying television's "negotiated and collective authorship."[8] Few television programs have been historicized and mythologized as often as *Saturday Night Live*, and a fascination with the program's creative processes was apparent even at the beginning of its run. In 1977, Avon Books published a companion to the program containing photographs of the cast and crew, reproductions of script pages, and fictional, comical correspondence among cast members, writers, guest hosts, and Michaels.[9] Two years later, *Rolling Stone* magazine published a compilation of its various stories about the program as well as some articles written solely for the book, including a backstage look at the first season's production, a short piece on the writers, and interviews with every cast member and O'Donoghue.[10] The subsequent years have seen several best-of video compilations and a handful of retrospectives, including *Saturday Night Live Backstage*, a two-hour special broadcast on NBC in February 2011.

While it overstates the case to suggest that O'Donoghue and *SNL*'s writers have been ignored in public discourse about the program, these historical and contemporary accounts usually present *SNL* as Michaels's property. Even as early as 1977, the popular press invested in auteurist mythmaking, with the *Washington Post* referring to Michaels as "the late-night Orson Welles of latter-day television."[11] More recently, the *Hollywood Reporter* referred to him as NBC late-night's "all-powerful Oz" ruling over his *SNL* "empire," and *Variety* named him one of American television's fifteen "movers and shakers" alongside individuals like David Sarnoff, Norman Lear, and Ted Turner.[12] Additionally, the 1995 coffee-table book *Saturday Night Live: The First Twenty Years* contains a foreword by Michaels,[13] and *Saturday Night Live Transcripts*, the unofficial online resource for transcriptions of *SNL* content, begins its summary of the program's genesis with "Lorne Michaels had a vision: to bring live late-night comedy/variety to television."[14] The now-definitive volume on the show, Tom Shales and James Andrew Miller's dishy oral history, *Live from New York*, closes with an entire chapter on Michaels even as its oral-history format provides a dialogic look at the inner workings of *SNL*. In this chapter, several figures associated with the program offer a range of thoughts and opinions on the executive producer. Even as this account presents an often complex and contradictory view of him, the theme of Michaels-as-father-figure is common.

Michaels was also ubiquitous in *SNL*'s typically self-mythologizing twenty-fifth anniversary special in 1999, although this particular special was notable for a *Saturday TV Funhouse* cartoon written by Robert Smigel that satirized Michaels's dominance over the program. In this sustained jab at his control of the show, an animated Michaels bores his audience with a speech about the history of the program, hawks *SNL* merchandise, and sings a song about his dictatorial reign. The cartoon ends with Michaels belting out the line "'Cause it's my show!" and holding the last word until the building collapses around him. An easy reading of this cartoon is that Smigel, an *SNL* writer and thus the very figure whom Michaels would overshadow, vented his frustrations in a scathing attack on Michaels's management of the show. However, the cartoon represents a highly contained form of attack. Just as *30 Rock*'s later jabs at NBCUniversal underline the ultimate power of the conglomerate and its network (insofar as NBC "allows" such material on the air in the first place), Michaels's tacit sanctioning of Smigel's piece finally reinforces the perception that Michaels does hold ultimate creative control over the program. It also proposes that he gamely accepts critique from his employees, further promoting a benevolent image.

Michaels's public image both as the craftsman who birthed and shaped the program and as the powerful force who keeps it existent and ostensibly relevant reflects two discourses familiar to discussions of television authorship: artistic creativity and executive management. Such an image is reminiscent of popular and academic discourse that long understood television as a "producer's medium." In the introduction to their book of interviews with television producers, Horace Newcomb and Robert Alley suggest that the producer is a combination of artist and business executive who oversees and ultimately controls all aspects of production in some manner while working collaboratively with the other members of that production.[15] While Newcomb and Alley eschew the worst excesses of auteurism in their acknowledgment of television's collaborative nature, they call these producers the "primary makers" of television and suggest that the successful ones carry a "vision," which "exceeds 'content,' or 'ideas,' exceeds the notion of a 'message.' The vision encompasses all these things and recognizes the best ways to express them *as television.*"[16] Caldwell notes that in the 1980s, television producers and directors with name recognition held the position of "showcase producers" based on their roles as promoters and "banner-carriers."[17] More recently, such producers-showrunners-auteurs have become "brand managers" who, in addition to providing or steering the program's creative content, oversee a franchise that extends beyond the television screen.[18] Especially since his post-hiatus return to the show in 1985, Michaels's public image has increasingly come to signify the figures of "showcase producer" and "brand manager." Frequently and increasingly appearing onscreen to parody his laconic, aloof backstage persona, he has come to serve as the de facto "face" of the program. In this role, Michaels has helped to promote an image of *SNL*'s backstage culture that is highly contained, censored, and self-serving.

Even if, as Derek Kompare suggests, "the prominence of the showrunner-as-author reminds us that television is indeed *made:* the result of intense collaborative, capitalist, and exploitative labor,"[19] Michaels's role as banner carrier and brand manager veils the messier elements of *SNL*'s week-to-week production even while gesturing toward its behind-the-scenes creative processes. As Michael Z. Newman and Elana Levine note, the contemporary practice of seeing television "showrunners" as auteurs "obscures the conditions of industrial media production and substitutes for collaborative notions of authorship a Romantic vision of the autonomous individual."[20] Although the variegated flow of a sketch program represents authorial collaboration and fragmentation *textually,* Michaels's current and retroactive wrangling of *SNL* (both in its production practices and in much of the discourse surrounding its backstage history) serves to manage the genre's variety. Namely, Michaels's ability to take public control of *SNL* over the years has coincided with a solidification of the program's format, a process that in turn contains the program as a more easily recognizable, and thus promotable, cultural institution. The overseeing producer who shepherds the "fragmented, joke-based"[21] practice of comedy writing and the ebb and flow of *SNL*'s quality into one coherent brand serves to inoculate the program against stylistic and authorial excess. Further, even when such excess is acknowledged, Michaels often gets much of the credit.[22] However, as a live showcase of different pieces, each bearing a presumably different authorial origin (but, significantly, almost never explicitly attributed to a particular writer on the program), the sketch genre invites a more complex understanding of television authorship than the Michaels-led franchise generally offers. A closer look at some of the program's early sketches highlights a less uniform, and more obviously subversive, *Saturday Night Live*.

MICHAEL O'DONOGHUE AND HIS HUMOR

In the fall of 1975, Michaels and NBC's head of late-night programming, Dick Ebersol, hired O'Donoghue as *Saturday Night's* first head writer. From 1975 to 1978, O'Donoghue led a writing staff that included performers and comics such as Dan Aykroyd, Anne Beatts, John Belushi, Chevy Chase, Tom Davis, Jim Downey, Al Franken, Marilyn Suzanne Miller, Bill Murray, Tom Schiller, Rosie Shuster, and Alan Zweibel. A former writer and editor for *National Lampoon* and co-creator of *The National Lampoon Radio Hour* (1973–1974), O'Donoghue helped bring a malevolent, mordant sense of humor to the program before leaving the show in 1978.[23] After Michaels's initial exit from the program in 1980 and a poorly received 1980–1981 season produced by Jean Doumanian, new executive producer Ebersol brought O'Donoghue back as head writer in order to create a link to *SNL*'s heyday. O'Donoghue later claimed he was attempting to sabotage the program during this period,[24] and popular accounts point to three of his never-aired sketches that led to his final exit. "The Last Ten Days in Silverman's Bunker" dramatizes the last days of recently fired NBC president Fred Silverman's tenure as "Fuhrer" of the "Nazional Broadcasting Company."[25] Despite Ebersol's support of the sketch, NBC chair Grant Tinker nixed it. In "The Good Excuse," Allied forces liberating Auschwitz encounter a Nazi soldier. When asked how he could help commit such brutal crimes, the soldier replies, "We had a good excuse." Inaudible to the audience, the excuse is whispered to several Allied soldiers throughout the sketch, and the soldiers are ultimately satisfied and agree with its logic. Although the joke only works because the notion of a "good excuse" for the Holocaust is so absurd, the sketch never made it on air. The final piece required the construction of a blowhole to be attached to the father of a family that lived too close to a nuclear power plant. O'Donoghue's final design for the blowhole resembled a vagina with teeth and was thus never shown onscreen.[26] Later in 1981, he was fired from the program.

If a hostile relationship with the powers that be at *SNL* and NBC is apparent in the stories surrounding his dismissal from the show, such an attitude is also evident in some of his *SNL* material. Sketches attributed directly to O'Donoghue as writer divide roughly into two areas: longer, narrative pieces starring the program's cast and short monologues performed by O'Donoghue. The former include the traditional trappings of theatrical sketches (e.g., multiple characters, sets, a brief plot), whereas the latter involve direct addresses to the audience and often lack the longer pieces' gestures toward theatricality or narrative. One of O'Donoghue's best-known longer sketches is a parody of *Star Trek* (NBC, 1966–1969) that aired during the first season. Though it begins as a relatively straightforward send-up with John Belushi as Captain Kirk, Chevy Chase as Mr. Spock, and Dan Aykroyd as Dr. McCoy, an NBC executive (played by Elliott Gould) eventually boards the *Enterprise* and informs the cast that *Star Trek* has been canceled. After stagehands begin to break down the set, Belushi/Kirk says, "We have tried to explore strange new worlds, to seek out new civilizations, to boldly go where no man has gone before. And except for one television network, we have found intelligent life everywhere in the galaxy." The piece is an example of televised sketch comedy's long tradition of self-reflexively exposing "the limits of conventional TV formats" and linking "their absurd arbitrariness to institutions and representatives of institutional power."[27] In this case, O'Donoghue and *Saturday Night* mock the cold, mindless efficiency of NBC executives, a bite-the-hand-that-feeds approach that would become a significant characteristic of *SNL*'s humor and would eventually overflow to Tina Fey's *30 Rock*.

If the *Star Trek* sketch takes an amusing, but ultimately mild, swipe at NBC, many O'Donoghue-penned parodies exhibit a more disturbingly violent sensibility. The first season's final episode contained "Police State," a parody of television cop shows that also satirized the abusive and racist practices of institutions like the Los Angeles Police Department. In this piece, Chase and Aykroyd play two police offers who immediately shoot and kill anyone they confront. In one instance, they yell at the suspect to "freeze" while he lies dead on the floor, and in another they read the Miranda rights to a suspect they have already killed. Throughout, the two cops banter about where they want to eat: "How about Italian? Nah, how about Indian? You want to eat Indian?" At the end of the sketch, the exchange morphs into "How would you feel about Mexican? You'd like to kill Mexican tonight?" O'Donoghue's practice of transforming ostensible protagonists into violent sociopaths is also present in his *Citizen Kane* parody from the tenth episode of season one. Aykroyd played Kane as a megalomaniac who murders civilians and prints the stories of their deaths in his paper. Though these critiques of police officers and cinematic sacred cows represent satiric and parodic practices familiar to sketch comedy, they evince a nihilistic approach that strips away appeals to more traditional comedic forms or topical satire and either subverts them or ignores them altogether.

O'Donoghue's nastiest humor is found in a series of fables known as "Mr. Mike's Least-Loved Bedtime Tales," which usually took the form of a starkly lit O'Donoghue narrating a gruesome story directly to the audience. The "moral" at the end of each bedtime tale was simply a bleak non sequitur, such as "Love is a death camp in a costume," or "It's all very easy to laugh at yourself. The difficult thing is learning to laugh at others." Where "Police State" offers a surprisingly cutting attack on urban police departments, the bedtime tales' engagement with social politics forgoes biting satire for, as Mr. Mike put it, "random acts of meaningless violence." A typical example occurred during the eighteenth episode of season two, hosted by civil rights activist and politician Julian Bond. In the sketch, Mr. Mike pays a visit to Uncle Remus, played by Garrett Morris, and begins telling Remus a variation on the Br'er Rabbit tale wherein the titular rabbit is skinned alive and the Tar Baby is used to "repair a pothole." Mr. Mike narrates, "Toward the end, when they were separating the ears from the side of the skull, he started screaming, 'Throw me in the briar patch! Throw me in the molten glass furnace! Anything but this!'" At the end of the sketch, O'Donoghue tells Remus he found the Bluebird of Happiness dead outside his cabin and sets the bird's corpse on Remus's shoulder before leaving. The result is a cracked-mirror version of racial humor, in which familiar signifiers of racialized content are present, but the focus of the attack deflects away from either African American stereotypes or *Song of the South*'s (1946)racism and moves instead to a small rabbit. O'Donoghue demystifies the allegorical and ideologically loaded figures of Br'er Rabbit and Tar Baby by treating them as

Figure 3.1. Mr. Mike (Michael O'Donoghue) tells Uncle Remus (Garrett Morris) a "Least-Loved Bedtime Tale."

their original forms (a rabbit and a lump of tar, respectively), thus unmooring these signifiers from their traditionally raced connotations.[28]

Whereas the Uncle Remus parody gestures toward racial satire before moving in a different direction, most of "Mr. Mike's Least-Loved Bedtime Tales" bypass topical political satire completely and, in general, eschew more familiar comedic forms. The brutality in the "Least-Loved Bedtime Tales" functions quite differently than the "violent" slapstick gags one might otherwise see in Hollywood films, comic theater, or television sitcoms. Jerry Palmer's explanation of comedic gags in film and television sheds light on the functions of violence in these contexts, which in turn highlights the ways O'Donoghue's humor diverged from this mode. Palmer outlines two crucial functions of a gag's construction: (1) "a shock or surprise" and (2) the contradictory result of this shock or surprise, which is at once implausible and (to a lesser extent) plausible.[29] He illustrates this process with a gag from Laurel and Hardy's *Liberty* (1929) in which a police officer is seemingly crushed by an elevator (the surprise) but instead emerges as a little person in a police officer's uniform (the contradictory result). This portion of the gag contains the combination of implausibility and plausibility since it is implausible that the officer would survive, but there is a measure of plausibility in the fact that crushing an object makes it smaller. As Palmer points out, "The essence of the second moment of the gag is that it is characterized by the simultaneous presence of both modes of reasoning, which are maintained in tension, or balance with each other."[30]

In the ninth episode of season two, O'Donoghue told host Jodie Foster a story called "The Little Engine That Died" in which the titular train, on its way up the side of a mountain, has a heart attack and dies. The train begins rolling back down the mountain, and the story continues:

> Now, in the valley, who should be sitting on the tracks but Freddy the Frog? And wouldn't you know, he's facing the wrong way, so he never sees the train coming at him at 180 miles an hour. Fortunately, Freddy hops off the tracks just in time, and the train misses him, hitting, instead, a school bus, killing 150—no one over age nine. Now, when the state police arrive at the scene, one of them looks around at the carnage and grizzly mutilation, spots Freddy and says, "You know, it's wrong that so many human beings should be dead, and this frog should still be alive." And so, they beat him to death with a softball bat.

Returning to Palmer, the "Least-Loved Bedtime Tales" never contain the balance between plausibility and implausibility necessary for violent comedy to function properly. In O'Donoghue's hypothetical version of the Laurel and Hardy gag, the officer would likely be "just mashed," as Mr. Mike so often described his protagonists' fates. Without the implausible event, in which the protagonist survives the act of violence, we are merely left with the shock and surprise and a horribly plausible and straightforward scenario that leads inevitably to carnage—or in the case of "The Little Engine That Died," several surprises and plausible acts of violence that follow each other. Palmer suggests that audiences that find the violence in comedies upsetting are perhaps focusing too heavily on the plausible event and ignoring its tension with the implausible one. It thus follows that if the plausible violence and consequences are all that remain, viewers may be more likely to find humor like O'Donoghue's to be "excessively abrasive," as Palmer puts it.[31]

O'Donoghue's other major role on the show presented a similarly violent twist on a familiar mode of entertainment: the celebrity imperson-

Figure 3.2. O'Donoghue demonstrates the length of a needle before doing his impression of Mike Douglas.

ator. On several occasions, O'Donoghue portrayed himself as an impressionist who only mimicked celebrities jamming needles into their eyes, a role that he originated on *The National Lampoon Radio Hour*. Making no attempts to offer a mimetic impersonation of the celebrities, O'Donoghue's entire act was composed of identical impressions wherein he would cover his eyes, scream horribly, and flail about onstage. That his targets were Elvis Presley, Mike Douglas, Tony Orlando and Dawn, and the Mormon Tabernacle Choir suggests an attack on sacred cows, mass culture, and symbols of holy reverence. As indebted to *Un Chien Andalou* (1929) as to sketch comedy, O'Donoghue's simulated ocular violence offered a mordant take on the celebrity impression, one of *SNL*'s oldest standbys. If, as David Marc argues, one of the program's greatest assets is the "perfect imitation" that "self-destructs by placing itself in an impossible context that undermines and tests belief,"[32] O'Donoghue's impressions jettison the "perfect imitation" in service of a simpler, crueler joke.

The "perfect imitation" is just one of many elements that comprise the program's formula under Michaels—a decades-old format that has been both critiqued for its inflexible nature and celebrated for its longevity and ability to launch careers. Relying heavily on a consistently ordered combination of cold opens, host monologues, commercial parodies, the news parody "Weekend Update," catchphrase-reciting recurring characters that can be easily spun off for feature films, celebrity impersonations, musical guests, and the occasional "surprise" celebrity walk-on, *SNL* maintains a relatively consistent week-to-week aesthetic. One of the bitterest criticisms of this approach comes from a 1995 *New York* excoriation of the program. Although the piece levies a broader critique at the program's backstage culture, a common theme is that the program, its formula, and its creator are tired, out of touch, and suffering from "institutional decay."[33] In promoting the program, however, Michaels admits that the formula is key to *SNL*'s success. In a book celebrating the program's twentieth anniversary, he laments that in the show's early days, "we had the ingredients, we didn't have the recipe."[34] A more recent *Hollywood Reporter* profile of Michaels suggests more favorably that *SNL* represents "the very model of the modern variety show."[35] For good or ill, the program is known for a weekly, ninety-minute sketch comedy experience that sticks to its influential blueprint.

Given *SNL*'s settlement into predictability, revisiting O'Donoghue's humor unearths approaches to comedy at odds with today's version of the program. For one, his "Least-Loved Bedtime Tales" and celebrity impressions both lacked certain signifiers of "metacommunication" crucial to signaling comic intent.[36] Violence needs what Palmer calls "comic insulation" in order to read as funny, since the audience must be able to tell that the violence is, in fact, only a joke.[37] Whereas Palmer's Laurel and Hardy example invokes a more obviously comic address through the metacues and syntax of silent farce, O'Donoghue's short monologues mock and undermine such conventions. Furthermore, since audience members bring a wide variety of tastes and social experiences to the reception of comedy, not every member of the audience will get the joke. Still, since O'Donoghue was performing on a sketch comedy program, it would of course be incorrect to claim that there is *no* comedic insulation. Mills points out that comic forms and genres (in particular the sitcom) communicate their comic intent through the generic codes that distance potentially upsetting material from verisimilitude.[38] Even in this context, however, there tended to be very little laughter from the studio audience during O'Donoghue's more violent bits. As Mills indicates, television comedy's laugh track or studio audience "doesn't just suggest that something is funny; it suggests something is obviously, clearly, unarguably, unproblematically funny, and that such responses are collectively defined and experienced."[39] If *SNL*'s studio audience did not express these responses, O'Donoghue's performances were difficult to read as comedy—particularly for viewers used to the version of *SNL* that bears the more apparent stamp of Lorne Michaels.

Thus, insofar as O'Donoghue traded in violent humor that emphasized the violence over the humor, his most significant transgression may have been against traditional forms of television comedy. In breaking social and televisual taboos surrounding death and suffering through his gory descriptions of human and animal carnage, his closest comedic relative is postwar America's "sick comedy," which "flourished as a popular response to less politically overt—but particularly American—social repressions."[40] To be sure, O'Donoghue's take on sick comedy saw more value in the "sick" than it did the "comedy." As Bob Tischler, one of *SNL*'s later head writers, recalls, "[O'Donoghue] was most interested in shocking the audience. I don't mind shocking the audience, but you have to make them laugh too, and entertain them. He was really just into the shock value, or doing something that was weird and boring."[41] If O'Donoghue's "anti-humor" undermined the forms and traditions by which comedy functions, he sought paradoxically to be funny by being unfunny—a contradictory mode of performance shared, albeit in different forms, by anti-comedians Andy Kaufman, Chris Elliott, and Neil Hamburger. As O'Donoghue pointed out, in a quip relayed in his 1994 *Village Voice* eulogy, "Things can be both funny and not funny at the same time."[42]

While O'Donoghue's sketches often stand out as markedly different in form and tone from much of the rest of the program's content, *SNL*'s 1970s aesthetic was too diverse to categorize. While the "cold open, monologue, sketches, musical guest" configuration has become essential to *SNL,* the program's structure in its first years was far more pliable. A given episode might include short films by Albert Brooks or Gary Weis; adult-oriented sketches featuring the Muppets; a performance by Andy

Kaufman, Toni Basil, or Ricky Jay; or one-off gimmicks such as a live remote of the cast skating on Rockefeller Center's ice rink. Furthermore,
O'Donoghue's performances as Mr. Mike provided examples of the writer's public persona in the text, and his monologues offered a carefully
crafted, self-reflexive, and highly public pronouncement of O'Donoghue's
own authorship of the program. Thus, when considering *SNL* and some
of its more experimental moments, it is worth considering the writer—
and not just O'Donoghue—and his/her place in the show's behind-the-
scenes production. Exemplary of the variegated nature of the program's
early aesthetic, O'Donoghue's writing and performance represents a
crack in the subsequent construction of *Saturday Night Live* as a singular,
and singularly authored, text.

CONCLUSION

Understanding O'Donoghue's work as both experimental in performance
and aesthetics *and* indicative of a broader problem in television authorship challenges traditional conceptions of what American television
comedy looks like and who controls the historical narrative of *SNL's*
creative processes. It is worth emphasizing that in order to provide a better understanding of O'Donoghue's contributions to *SNL's* early years,
my goal has not been to supplant Michaels with O'Donoghue as another
authorial hegemon. Rather, I use his work to analyze part of the program's early aesthetic and to interrogate the myth of Michaels as *SNL's*
auteur. Put another way, O'Donoghue represents an analytical chisel
with which to pick away at the calcified myths of Michaels's dominance
behind the scenes at Rockefeller Center's Studio 8H. Though I have provided examples of O'Donoghue's work "in the text" (both as writer and
performer), perhaps opening this chapter to the charge of working in the
"humanist literary tradition that ascribes authorship to a single writer
based on whether or not his/her work registers a modernist intervention
in the dominant hegemonic tendencies of the mass media,"[43] I am less
interested in indicating and celebrating O'Donoghue's singular vision
than I am in locating fissures in Michaels's now taken-for-granted auteur position. In sum, the political goals of such an approach are perhaps
best symbolized by a line from *SNL* writer Anne Beatts, which closes

Shales and Miller's *Live from New York:* "But enough about Lorne. What about me?"[44]

Notes

1. I use the common abbreviation *SNL* to refer to both *NBC's Saturday Night* and *Saturday Night Live*. The program changed its name from the former to the latter in 1977.

2. Mohr, *Gasping for Airtime*; Davis, *Thirty-Nine Years of Short-Term Memory Loss*.

3. Felicia E. Henderson calls this space "half-hour comedy's creative ground zero," where "quasi-familial and organizational rules structure conventionalized socioprofessional activities that overdetermine the manner by which television's on-screen texts are authored. In this space, ideas are negotiated, consensus is formed, and issues of gender, race, and class identities play out and complicate the on-screen narratives that eventually air on network and cable television" ("The Culture behind Closed Doors," 146). Though Henderson refers, here, to the half-hour sitcom writers room, her description characterizes much of what has been written about *SNL*'s backstage environment, particularly in unsanctioned and "uncensored" histories of the show.

4. Caldwell, *Production Culture*, 205.

5. See Shales and Miller, *Live from New York*, 154–157; Carmon, "*The Daily Show*'s Woman Problem"; Henderson, "The Culture behind Closed Doors," 148–151; Caldwell, *Production Culture*, 214–215.

6. Shales and Miller, *Live from New York*, 223.

7. Tucker, *Kissing Bill O'Reilly, Roasting Miss Piggy*, 157.

8. Caldwell, *Production Culture*, 199. Though Caldwell primarily analyzes contemporary film and television production cultures, many of his descriptions of contingent, fast-paced production aptly describe the publicly disclosed tales of *SNL*'s backstage environment.

9. Beatts and Head, *Saturday Night Live*.

10. Partridge, *Rolling Stone Visits Saturday Night Live*.

11. Shales, "*Saturday Night*: A Show the Peacock Can Crow About."

12. Wilson, "A Rare Glimpse inside the Empire of *SNL*'s Lorne Michaels"; Adalian, Levine, and Schneider, "TV Movers and Shakers."

13. Cader, *Saturday Night Live*, 7–8.

14. "Season 1: 1975–1976," *Saturday Night Live Transcripts*.

15. Newcomb and Alley, *The Producer's Medium*, 12.

16. Ibid., xiii.

17. Caldwell, *Televisuality*, 15.

18. Mann, "It's Not TV," 99.

19. Kompare, "More 'Moments of Television,'" 98. While Michaels is not often labeled a "showrunner" per se, his management of *SNL* and his status as the steadily recognizable face of the program suggest that he fulfills a similar role within public discourse about the program.

20. Newman and Levine, *Legitimating Television*, 53.

21. Caldwell, *Production Culture*, 212.

22. See, for example, Plasketes, "The Comic and Artistic Vision of Lorne Michaels."

23. For more on *NBC's Saturday Night/Saturday Night Live*'s early history, see Partridge, *Rolling Stone Visits Saturday Night Live;* Hill and Weingrad, *Saturday Night;* Perrin, *Mr. Mike;* Shales and Miller, *Live from New York;* and Miller, "What Closes on Saturday Night."

24. Hill and Weingrad, *Saturday Night,* 455.

25. See Perrin, *Mr. Mike,* 383–385; Shales and Miller, *Live from New York,* 231; Rosenberg, "Silverman Spoof Too Hot to Handle."

26. Hill and Weingrad, *Saturday Night,* 455–456.

27. Neale and Krutnik, *Popular Film and Television Comedy,* 202.

28. I have developed this analysis from some of my earlier thoughts on O'Donoghue's humor. See Elkins, "Michael O'Donoghue, *SNL,* and the Comedy of Cruelty."

29. Palmer, *The Logic of the Absurd,* 43.

30. Ibid.

31. Ibid., 57.

32. Marc, *Demographic Vistas,* 153.

33. Smith, "Comedy Isn't Funny," 32.

34. Cader, *Saturday Night Live,* 7.

35. Wilson, "A Rare Glimpse inside the Empire of *SNL*'s Lorne Michaels."

36. Mills, "Comedy Verite," 67.

37. Palmer, *The Logic of the Absurd,* 45.

38. Mills, "Comedy Verite," 67–68.

39. Mills, *The Sitcom,* 81.

40. Thompson, *Parody and Taste in Postwar American Television Culture,* 24.

41. Qtd. in Shales and Miller, *Live from New York,* 225.

42. James, "Goodbye, Mr. Mike."

43. Mann, "It's Not TV," 102.

44. Shales and Miller, *Live from New York,* 600.

Works Cited

Adalian, Josef, Stuart Levine, and Michael Schneider. "TV Movers and Shakers." *Variety,* October 17, 2005.

Beatts, Anne, and John Head, eds. *Saturday Night Live.* New York: Avon, 1977.

Cader, Michael, ed. *Saturday Night Live: The First Twenty Years.* Boston: Cader Books, 1995.

Caldwell, John Thornton. *Production Culture: Industrial Reflexivity and Critical Practice in Film and Television.* Durham, NC: Duke University Press, 2008.

———. *Televisuality: Style, Crisis, and Authority in American Television.* New Brunswick, NJ: Rutgers University Press, 1995.

Carmon, Irin. "*The Daily Show*'s Woman Problem." *Jezebel,* June 23, 2010, http://jezebel.com/5570545/comedy-of-errors-behind-the-scenes-of-the--daily-shows-lady-problem.

Davis, Tom. *Thirty-Nine Years of Short-Term Memory Loss.* New York: Grove, 2009.

Elkins, Evan. "Michael O'Donoghue, *SNL,* and the Comedy of Cruelty." *FlowTV,* March 20, 2009, http://flowtv.org/2009/03/michaelo'donoghue-snl-and-the-comedy-of-cruelty-evan-elkins-university-of-texas-austin.

Henderson, Felicia E. "The Culture behind Closed Doors: Issues of Gender and Race in the Writers' Room." *Cinema Journal* 50(2) (Winter 2011):145–152.

Hill, Doug, and Jeff Weingrad. *Saturday Night: A Backstage History of Saturday Night Live*. New York: Beech Tree, 1986.

James, Darius. "Goodbye, Mr. Mike: Michael O'Donoghue, 1940–1994." *Village Voice*, November 29, 1994.

Kompare, Derek. "More 'Moments of Television': Online Cult Television Authorship." In *FlowTV: Television in the Age of Media Convergence*, edited by Michael Kackman et al., 95–113. New York: Routledge, 2011.

Mann, Denise. "It's Not TV, It's Brand Management TV: The Collective Author(s) of the *Lost* Franchise." In *Production Studies: Cultural Studies of Media Industries*, edited by Vicki Mayer, Miranda J. Banks, and John Thornton Caldwell, 99–114. New York: Routledge, 2009.

Marc, David. *Demographic Vistas: Television in American Culture*, rev. ed. Philadelphia: University of Pennsylvania Press, 1996.

Miller, Jeffrey. "What Closes on Saturday Night." In *NBC: America's Network*, edited by Michele Hilmes, 192–208. Berkeley: University of California Press, 2007.

Mills, Brett. "Comedy Verite: Contemporary Sitcom Form." *Screen* 45(1) (Spring 2004):63–78.

———. *The Sitcom*. Edinburgh: Edinburgh University Press, 2009.

Mohr, Jay. *Gasping for Airtime: Two Years in the Trenches at Saturday Night Live*. New York: Hyperion, 2004.

Neale, Steve, and Frank Krutnik. *Popular Film and Television Comedy*. London: Routledge, 1990.

Newcomb, Horace, and Robert S. Alley. *The Producer's Medium: Conversations with Creators of American TV*. Oxford: Oxford University Press, 1983.

Newman, Michael Z., and Elana Levine. *Legitimating Television: Media Convergence and Cultural Studies*. New York: Routledge, 2012.

Palmer, Jerry. *The Logic of the Absurd: On Film and Television Comedy*. London: BFI Publishing, 1988.

Perrin, Dennis. *Mr. Mike: The Life and Work of Michael O'Donoghue*. New York: Avon, 1999.

Plasketes, George M. "The Comic and Artistic Vision of Lorne Michaels and the Production of Unconventional Television." In *Making Television: Authorship and the Production Process*, edited by Robert J. Thompson and Gary Burns, 185–201. New York: Praeger, 1990.

Rosenberg, Howard. "Silverman Spoof Too Hot to Handle." *Los Angeles Times*, December 25, 1981.

Sacks, Mike. *And Here's the Kicker: Conversations with 21 Top Humor Writers on Their Craft*. Cincinnati, OH: Writer's Digest Books, 2009.

Saturday Night Live Transcripts. http://snltranscripts.jt.org (accessed July 8, 2011).

Shales, Tom. "*Saturday Night:* A Show the Peacock Can Crow About." *Washington Post*, September 28, 1977.

Shales, Tom, and James Andrew Miller. *Live from New York: An Uncensored History of Saturday Night Live*. Boston: Little, Brown, 2002.

Smith, Chris. "Comedy Isn't Funny." *New York*, March 13, 1995.

Thompson, Ethan. *Parody and Taste in Postwar American Television Culture*. New York: Routledge, 2011.

Tucker, Ken. *Kissing Bill O'Reilly, Roasting Miss Piggy: 100 Things to Love and Hate about TV*. New York: St. Martin's, 2005.

Wilson, Stacey. "A Rare Glimpse inside the Empire of *SNL*'s Lorne Michaels." *Hollywood Reporter*, April 22, 2011.

PART TWO

Staying Alive on Saturday Night

Politics and the Brand: *Saturday Night Live*'s Campaign Season Humor

JEFFREY P. JONES

From Chevy Chase's thin but arresting impersonation of President Gerald Ford in 1975 to Tina Fey's spot-on caricature of vice presidential candidate Sarah Palin in 2008, *Saturday Night Live* has been the go-to location in U.S. culture for humorous television commentary on presidents, presidential candidates, and election events. Despite the popularity of new forms of political satire such as *The Daily Show with Jon Stewart* (1999–present) and *The Colbert Report* (2005–present) that now appear on cable channels, *Saturday Night Live*—given its status as the longest-running U.S. television show offering political satire—still retains an important presence as a television location for critical political commentary, especially during campaign season. Part of the reason is its format as a weekly live sketch comedy program, which allows commentary that other comedy formats don't. While late-night talk show monologues and fake newscasts offer humorous reflections on daily political events, *SNL*'s live sketch comedy format and regular weekly appearance allows audiences to see major campaign events humorously "reenacted" each week, providing a comedic commentary during the campaign season. Given its place as one of the only locations for satirical political humor on television for much of the show's run, *SNL* occupies a special role as comedic commentator on electoral politics, as well as a privileged position because of the broader mass audience's familiarity with its style of explaining and commenting on politics through popular culture.

Campaign humor reasserts the program's cultural relevance, taking a show that has, over the years, periodically floundered with lackluster casts and poorly written sketches, and encouraging audiences (especially those outside its core youthful demographic) to care enough once again to watch, to share clips, and to use it for water cooler talk. Journalists also have a role in this process, crafting articles and news stories that explicitly proclaim to readers and viewers how and why *SNL* still matters. This assertion of cultural relevance is important to the revival and perpetuation of the franchise itself.

This chapter explores how political comedy and satire are central to the *SNL* brand in four distinct ways: (1) by establishing the show as a significant site for mass audiences to engage with political humor during presidential campaign seasons; (2) as a narrative strategy in the historical development of the show and in establishing the show's standout star personas; (3) as a means of periodically reasserting and reaffirming the program's cultural relevance; and (4) as popular content that is highly conducive to repackaging for prime-time broadcast specials and aftermarket sales. Although political comedy, more broadly construed, has permeated the show's skits and segments across the entirety of *SNL's* run, it is the show's focus on campaign season humor that is of interest here. Given the recurring nature of presidential electoral contests, and the political and social significance of them (including rapt public attention to the presidential race), the program uses such piggyback programming to reassert itself as a popular location for humorous political critique. Finally, I argue that through memorable impersonations and caricatures—and their repetition across time and programming spaces—the program plays a significant role in shaping public memory about presidents and presidential candidates, including creating its own political televisual heritage through such caricatured renderings.

For many viewers, politics is intimately linked to the *SNL* brand because it is one of the most consistent and longest running features of the program's comedy, dating back to its first season. Outside of news and fictional prime-time programming, such as cop shows and courtroom dramas, politics was not a prevalent topic on network television when *SNL* appeared in late 1975. What is more, the use of political humor (much less satire) was largely nonexistent outside of one-liner jokes on programs such as *The Tonight Show* (1954–present) and *Rowan & Martin's Laugh-In* (1968–1973) or the occasional political statement or controversial musical act on *The Smothers Brothers Comedy Hour* (1967–1969).[1] As Gray, Jones, and Thompson recount, television in the network era was an unwelcoming place for political satire, which is what made original cast member Chevy Chase's impersonation of Ford all the more remarkable in the fourth episode of the first season of *SNL*.[2] While comedians such as Rich Little had perfected presidential caricatures as stand-up routines, Chase's simple assertion that he *was* the president in a comedy sketch—despite no attempt to look, sound, or even act like Gerald Ford—meshed perfectly with the show's edgy and youthful approach to comedy and to politics.[3] Lorne Michaels, the show's longtime executive producer, notes that the edgy approach to politics was a product of the time: "Politics was something everyone knew and talked about. I think we defined ourselves as a generation in that way."[4] Thus, using politics as a programming strategy to target baby boomers made sense. The sketch format also allowed for politics to be done differently from elsewhere on television, marking the show as original and distinct. As one longtime writer of many *SNL* political sketches, Jim Downey, reflects, "By actually presenting little scenes, with actors portraying the political figures and no actual commentary—letting the scene speak for itself—it was a different way of doing [political humor]."[5] Again, such reenactments allowed television audiences to experience political humor in a new way. With the impersonation of a sitting president, the sketches became a standout and defining feature of the new show, and since that time, political sketches about presidents and presidential candidates have been a recurring and popular element of the program.

The Ford sketches were also the first incarnation of what would become a central strategy of blending content with star development. In their analysis of *SNL*'s "Weekend Update" segment, Amber Day and Ethan Thompson argue that the show has tended to emphasize particular cast members as breakout stars, letting them craft character types that define their comedic personas.[6] In portraying Ford as a bumbling and scatter-brained president, Chase was not impersonating Ford as much as constructing his own comedic persona, one that would be used time and again in movies such as *Foul Play* (1978), *National Lampoon's Vacation*

(1983), and *Fletch* (1985). The show's political humor, then, is less about its purported subject matter than it is a narrative strategy linking comedians to character types that encourage repeated viewing for audience engagement with these characters—as opposed to new scenarios and new characters week after week, as occurs through much of the show's other content. Thus, the way *SNL* uses topical material—in this instance, politicians, and for Day and Thompson, news—is as much about developing the show itself as it is about offering critical political commentary. With Chase's recurring appearances as Ford, the show announced that audiences should tune in to see how the president would be interpreted each week, but also to enjoy the hot new star of physical humor, Chevy Chase.

Politicians took notice of this change in the televisual landscape, and Ford dispatched his press secretary, Ron Nessen, to appear on the show in the spring of the first season. For that same episode, President Ford actually recorded the "Live from New York" opener from the Oval Office. With a tweak back at Chevy Chase—who had created a signature line as his opening for the "Weekend Update" segment that he anchored, "Good evening. I'm Chevy Chase, and you're not"—Ford taped a segment saying, "Good evening. I'm Gerald Ford, and you're not."[7] This was the first instance (with many to follow) of politicians recognizing that a comedy show was crafting a powerful and widely commented-on political interpretation, one they had best laugh along with or participate in directly.[8]

Thus, over the years, a bevy of politicians have appeared (live or via tape, some as hosts, and some actually during their campaigns), including George McGovern, Jesse Jackson, Bob Dole, Bruce Babbitt, Al Gore, George W. Bush, Steve Forbes, Ralph Nader, Ross Perot, John McCain, Al Sharpton, Barack Obama, Hillary Clinton, and Jon Huntsman.

Yet part of their willingness to appear on the show comes from the realization that the type of political humor *SNL* produces is, in most cases, harmless—or certainly not critical or offensive enough to merit an antagonistic relationship to the show. Elsewhere, I have criticized *SNL's* presidential caricatures because of how rarely the show engages in what could be considered genuine political satire—critiques that comment on the powerful for their policies or behaviors as political actors in public life.[9] As one critic in the popular press also notes, "This isn't hard-hitting political satire. In fact, most of it isn't political satire at all, in the strict sense."[10] The show's political humor is, instead, largely apolitical, focusing most intently on politicians' behaviors or personality tics, such as the funny ways in which they speak or their sexual peccadilloes, to garner laughs. As Lorne Michaels notes about the show's sketches, "[They] are gentle, not vicious. They are the silly take, which in my opinion is also the smart take."[11] It is largely this approach to political comedy as "good-natured" humor that politicians feel comfortable in playing along with, if not supporting outright.

Moments in which this good-natured approach *and* biting satire become one and the same do occasionally occur, though typically out of coincidence more than intent. For instance, in representing candidates George W. Bush in 2000 and Sarah Palin in 2008, the show seized upon the outlandish personal tics of the candidates, yet this was exactly where the satiric critique belonged. Bush and Palin were newcomers to the national scene, and their personal attributes—dim-witted and arrogant, with a desire to charm their way into power—were also key to understanding them as politicians. The comedy that emerged was particularly brutal because the satire pointed out these features clearly. As cutting as the portrayals were, however, it is difficult to ascertain what the caricatures' actual effect on voters' opinions may have been, since Bush went on to win two terms in office, while Palin went on to electoral defeat but eventual media and pop culture stardom.[12] The satirical portrayal did further Will Ferrell's already skyrocketing career by becoming part of his comedic persona: he continued to deploy his impersonation of Bush after he left the show, first through his comedy website, *Funny or Die,* and later in the 2009 one-man Broadway production and HBO special, *You're Welcome America: A Final Night with George W. Bush.*

One of the less explored aspects of *SNL's* political comedy is not how it works against politicians through reductive or demeaning portrayals, but rather how it makes the candidates more likable, perhaps even popular—flaws and all. People ritually turn to *SNL* during campaign season to see what interpretation of the candidates and campaign events the show will make. Citizens are constantly searching for political meaning through news programs, but also increasingly through comedy shows.[13] Comedic caricature is about essence, reducing numerous competing narratives to a particularly arresting one. These narratives bestow upon a politician a popular persona, something people can identify

Figure 4.1. Will Ferrell cracks open a beer in *You're Welcome America: A Final Night with George W. Bush.*

with, even if in mocking ways. At times they reduce politicians to the level of the people and make them understandable, in particular by crafting a narrative of who the person is and what makes him or her tick, including his or her personal drives and motivations, however reductive. While it might seem on the surface that such narratives are demeaning, we should consider how they actually make the politician more human, even likable, all the more so because the "critique" is wrapped in the language and affect of "all-in-good-fun" humor. As one Democratic strategist noted about *SNL*'s take on George W. Bush, "I think the caricature of Bush as bumbler has helped him more than it's helped us."[14] Lorne Michaels agrees, attributing this outcome to the audience's affection for the cast member and the character he or she has created. "So much of it is casting," he contends. "If Will Ferrell plays George Bush, they like Bush more. 'Strategery' was entirely forgivable because he seemed like a guy they liked."[15] And an actor like Ferrell recognizes the affection in the portrayal, leading him to incorporate this persona as part of his continuing comedic repertoire, thus building his own brand both during and after his employment by *SNL*.

Take, for instance, Dana Carvey's portrayal of George H. W. Bush. A career politician of patrician upbringing, Bush's generally moderate politics and bland style did little to give him much in the way of a popular persona, especially since his predecessor was a charismatic former movie star. When Carvey crafted a caricature that focused on Bush's seemingly strange lexical choices and awkward manner of speaking, he served up Bush as someone recognizable, familiar, and unthreatening—a wacky neighbor or uncle who should be laughed at more than scorned. The portrayal was so benign that Bush himself embraced it, at times parodying the parody by repeating the lines that Carvey made popular and eventually having Carvey appear alongside him at public and private events in his retirement. Yet SNL has not found a successful narrative interpretation of President Barack Obama. As one critic put it, "In [the show's] long history of mocking presidents, no impression has made less of one."[16] And in that regard, the show has probably done itself and the president a disservice. While Obama has suffered politically from negative and demeaning portrayals by his right-wing political opponents (such as the commentary on Fox News), there are few affectionate counterweights to such ideologically driven narratives in popular culture to offset the negativity.

The show's portrayal of President Bill Clinton is another example of how a popular narrative can contribute to a popular imaginary that can help a politician. Phil Hartman's caricature of Clinton was as a smart and friendly common man who was interminably hungry for junk food. When Darrell Hammond took over the role, the portrayal of insatiability morphed into rapaciousness for women and sex. The show thus took Clinton's foibles—which were significant enough to have him impeached—and used them to construct a more fun-loving and harmless character, at least for those willing to embrace the sexualized persona of both the real-life and comedic actors.

SNL, then, plays a particularly significant role in U.S. political culture by generating a popular interpretation of presidents and presidential aspirants, ritually establishing a portrayal that (as one news report put it) "can seem more vivid than their real-life counterparts."[17] It is that vividness that allows SNL to establish and cement political portraits in the public consciousness, as was done so well by editorial cartoonists in previous eras.[18] With depictions of Richard Nixon as paranoid and brooding, Gerald Ford as bumbling, Jimmy Carter as smarter-than-thou, Ronald Reagan as a secret mastermind, the elder George Bush as an awkward public speaker, Bill Clinton as sex obsessed, and the younger George Bush as dim-witted and arrogant, these particular caricatures have become part of American cultural memory, in some ways becoming central to, if not defining of, each president's popular persona. This is all the more true as popular sketches are aired repeatedly in the various retrospectives the show runs every four years, not to mention the after-market packaging in DVD sales and their presence in archived databases such as Hulu and Yahoo. And in the absence of alternative images (such as news footage), which are much less visible once presidents leave office, these portrayals become all the more powerful through their repetition and public affection for them.

Thus, the caricatures, in many ways, *become* the president or presidential candidate in the popular imagination, quickly conjured or referenced, and easily packaged for repeated public consumption. One instance of this was seen when Will Ferrell brought former *SNL* presidential impersonators together on his *Funny or Die* website to advocate for passage of a proposed consumer protection bill in 2009. He assembled Dana Carvey performing the elder Bush, Darrell Hammond as Clinton, Dan Aykroyd as Carter, Chase as Ford, Fred Armisen as Obama, Jim Carrey substituting as Reagan, and himself as the younger Bush—again representing how, across these actors, the political caricatures they developed on the show are intimately intertwined with each comedian's own comedic persona. In the sketch, the characters are seen infiltrating Obama's dream (as ghosts of presidents past), advocating a course of presidential action while offering their now-familiar caricatured quips. These representations have become part of the cultural landscape and are easily mobilized as recognizable and familiar figures. They are the "presidents we imagine," as scholar Jeff Smith notes about representations of presidents in popular culture—in this instance, with the help of *SNL*.[19]

The conjoining of real and fictional political personas can also occur because the sketches may not venture too far from the ridiculousness of political reality itself, using the raw material of the actual words and events that arise each week. A particularly powerful example occurred in 2008 when the show's writers used many of Sarah Palin's words verbatim from a news interview, with occasional satiric additions and comedic inflections to drive the point home. Overall, though, much of the humor comes from taking the natural hilarity that is somewhat obscured

Figure 4.2. A number of *SNL* alumni gather to impersonate U.S. presidents in a short for the *Funny or Die* website.

by the seriousness of the news genre and transposing it into the comedy genre.[20] Similarly, *SNL* head writer Seth Meyers notes, "It's the best for a writer when 70 million people see a debate because everyone knows the lines."[21] Such was the case in the 2000 election, when Al Gore's repeated assertions of a "lockbox" in the actual presidential debate became central to *SNL*'s damning debate skit a few days later. The humor didn't have to be explained to viewers, for Gore's annoying repetition of the word was fresh in viewers' minds, and thus Gore had already set up the joke perfectly. In this way, it becomes easy for viewers to meld the fictional and nonfictional into a seemingly unitary whole, with the humorous and fictional extensions and exaggerations now seen as part of the overall imagined persona.[22]

Journalists too have a role to play in the popularization, repetition, and circulation of these memorable scenes and characters, and they often unintentionally establish and maintain *SNL*'s particular contributions to the cultural lexicon. Key phrases that have arisen from *SNL*'s campaign and presidential sketches—which are then routinely circulated in news articles every four years by journalists—include "strategery," "lockboxes," "Not gonna do it," "Stay the course," "I can't believe I'm losing to this guy," "You going to finish these fries?," "It was my understanding that there would be no math," "The question is moot," and "I can see Russia from my house." With each campaign season, as *SNL* routinely ventures into political caricature, journalists and television critics hype the show and repeat these cultural moments, thus explicitly asserting a cultural relevance that isn't to be missed, and implicitly encouraging the ritual return to viewing.

In 2008, when there was an unusually intense competition for the Democratic Party's presidential nominee and then the appearance of the charismatic Palin, *SNL* rode the popular interest in the election with inspired sketches by Tina Fey and Amy Poehler. Journalists were quick to notice, with one proclaiming, "Fey's take on Palin has become such a pop culture touchstone that it seems as if the whole nation is waiting to see what she'll do next."[23] Other publications announced an "*SNL* revival," called 2008 a "comeback year," exclaimed that the show had "become even more relevant," and labeled *SNL* "the real winner" of the 2008 election season.[24] Although *SNL* is one of the longest running comedy programs in U.S. television history, journalists are nevertheless central to the re-establishment of the show's cultural relevance. They remind viewers that, once again, *SNL matters*, and that audiences should be watching. They craft pieces titled "Amid Campaign, *SNL* Must-See Status Returns,"[25] and broadcast segments that proclaim how the show has "entered the national consciousness [and] certainly the national conversation."[26] And they circulate clips within their own television news coverage, garnering additional national exposure for the show.[27] Thus, politics is central to the brand, part of what *SNL* has been and what audiences expect it to provide. As Michaels maintains, "In an election year, we tend to get more people coming around because it's one of the things that we do really well."[28]

The economic benefits of the political sketches are substantial, as the 2008 season demonstrated. When Fey's first impersonation of Palin became a popular sensation, subsequent sketches increased viewership dramatically. By early October, ratings were up 50 percent for the season.[29] On October 18, the show attracted 14 million viewers, its highest rated show in fourteen years, even besting most of the shows that aired in prime time that week. What is more, clips that aired on the Internet archive Hulu drew 14.3 million viewers for the first sketch caricaturing Palin and 11.1 million viewers for the second.[30] Some of that draw was related to the brilliance of the sketches and the impersonation, some because of interest in the campaign more generally, and some because of Palin's appearance on the final show. Regardless, the pull on viewers was enormous, and as one report contends, "more Americans watched the parodies on *SNL* broadcasts—and their extended lifespan on the Internet—than the actual network news interviews of the real Palin."[31] As this quote suggests, for many Americans, their engagement with politics may happen as much in the realm of popular culture as it does through other, more traditional realms of civic information and engagement.[32]

Another benefit for the show is that politics provides recognizable and familiar faces as guests. While perhaps not as popular in drawing the show's youthful core demographic, such guests, as we have seen, help (re)legitimate the show in critical circles, thus making it worthy of journalistic publicity—something that is much less the case when celebrities headline. Even as make-believe political guests (that is, when only the political caricature appears), the program nevertheless possesses the gravitas of having the "president of the United States" opening the show. Political sketches during campaign season are also typically used as cold opens, that is, they form the transition into the show from advertisements or previous programming before the show's title, music, and announcer appear, thus making the sketches seem even more like real news events. Politics' topicality, then, provides an important narrative break from repeated gag sketches derived from pop culture references or the pure imaginary. Politics grounds the show in reality, while providing a new cast of characters for the show's writers to exploit and the show's audience to become familiar with.

Finally, the show's producers have established the economic value of such portrayals by recycling old sketches, packaging them as election year specials and as DVDs for aftermarket sales. In 1992, *SNL* created its first *SNL Presidential Bash*, with repeated events in 2000 and 2004. In 2008, political interest allowed the program to expand into prime time on Thursday nights, and the show ran three specials—*Saturday Night Live Weekend Update Thursday*—leading up to the election. An *SNL Election Special* also aired on the Monday night before the election. In 1995, the program packaged its political material in *The Best of Saturday Night Live: Presidential Bash*, a VHS offering, and did the same with *Presidential Bash 2000* on DVD. Other compilations include *SNL Presents: The*

Clinton Years (1999) and a *Saturday Night Live Goes Political* CD-ROM in 1996 (which also included a video game). In short, politics has proven to be a steady, consistent, and commodifiable property for the show, with value outside the sketches' original airings. And again, through such repetition, the show plays a particularly important role in the construction of Americans' popular memory of these candidates and presidents.

In conclusion, *SNL*'s political sketches should be examined beyond their role as political commentary that affects voting or campaign dynamics.[33] As I have argued, *SNL*'s campaign season political humor has both cultural and economic effects. Culturally, caricatures are an important contributing factor in how citizens conceive of politicians, both during and after they have left the political stage. But we shouldn't assume that such reductive portrayals are, as they seem on the surface, damagingly negative. They also have positive value in shaping the public's relationship to politicians through narratives that humanize or that bring politicians and their overly crafted and managed public personas down to the level of the people. This, we can suggest, is one important reason that *SNL* retains its popularity as a ritualized spot for politics during presidential campaign seasons—that crucial moment when many Americans start paying attention to politics once again. The show also crafts political caricatures that have proven enduring in their longevity, and thus the show participates in crafting a form of televisual heritage associated with politicians in the popular imagination.[34] While more biting and critical satire such as that found on *The Daily Show with Jon Stewart* and *The Colbert Report* is now available, *SNL* still retains its popularity with mass audiences. Finally, another reason for the continuing popularity of the show's political skits relates to the ways in which sketch reenactments allow for a different form of "play" with politics than that offered by fake news and fake punditry. This occurs at the level of political imagining (e.g., its good-natured quality), but also at the level of character: the show transforms politicians into people whom we are pleased to be around—or, at the least, into people we enjoy laughing at rather than being angry with much of the time.

Economically, the centrality of politics to the brand means that, like politics itself, the sketches can stand on their own, able to be repackaged and having economic value. The recycling, and the affection these repeated viewings extract from audiences, helps reassert the program's cultural relevance. When Lorne Michaels left the show from 1980 to 1985, the political content atrophied. With discussions that the program might be canceled, Michaels returned to the show, but announced that he would return to the "emphasis on political humor that characterized the early seasons."[35] *SNL* recognizes that it needs politics, and that politics is what people (including journalists) have come to expect from the show. Given that political life typically offers up real-life characters that are as interesting as anything fiction and comedy writers can conjure, political sketches can—as seen with Sarah Palin and Al Gore, for instance—almost write themselves. And thus audiences wait for each campaign season when they will be introduced to a new set of political characters on *SNL,* ones that they may or may not be engaged with for another four years, but ones that almost always and consistently draw a laugh through this particular form of popular identification with politics.

Notes

The author wishes to thank Jessica Weaver for her invaluable research assistance with this project.

1. Bodroghkozy, *Groove Tube,* 123–163.
2. Gray, Jones, and Thompson, "The State of Satire."
3. Shales and Miller, *Live from New York.*
4. Qtd. in Purdham, "*Saturday Night Live* Mocks Politics."
5. Ibid.
6. Day and Thompson, "Live from New York."
7. Purdham, "*Saturday Night Live* Mocks Politics."
8. Even Richard Nixon recognized the importance of television, especially to more youthful audiences, when he appeared briefly on *Rowan & Martin's Laugh-In* during the 1968 presidential campaign, offering up the show's signature comedic quip (though in question form): "Sock it to me?" Liebovich, "Laugh, or the World Laughs at You"; Kolbert, "Stooping to Conquer," 116.
9. Jones, "With All Due Respect"; see also Day and Thompson, "Live from New York."
10. Sanneh, "Laughing Matters," 94.
11. Qtd. in Peyser, "Al and Dubya," 38.
12. Stanley, "On *SNL* It's the Real Sarah Palin."
13. Jones, *Entertaining Politics.*
14. Zengerle, "The State of the George W. Bush Joke," 1.
15. Qtd. in Carter, "An Election to Laugh About," C1.
16. Zinoman, "Comedians in Chief."
17. Purdham, "*Saturday Night Live* Mocks Politics."

18. Lamb, *Drawn to Extremes.*

19. Smith, *Presidents We Imagine.*

20. There is an integrated rendering of the news and comedy performances: "Tina Fey Quotes Sarah Palin Word for Word," http://www.youtube.com/watch?v=vgRA80Tk8ig &feature.

21. Qtd. in Carter, "An Election to Laugh About."

22. Michael Delli Carpini and Bruce Williams have demonstrated the ways in which citizens engage in this blending of fiction and nonfiction in their understanding of public and political figures. See Delli Carpini and Williams, "Constructing Public Opinion."

23. Hartlaub, "I Resemble That Remark!," E1.

24. Kinon, "Political Grist," 6; Lafayette, "Political Parodies Pay," 1; Strachan, "Parody Goes On," C9.

25. "Amid Campaign."

26. Williams, "*SNL* Becomes Player."

27. Rutenberg, "Live, from New York," E1.

28. Qtd. in Kinon, "Political Grist."

29. Carter, "An Election to Laugh About."

30. Stelter, "Web Site's Formula." See also Carter, "Candidate Delivers."

31. Flowers and Young, "Parodying Palin," 62.

32. Jones, *Entertaining Politics.*

33. Smith and Voth, "The Role of Humor"; Flowers and Young, "Parodying Palin"; Miller, Peake, and Boulton, "Testing the *Saturday Night Live* Hypothesis"; Young, "Political Entertainment."

34. See Kompare, *Rerun Nation.*

35. Belkin, "A Decade Old," 27.

Works Cited

"Amid Campaign, *SNL* Must-See Status Returns." *All Things Considered,* National Public Radio, October 9, 2008.

Belkin, Lisa. "A Decade Old, *Saturday Night Live* Looks to Fresh Faces." *New York Times,* November 3, 1985, Arts and Leisure, 27.

Bodroghkozy, Aniko. *Groove Tube: Sixties Television and the Youth Rebellion.* Durham, NC: Duke University Press, 2001.

Carter, Bill. "Candidate Delivers a Ratings Boost." *New York Times,* October 19, 2008.

———. "An Election to Laugh About." *New York Times,* October 8, 2008.

Day, Amber, and Ethan Thompson. "Live from New York, It's the Fake News!: *Saturday Night Live* and the (Non)Politics of Parody." *Popular Communication* 10(1–2) (2012):170–182.

Delli Carpini, Michael X., and Bruce A. Williams. "Constructing Public Opinion: The Uses of Fictional and Nonfictional Television in Conversations about the Environment." In *The Psychology of Political Communication,* edited by Ann N. Crigler. Ann Arbor: University of Michigan Press, 1996.

Flowers, Arhlene A., and Cory L. Young. "Parodying Palin: How Tina Fey's Visual and Verbal Impersonations Revived a Comedy Show and Impacted the 2008 Election." *Journal of Visual Literacy* 29(1) (2010):47–67.

Gray, Jonathan, Jeffrey P. Jones, and Ethan Thompson. "The State of Satire, the Satire of State." In *Satire TV: Politics and Comedy in the Post-Network Era,* edited by Jonathan Gray, Jeffrey P. Jones, and Ethan Thompson, 3–36. New York: New York University Press, 2009.

Hartlaub, Peter. "I Resemble That Remark!: Tina Fey's Eerily Spot-On Sarah Palin a Top Candidate among Presidential Impersonations." *San Francisco Chronicle,* October 14, 2008, E1.

Jones, Jeffrey P. *Entertaining Politics: Satiric Television and Political Engagement,* 2nd ed. Lanham, MD: Rowman and Littlefield, 2010.

———. "With All Due Respect: Satirizing Presidents from *Saturday Night Live* to *Lil' Bush.*" In *Satire TV: Politics and Comedy in the Post-Network Era,* edited by Jonathan Gray, Jeffrey P. Jones, and Ethan Thompson. New York: New York University Press, 2009.

Kinon, Cristina. "Political Grist for Comedy Mill." *Daily News,* October 26, 2008, Sunday Now, 6.

Kolbert, Elizabeth. "Stooping to Conquer: Why Candidates Need to Make Fun of Themselves." *New Yorker,* April 19, 2004.

Kompare, Derek. *Rerun Nation.* London: Routledge, 2005.

Lafayette, Jon. "Political Parodies Pay in Election Year." *Television Week,* October 6, 2008, 1.

Lamb, Chris. *Drawn to Extremes: The Use and Abuse of Editorial Cartoons.* New York: Columbia University Press, 2004.

Liebovich, Mark. "Laugh, or the World Laughs at You." *New York Times,* October 5, 2008.

Miller, Melissa K., Jeffrey S. Peake, and Brittany Anne Boulton. "Testing the *Saturday Night Live* Hypothesis: Fairness and Bias in Newspaper Coverage of Hillary Clinton's Presidential Campaign." *Politics and Gender* 6 (2010):169–198.

Peyser, Marc. "Al and Dubya after Hours." *Newsweek,* October 30, 2000.

Purdham, Todd S. "*Saturday Night Live* Mocks Politics with Bi-Partisan Gusto." *Politico,* April 29, 2011, http://www.politico.com/news/stories/0411/53754.html.

Rutenberg, Jim. "Live, from New York, It's George Bush!" *New York Times,* January 25, 2001, E1.

Sanneh, Kelefa. "Laughing Matters: Saturday-Night Politics." *New Yorker,* October 27, 2008, 94.

Shales, Tom, and James Andrew Miller. *Live from New York: An Uncensored History of Saturday Night Live.* New York: Little, Brown, 2002.

Smith, Chris, and Ben Voth. "The Role of Humor in Political Argument: How 'Strategery' and 'Lockboxes' Changed a Political Campaign." *Argumentation and Advocacy* 39 (Fall 2002): 110–129.

Smith, Jeff. *The Presidents We Imagine: Two Centuries of White House Fictions on the Page, on the Stage, Onscreen, and Online.* Madison: University of Wisconsin Press, 2009.

Stanley, Alessandra. "On *SNL* It's the Real Sarah Palin, Looking Like a Real Entertainer." *New York Times,* October 20, 2008.

Stelter, Brian. "Web Site's Formula for Success: TV Content with Fewer Ads." *New York Times,* October 29, 2008.

Strachan, Alex. "The Parody Goes On: Poking Fun at the Political Scene Still Gets Laughs for 33-Year-Old TV Show." *Times Colonist* (Victoria, BC), July 23, 2008, C9.

Williams, Brian. "*SNL* Becomes Player in Campaign 2000." *The News with Brian Williams,* MSNBC, October 13, 2000.

Young, Dannagal G. "Political Entertainment and the Press's Construction of Sarah Feylin." *Popular Communication* 9(4) (2011):251–265.

Zengerle, Jason. "The State of the George W. Bush Joke." *New York Times,* August 22, 2004, sec. 2, 1.

Zinoman, Jason. "Comedians in Chief Mustn't Be Prudent." *New York Times,* December 5, 2011.

Speaking Too Soon: *SNL*, 9/11, and the Remaking of American Irony

MATT SIENKIEWICZ

Cultural critics have long shown a proclivity for dabbling in other areas of intellectual practice including, on occasion, the coronary sciences. There is, it seems, a considerable sense of satisfaction in the finality of declaring the death of various abstractions. Such statements rarely look prescient retrospectively, but this has not stopped a string of eminent Western thinkers from announcing that all sorts of intangible things have forever departed from the realm of the living, or at least of the relevant. G. W. F. Hegel declared "history" to be over in 1806. Friedrich Nietzsche boldly announced the death of God in 1882. Francis Fukuyama, building on Hegel's declaration, in 1992 once more proclaimed the "end of history" after the fall of Soviet communism.[1] And, according to many, irony took its final breaths on the smoke-filled morning of September 11, 2001.

On September 12, Andrew Coyne of the Canadian *National Post* wrote, "The Age of Irony died yesterday," a claim that has been frequently repeated and mocked ever since.[2] *Vanity Fair*'s Graydon Carter took up the same notion a week later, stating flatly, "It's the end of the age of irony."[3] *Time*'s Roger Rosenblatt wrote an oft-cited article entitled "The Age of Irony Comes to an End," claiming, among other things, that 9/11 would forever end a prevalent cultural attitude that failed to distinguish "a joke from a menace."[4] However unlikely, the events of 9/11, it seems, helped to place a concept generally relegated to the intellectual realms of philosophy and literary criticism squarely within mainstream public discourse. In hindsight, this connection may seem rather strange, if not outright foolish. Nonetheless, there is no denying the seriousness with which it was taken at the time.

Coyne, Carter, Rosenblatt, and others who supported the death-of-irony thesis have been met with the same skepticism and occasional derision visited upon those who had argued for the death of God and history before them. Despite the solemnity that swept over the United States and much of the world in the wake of 9/11, people have not ceased to enjoy sarcastic or politically skeptical humor. In fact, shows like *The Daily Show with Jon Stewart* (1999–present), *The Colbert Report* (2005–present), *South Park* (1997–present), and others have arguably brought this mode of comedy to new heights in terms of both artistry and popularity.

What, precisely, would it mean to say that American irony died on 9/11? The interpretations implied by most contemporary popular commentators on the subject suggest that the mere existence of humor since the fall of the Twin Towers proves the ineptitude of cultural undertakers like Carter and Rosenblatt. *Newsweek,* in its celebration of the young century's greatest misjudgments, quite uncharitably suggests that Carter's statement was meant to communicate that the United States would "stop laughing" altogether after the tragedy. Pointing to the release of the comedic film *Zoolander* (2001), the magazine rests its case.[5] If irony is equated with comedy, then it is silly to suggest that irony did, or ever could, die.

Of course, both popular commentators and scholars have put forth more nuanced understandings of the death of irony. Writing for the comedy commentary website *Splitsider* nearly a decade after 9/11, A. J. Aronstein thoughtfully reappraises the death-of-irony thesis, suggesting that it really identified the demise of a certain "postmodern" sensibility that stood in contrast with cultural authenticity.[6] Media scholars Jonathan Gray, Jeffrey P. Jones, and Ethan Thompson point to a post-network era marked by the incisive satire of *The Daily Show, The Colbert Report, Saturday Night Live,* and *South Park,* arguing that now "humor is able to deal powerfully with serious issues of power and politics" and drawing a sharp distinction between productive irony and the "light, frivolous" variety that people such as Carter and Rosenblatt pronounced dead.[7] Amber Day, in a book-length treatment of the subject of comedy and politics, argues that the death-of-irony thesis was largely underpinned by an assumption that irony is inherently opposed to authenticity and that a better conceptual frame sees "irony as a mode of engagement rather than . . . [as a] cynical dismissal of politics."[8] Correcting this misunderstanding of irony, she suggests, will help explain why irony did not die with 9/11.

In this chapter I consider the question of irony and 9/11 via a close look at *SNL*'s comedic tendencies both before and after that tragic day. Although I cannot go as far as to reaffirm the overwrought mortuary declarations of Carter and Rosenblatt, I do wish to take seriously the possibility that a real change in ironic modes of comedy took place around this time. To do so, I offer two separate, though not entirely unrelated, conceptions of irony. In discussing pre-9/11 *SNL*, I draw upon the literary and philosophical work of Søren Kierkegaard, particularly his notion of "the ironist." According to Ronald Schleifer, this character embraces "infinite negativity," and thus "is absolutely negatively free in total possibility."[9] By Kierkegaardian irony, I mean a view that approaches the world with the sense that all meaning is ultimately artificial and thus nothing ought to be taken seriously. This view denies that anything is, in a fundamental sense, important and thus embraces a perspective through which surface-level aesthetics are allowed to replace traditional ethical and religious understandings of the meaning of life. Engaging with popular critic Jedediah Purdy, I suggest that pre-9/11 *SNL* can be productively viewed as embracing a mode of comedy akin to the irony Kierkegaard describes (but, it must be said, does not like).

I then consider the moment directly following 9/11, suggesting that, for a brief time, *SNL*, like much of American television, really did attempt to portray sincerity and shied away from irony of any kind. However, this irony-free moment quickly passed. Considering post-9/11 *SNL*, I suggest that, for a variety of reasons, the program turned away from the Kierkegaardian sense of irony and toward a more classical, Socratic approach. Described in the *Oxford Dictionary of Philosophy* as "Socrates's irritating tendency to praise his hearers while undermining them," Socratic irony is a mode of address in which a specific meaning may be twisted, but only in the service of asserting a sincerely held alternative meaning.[10] As opposed to Kierkegaard's ironist, who speaks in a manner that negates the possibility for any true meaning, Socratic irony says one thing in order to passionately argue for its opposite. It is something akin to sarcasm in the common sense, but it is a sarcasm that is meant to prove a specific point. Through a careful analysis of a variety of *SNL* sketches as well as a consideration of the program's industrial and cultural contexts, I argue that although irony did not disappear on 9/11, the moment did mark a turning point at which the dominance of a nihilistic, Kierkegaardian form of irony began to slip away and a Socratic, more politically and socially committed mode of ironic address took its place.

SNL'S PURDIAN/KIERKEGAARDIAN PRE-9/11 IRONY

Though those declaring the death of irony at the time of 9/11 never addressed his work directly, the person most closely associated with the definition of irony that circulated widely during the 1990s is Jedediah Purdy. In his bestselling work *For Common Things*, Purdy crafts a jeremiad against contemporary American society, declaring it to be high on cynicism and distrust and very low on sincerity and commitment, intellectual or otherwise. The diagnosis he puts forth is that Americans have suffered from an excess of irony and, accordingly, they have cultivated an inability to authentically engage in anything sincere. Purdy came under considerable fire for suggesting that the United States was incapable of taking anything seriously just a few years before the rise of Jon Stewart, Stephen Colbert, and a more politically oriented *SNL*. In large part this negative critical attention is due to a perceived imprecision and curmudgeonliness in his writing. Day provides a highly critical reading of Purdy, which implicitly blames his writing for the confusion over the concept of irony that has proliferated since 9/11. According to Day, the problem stems largely from Purdy's use of irony as a stand-in for an imprecise "cluster of contemporary attitudes." Day understands Purdy's notion of irony as "smirking cynicism," a definition that, she argues, serves to devalue any type of address that fails to conform to traditional, unfunny modes of rhetoric and communication.[11]

I would like to reconsider the utility of Purdy's analysis. His notion of the ironic may not be precise enough to meet the highest standards of academic rigor, but it is not as vague or conceptually impotent as many of his critics have suggested. In order to ground his rather abstract ideas, Purdy focuses on Jerry Seinfeld, who he believes incarnates the distanced,

SPEAKING TOO SOON   97

uncommitted worldview that dominated American life throughout the 1990s. Seinfeld, Purdy writes, "resists disappointment or failure by refusing to identify strongly with any project, relationship, or aspiration."[12] Above all, this brand of irony denies the value in, or perhaps even the possibility of, "earnest speech."[13] In essence, what Purdy seems to be arguing is that 1990s American popular culture was marked by an insistence on undermining itself. Television like *Seinfeld* (1990–1998) and *Saturday Night Live*'s "Wayne's World" sketches, he argues, could only find meaning in denying the possibility that depth could be achieved in any form, let alone in popular culture.

For Purdy, 1990s American irony is nihilistic and inherently hostile to any notion that humor could serve a productive social function. In this regard, it draws upon an important Kierkegaardian conception and denunciation of irony. Purdy's reading of Jerry Seinfeld and Wayne and Garth suggests that during this time Americans had become attracted to what Søren Kierkegaard (also unsympathetically) understands as the ironic or "aesthetic" mode of existence. The ironist, or aesthete, as described in Kierkegaard's *The Concept of Irony*, is a figure who, seeing the absurd seriousness with which society can treat ultimately trivial matters, resorts to a playful existence that, while light and free on the surface, conceals an "infinite negativity" at its core.[14] The ironist, for both Kierkegaard in the 1840s and Purdy in the 1990s, is someone who denies that real ethical and political values can exist and thus chooses to make up her own, knowing full well that these self-created values will not stand up to any kind of serious scrutiny.

Though Purdy does not engage with Kierkegaard's ironist in his critique, his brief treatment of *SNL*'s "Wayne's World" suggests that it is this particular vision of the ironic that he sees dominating American culture before 9/11—a situation he feels is detrimental to U.S. society's political and ethical health. The catchphrase-laden "Wayne's World" sketches and films, Purdy argues, mimic a society in which "we find ourselves using phrases that are caught up in a web we did not weave."[15] According to Purdy, in the 1990s Americans felt there was little to be gained or lost on the level of fundamental moral and political issues. As a result, mainstream culture became content to play the game of constant self-reference. The collage of song lyrics, catchphrases, and obsession with the superficial culture of heavy metal music in "Wayne's World" never gets around to saying anything meaningful about the kinds of issues essential to a morally functioning society—what Purdy might call "authenticity."

A close look at the *SNL* episodes immediately preceding and following 9/11 provide a useful vantage point to apply Purdy's Kierkegaardian understanding of irony in a concrete fashion. In an apparent coincidence, both episodes began with a segment centering on New York mayor Rudy Giuliani. The final episode of the 2000–2001 *SNL* season opens with a shot of Giuliani's Gracie Mansion. The scene then cuts to Darrell Hammond doing his impression of the mayor, sitting in a leather chair and addressing the camera. He introduces the audience to his "friend" Judith Nathan, a woman well known at the time as Giuliani's mistress. Nathan, played by Rachel Dratch, hides playfully behind a plant as Giuliani describes the unfairness of his wife's refusal to allow Nathan to visit the mansion. For the remainder of the sketch, Giuliani's wife chases Nathan around with a baseball bat while the mayor makes repeated references to rumors of his sexual dysfunction. Rather than providing a cogent critique of Giuliani's politics, the sketch's text is an exercise in the sort of free play and superficial referentiality that Purdy attributes to the ironist's worldview, albeit with a disturbing twist. In the midst of a series of jokes about his wife's attacks on him and his own obsession with Nathan, Giuliani offhandedly commends Robert Blake for "taking things into his own hands" the previous week—a reference to Blake's recent arrest for the murder of his wife, Bonnie Lee Bakley. The joke, which elicited groans from the studio audience, represents the very sort of cultural moment that Purdy bemoans and that Carter and Rosenblatt wished dead after 9/11. Absent from the sketch is any explicit connection to how Giuliani's personal foibles relate to the politics of New York City or his ability to successfully govern. Having spent some years providing a seemingly endless supply of Clinton-Lewinsky jokes, *SNL* seemed to be invoking Giuliani as a way of reinstating a discourse in which political scandal is primarily associated with soap-opera storylines as opposed to legitimate public concern.

Certainly, some readers may have read this scene as being politically engaged. Giuliani's conspicuously conservative approach to sex and crime in New York City could have served as a bridge from the sketch's content to more serious matters of public policy and morality. However,

Figure 5.1. Darrell Hammond plays Mayor Giuliani in *SNL*'s last pre-9/11 show.

there is little evidence that this is the preferred meaning of the scene. No joke is made of Giuliani's ability to govern New York City or the political ramifications of his infidelities. The punch lines are fully personal and apolitical, including the culminating line in which Giuliani rejoices he's "fifty-seven with a comb-over and a broken penis and the ladies still fight over" him. Dropped directly into the middle of this ironic (in the Kierkegaardian sense) play is the serious allusion to the murder of Bakley. Played for nothing more than a cheap laugh, this reference is an example par excellence of Purdy's understanding of pre-9/11 irony. The Blake-Bakley murder story is treated exclusively as a signifier, quickly dropped into the scene in connection to Giuliani's frustration over his wife's refusal to accept his mistress. Whether or not it is funny is somewhat beside the point. There were certainly ample opportunities for the sketch to skewer Giuliani's policies as well as his personality. As a law-and-order Republican who made a great show of banning "sex-oriented businesses" in New York City, Giuliani's personal foibles perhaps say a great deal about the relationship between public and private sexuality.[16]

Jokes about violence may well have been connected to issues of domestic abuse or police brutality. And perhaps some viewers made these connections. The sketch, however, fails to provide them in a way that suggests the producers were concerned with the political ramifications of the sex-comedy of errors they were skewering. The bit exemplifies Jones's observation that *SNL*'s political impressions place "an emphasis on physical or phonetic resemblance that focuses on the politician's presentation of self" as opposed to taking seriously the relationship between satire and matters of true political importance.[17] As Purdy might put it, the Giuliani sketch does not appear to be committed to the notion that it has an important role to play in public discourse.

A sketch later in the same episode brings this very issue to the forefront, asking the audience to confront, and perhaps embrace, the fact that a program like *SNL* does not do anything useful in an ethical or political sense. In an animated segment of *TV Funhouse* produced by Robert Smigel, a character representing Lorne Michaels sits watching a cartoon within the cartoon. Titled "The Anatominals Show," it features classic Hanna-Barbera characters drawn with exaggerated breasts and testicles and discussing various ailments, including Boo-Boo's hemorrhoids. Eventually, Michaels has seen enough. He calls in Satan and tells him "the deal is off." He knew that producing TV was not meaningful work, but he had no idea "it would get this bad." Satan agrees to rescind Michaels's apparent pact with him, sending Michaels off to the life he would have lived without *SNL*. Michaels, wearing a ponytail and tie-dyed shirt, finds himself magically transported to Africa, delivering medical supplies. For a moment he is pleased, self-satisfactorily describing his new life as "noble" and "the road less traveled." Seconds later he is terrorized by a giant mosquito and panics when he can't find bottled water. When an angel appears and offers to show him all of the good this version of himself could do, he refuses and begs the devil to return him to New York. In the last scene of the cartoon, he looks approvingly at "The Anatominals Show," remarking that the bit could be a "new hook" for *SNL*.

The cartoon supports Purdy's case, making the claim that *SNL* in May 2001 bore no relation to the sort of things that are truly important. This *SNL* bit revels in its own moral irrelevance and mocks the very notion that a meeting point might be found between the comedy TV pro-

Figure 5.2. "The Anatominals Show."

ducer and the ethically driven individual. In some ways the sketch might be implying that this is a bad state of affairs, but it does not in any explicit way challenge the underlying distinction that it makes between TV comedy and positive social change; in its logic, being a television comedy producer and working toward the social good are incompatible activities. While this assumption may be accepted by some, the many academic and popular commentators who have devoted their work to spelling out the political, cultural, and social implications of *SNL, The Daily Show, The Colbert Report,* and other programs would resist the idea that TV comedy cannot serve as a vehicle for a sincere engagement with the social good. Furthermore, post-9/11 comedy writers and comedians have made concerted efforts to place themselves directly in the field of citizen action. While Colbert and Stewart's "Rally to Restore Sanity and/or Fear" best exemplifies these attempts, *SNL* has also aimed to break down the wall between comedy and committed political and ethical positions. This was perhaps most famously seen in Tina Fey's feminist "Bitches Get Stuff Done" monologue in support of Hillary Clinton. "The Anatominals"/ Michaels sketch, however, seems to be a gently self-mocking nod at the program's lack of engagement in anything beyond the realm of cultural play. As television and *SNL* changed during the first decade of the twenty-first century, this attitude would melt away, leading to a comedy world that was more likely to embrace a sense of social engagement and to eschew any notion that humor was somehow diametrically opposed to a worldview in which questions of right and wrong were no longer relevant.

STAGE TWO: GIULIANIAN AUTHENTICITY; OR, THE QUEST FOR APPROVAL

SNL's return to the air on September 29, 2001, also featured Giuliani. This time New York's mayor, now recognized as a national hero, played himself. Breaking the program's decades-old format, the episode opened with a somber, ten-minute prologue that featured an emotional musical performance by Paul Simon, a tribute to New York's firefighters, and a now-famous exchange between Lorne Michaels and Giuliani. Whereas in the show's twenty-sixth season Giuliani had been portrayed as little more than a collection of silly signifiers often attributed to a prototypical politician—selfishness, lustfulness, obliviousness—during season twenty-seven's opener his presence anchored the show's authentic commitment to honoring the victims of September 11. As the very serious opening segment came to a close, Lorne Michaels turned to Giuliani, embracing him as the embodiment of the pain and resilience of New York City. Then, Michaels asked the mayor if it was okay for the show to be funny from that point forward. Giuliani's response of "why start now?" has been noted by scholars such as Lynn Spigel and Amber Day as representing an official government sanctioning of post-9/11 laughter.[18] And it also marked the beginning of a period of transition in *SNL*'s comedy.

SNL's efforts at sincerity and its concern with asking permission went well beyond the opening segment with Giuliani. In her opening monologue for that first post-9/11 episode, host Reese Witherspoon offered a combination of promises and apologies, making clear to the audience that something about comedy had changed, at least for the time being. She began by expressing her appreciation for the audience's presence or, as one might interpret her remarks, their very existence. She then assured the crowd that, despite the circumstances, the cast and crew would "give it everything [they've] got." Finally, she asked permission to tell a joke, in much the way that Michaels had asked Giuliani. This time, however, the gatekeeper was the audience, which encouraged her to tell the joke, despite her admonition that it would contain a "bad word." The joke was not a particularly funny one, but it was delivered in a friendly, undeniably sincere fashion. The punch line involved a boy, apparently having been raised as a polar bear, remarking that he is "freezing [his] balls off."

The content of the humor, in many ways, had changed remarkably little from the episode preceding it. Both the pre- and post-9/11 episodes prominently included jokes that referenced animal testicles. But the mode of address used throughout the Witherspoon episode was very much changed, with moments of stressed, perhaps even forced, sincerity appearing at various intervals. The events of 9/11 had forced *SNL* to consider what role it might play in a world in which nothing, including comedy, would get a free pass with regard to moral significance. Before launching into her polar bear joke, Witherspoon acknowledged as much, saying that the cast and crew were still "figuring things out." This episode, as well as some of those that would follow, regularly broke out of comedic modes of address entirely, speaking sincerely to the audience, seemingly reminding viewers that *SNL* realized it now had to serve a purpose beyond just making people laugh. During the Witherspoon episode, "Weekend Update" featured an appeal for donations to the Twin Towers Fund, alongside a declaration by Tina Fey that "New York City is awesome." A few weeks later, Drew Barrymore would mix into her opening monologue an authentic-sounding account of her fears about traveling to New York during the anthrax scare that immediately followed the 9/11 attacks. While it was acceptable at this juncture to make jokes, a few of which even touched upon 9/11-related topics, such as Osama bin Laden, humor could no longer revel in its frivolousness. The specter of something that truly did matter, something that irrefutably existed beyond the realm of the aesthetic free play embraced by the ironist, demanded a new mode of comedic address, even if *SNL* did not have time to fully adapt to this new style. Though the show would later come to integrate this sense of meaning into its comedy, it began by occasionally interrupting its previous approach to humor with moments of reference to the serious situation surrounding the program's production in New York City.

Looking at this immediate post-9/11 moment, Lynn Spigel points to the brief popularity of "event TV" geared toward giving U.S. broadcasting a connection with national unity and, perhaps, providing a communal sense of injury that could underpin the coming war effort.[19] *SNL*, if only briefly, engaged in this mode of address as a bridge away from 9/11 and, I argue, ultimately toward a different, more politically engaged mode of comedy suited to the changing climate of the first decade of the twenty-first century. But while larger, more famous comedy institutions such as *SNL* and the network late-night talk shows were engaged in the type of unifying displays of authenticity described by Spigel, smaller, more nimble outlets took on the trauma of 9/11 directly. Most famously, *The Onion* held nothing back with its first post-9/11 issue, declaring in bold headline type "HOLY FUCKING SHIT: Attack on America." Paul Achter argues that *The Onion,* in contrast to the type of comedy on broadcast television, engaged deeply with the carnivalesque in order to "activate a rhetoric of healing."[20] The faux news stories in the issue put the terrorists through various hellish trials and tribulations, and in one article "the hijackers become food, sex toys, and receptacles for feces."[21] This approach to post-tragedy comedy was aimed at confronting the real, deeply angry feelings of Americans. Though meant to evoke laughter, it nonetheless was steeped in an authenticity that embraced the ethical possibilities of humor.

This strategy was not immediately embraced by *SNL*, which deployed its arsenal of humor in its return episode in order to craft seemingly risqué jokes about hemorrhoids and bestiality. Directly following Witherspoon's monologue, *SNL's* return episode featured a faux ad for Preparation H that mimicked the "extreme sports" marketing campaigns of products such as Mountain Dew. The first live sketch of the program involved a shipwrecked Will Ferrell becoming increasingly uncomfortable with the fact that a mermaid, though pleasingly featuring the top half of Reese Witherspoon, would nonetheless possess a fish's vagina. The sketch is carnivalesque in content, and it is far from clear that this mode of address is intended as any sort of significant commentary. Whereas *The Onion* employed the subversive elements of comedy and satire in order to give expression to the—perhaps conflicted—ethical intuitions of Americans, *SNL* began its post-9/11 life in a far more hesitant fashion.

STAGE THREE: *SNL*, STEWART, AND SOCRATES

A week later *SNL* took a step down the trail that *The Onion* had blazed and that would become a trademark of post-9/11 comedy. Apparently more comfortable now in taking a critical look at America's new cultural milieu, the second episode after 9/11 clearly displayed evidence of a new era of *SNL* that would feature a deeper sense of political engagement. The episode featured a variety of sketches that addressed questions of post-9/11 American life, and though they were far gentler than the humor found in *The Onion*, this material nonetheless featured a considerably more critical brand of comedy. In one of the season's best-known sketches, Will Ferrell arrives at work wearing a red, white, and blue thong in lieu of pants, claiming that in doing so he is the only person at the office displaying real patriotism. Whereas others have donned pins or kerchiefs with U.S. themes, he has chosen to wear nothing but the old stars and stripes. The sketch is carnivalesque in the extreme, flipping societal standards by replacing casual work attire with an outfit that prominently features Ferrell's bare buttocks and fuzzy paunch. The target of the comedy, it seems, is the issue of authentic patriotism and the relationship that certain surface expressions, such as verbal declarations and fashion statements, might bear to it. By parodying surface expressions, however, the sketch posits, or at least asks the viewer to consider, the possibility of a true, meaningful patriotism that might consist of other, more productive forms of expression. Such a reading of the sketch positions it in direct opposition to Purdy's idea of American irony before 9/11, which was premised on the notion that authenticity of any kind was not a goal worth pursuing.

A later sketch in the same episode takes on U.S. popular culture and perhaps even *SNL's* previous episode, skewering the over-the-top efforts at sincerity found on various 9/11 television specials and tributes. A parody of the red carpet preshow of 2001's famously delayed Emmy Awards ceremony, the sketch features impressions of celebrities competing for attention via increasingly overt displays of self-abnegating patriotism. Calista Flockhart loudly and repeatedly announces that the day was not about her but America, making a loud, self-glorifying scene in the process. Della Reese, played by Tracy Morgan, shows up wearing only a trash bag, suggesting that her fashion choice represents just the sort of self-effacement that such a somber occasion calls for. The joke throughout the sketch is that American popular culture in the weeks following 9/11 had claimed a sincere interest in helping the nation cope with the tragedy but had, in truth, used it as yet another ploy for attention. There were things that really needed to be done during this time, but the sketch suggested that popular culture, at least in certain high-profile ways, was failing to do so. There is a harshness that distinguishes it from the pre-9/11 "Anatominals" bit described above. The sketch ends with Joan Rivers crying in a desperate attempt to show her somber patriotism. Whereas "The Anatominals" embraced pop culture's inability to make a positive impact, this sketch mourns it.

These sketches, I argue, mark *SNL's* turn toward a different sort of irony—one that stands in strong contrast to the vision described by Purdy and that I have compared to Kierkegaard's ironist. Instead, this mode of comedy draws upon a more traditional, Socratic notion of irony. Whereas the aesthetic irony of Kierkegaard and Wayne and Garth aims to negate the possibility of real meaning by relegating all communication to the level of surface appearances, the Socratic, post-9/11 version attempts a far more targeted inversion. As opposed to putting in doubt the ultimate importance of addressing an issue, as I argue the pre-9/11 Giuliani sketch did, these bits say one thing in order to prove its opposite. In Platonic dialogues, this approach to irony is most evident when Socrates praises his opponent's intelligence or denigrates his own. In such cases he says one thing in order to eventually, more forcefully, compel his interlocutor to switch positions. Such is the case when Ferrell declares that wearing a patriotic thong is the essence of supporting your nation or Morgan says that wearing a trash bag is a sign of celebrity humbleness. These utterances do not mean what they say, but they do have a precise rhetorical intention. Most crucially, they do not deny the possibility of meaningful action; they simply aim to outline the parameters of such engagement by defining what is not appropriate or effective. In the world of contemporary comedy, this brand of irony is best instantiated by the persona of Stephen Colbert, whose endless irony is not meant to deny the possibility of meaning but instead to reinforce the absurdity of the positions he takes in order to argue for their opposites.

This is not to say that *SNL* never engaged in this form of comedy before 9/11 or always did after it. Clearly this is not the case. However, there was a marked turn in *SNL*'s approach to political and social engagement beginning with 9/11, even if it has subsided somewhat as memories of the tragedy have become more distant. Sketches in the immediate post-9/11 period had a tendency to focus on policies more and political personalities less than in previous eras, although, as Jones has argued, *SNL*'s presidential impressions will probably always rely on personal foibles and simple mimesis to some extent.[22] Increasingly, however, *SNL* after 9/11 began to take on the minutiae of governmental practice and to devote prime slots, particularly cold opens, to sketches that required an in-depth understanding of current events in order to be fully appreciated. By the second half of the decade following 9/11, viewers could expect *SNL* to provide very specific takes on public life that implied a need for seriousness through the use of ironic comedy. The merging of *SNL* and the importance of real public engagement reached its height with Tina Fey's scathing, uncanny impression of Republican vice presidential candidate Sarah Palin. Scholars Jody Baumgardner, Jonathan Morris, and Natasha Walth have gone so far as to describe a "Tina Fey effect," in which viewers were primed by Fey's *SNL* sketches and ultimately came to reject the viability of Palin's candidacy.[23] Though Fey and *SNL* never explicitly stated it, most came to read the sketches as making a direct statement on the appropriateness of Palin as a national political figure. Such a sense of sincere commitment stands directly opposed to the Purdian explanation of 1990s irony. And, perhaps just as interestingly, *SNL* has continued with this mode of engagement beyond election season.

For example, on September 17, 2009, *SNL* opened its special Thursday prime-time episode with an extended sketch dealing with a briefly famous congressional moment during which Senator Joe Wilson defied all notions of decorum and screamed "You lie!" during a speech by President Obama. The sketch opens with a meeting of Republican senators who in a brief moment of miscalculation, decide they will all scream "You lie!" at the president. At this point Wilson excuses himself from the room. The Republicans then quickly reconsider their decision, coming to the conclusion that to do such a thing would be preposterous. Wilson, of course, misses the change in plans. The sketch then cuts to after the speech, with Wilson reeling from the isolation and embarrassment of his lone wolf defiance of proper behavior.

The Wilson event was certainly newsworthy at the time, and during a previous era *SNL* might have featured it, perhaps as an item during "Weekend Update." However, by 2009 *SNL* had moved to a strategy of humor barely recognizable from the pre-9/11 days of softly handled parodies of the peccadilloes of the Clintons and Giulianis of the world. Instead, the sketch made a very specific critique that reinforced a clear sense of right and wrong. A plausible and, I would argue, producer-preferred reading of the sketch is that in crafting a ridiculous situation in which Wilson's outburst was perhaps somewhat understandable, the humor emphasizes the impossibility of any such justification. Although irony is the mode of address in the sketch, it is not being exercised for the purpose of negation or as a disavowal of the ultimate meaningfulness of comedy. Instead, following the Socratic mode of irony, it presented the opposite of the point it wished to make, not only to get a laugh, but also to make a claim about the direction of U.S. political life.

CONCLUSION

It is important to note that this shift in modes of comedic irony is not solely the result of 9/11. As Spigel argues, the trauma of 9/11 hardly served as the ultimate determinant of the shape that American television would take during the first decade of the twenty-first century. Despite a brief moment in which networks focused on national unity as a reaction to the tragic events, very quickly "the competitive environment of narrowcasting . . . gave way to the 'bottom line.'"[24] In the realm of comedy, this meant a field of play inundated with specifically targeted programming geared precisely at the younger audiences *SNL* had traditionally succeeded in courting. Producing a variety of comedy programs on a daily basis, Comedy Central and Cartoon Network have played a key role in shaping the comedic expectations of many viewers. At the same time, Internet outlets such as *The Onion* and *Funny or Die* have provided nonstop material, much of which is pitched in terms of political and social critique. Just as *SNL* would ultimately embrace web-friendly video segments in order to keep up with the comedy marketplace, the turn toward socially engaged, often politically motivated comedy can also be read as a move necessitated by marketplace expectations. Furthermore, there is a danger in overstating the extent to which *SNL* has devoted itself to the sorts of complex, politically engaged comedy described above. With an hour and a half to fill each week and a mass audience with varied political beliefs to attract, *SNL* by necessity often relies on the silly and the simple. As Jones notes in this volume, there remains a need for the show to mock the more superficial elements of U.S. life and politics.

Nonetheless, watching *SNL* episodes from before and after 9/11 does give the impression that something has changed with regard to the program's self-conception, at least in certain memorable moments. Even now, more than a decade after 9/11, the program shows a consistent willingness not simply to point out absurdities in the world, but also to make cogent—or at least provocative—points regarding right and wrong. And this approach has moved beyond the realm of politics. In the February 18, 2012, episode, the cold open took on the brief but impressive popularity of Asian American basketball player Jeremy Lin. During the sketch, three basketball analysts describe Lin in increasingly stereotypical terms without a sense of impropriety. The fourth makes parallel statements about African American players and is immediately reprimanded for being ignorant and racist. The bit, I would argue, is employing a Socratic mode of irony in order to point out the racist manner in which the American media has been willing to essentialize and make a novelty out of an Asian athlete. This is not a mere comedic point. It is an incisive critique and one that not only assumes a certain sense of right and wrong, but also suggests that a sketch comedy show ought to play a role in pursuing, or at least pointing to, the right. It is fruitless to claim such a sketch could never have been written before 9/11. Yet it is worth considering the ways in which it would have stood out during the 1990s and feels more natural in the show's current era. Irony did not die after 9/11, of course. It has always existed and always will exist in many different forms. The balance of those forms can change, however, and it is worth noting the ways in which the decade or so following one of America's greatest tragedies has led to a golden era for comedy willing to be ironic but also not afraid to make a point.

Notes

1. Fukuyama, *The End of History and the Last Man.*
2. Qtd. in Randall, "The 'Death of Irony.'"
3. Qtd. in Beers, "Irony Is Dead! Long Live Irony!"

4. Rosenblatt, "The Age of Irony Comes to an End."

5. Peyser, "Graydon Carter Proclaims the End of Irony."

6. Aronstein, "Comedy after 9/11."

7. Gray, Jones, and Thompson. "The State of Satire," 11.

8. Day, *Satire and Dissent,* 32.

9. Schleifer, "Irony, Identity and Repetition," 48.

10. Blackburn, *Oxford Dictionary of Philosophy,* 343.

11. Day, *Satire and Dissent,* 28.

12. Purdy, *For Common Things,* 14.

13. Ibid., 10.

14. Schleifer, "Irony, Identity and Repetition," 46.

15. Purdy, *For Common Things,* 11.

16. Myers, "Giuliani Proposes Toughening Laws on X-Rated Shops."

17. Jones, "With All Due Respect," 43.

18. Spigel, "Entertainment Wars," 236.

19. Ibid., 244.

20. Achter, "Comedy in Unfunny Times," 294.

21. Ibid., 293.

22. Jones, "With All Due Respect."

23. Qtd. in Kliff, "Wonkblog."

24. Spigel, "Entertainment Wars," 257.

Works Cited

Achter, Paul. "Comedy in Unfunny Times: News Parody and Carnival after 9/11." *Critical Studies in Media Communication* 25(3) (2008):274–303.

Aronstein, A. J. "Comedy after 9/11: Sincerity and Irony." *Splitsider,* September 8, 2011. http://splitsider.com/2011/09/comedy-after-911-sincerity-and-irony (accessed September 10, 2012).

Beers, David. "Irony Is Dead! Long Live Irony!" *Salon,* September 25, 2001. http://www.salon.com/2001/09/25/irony_lives/ (accessed September 10, 2012).

Blackburn, Simon. *Oxford Dictionary of Philosophy.* New York: Oxford University Press, 2008.

Day, Amber. *Satire and Dissent: Interventions in Contemporary Political Debate.* Bloomington: Indiana University Press, 2011.

Fukuyama, Francis. *The End of History and the Last Man.* New York: Free Press, 1992.

Gray, Jonathan, Jeffrey Jones, and Ethan Thompson. "The State of Satire, the Satire of State." In *Satire TV,* edited by J. Gray, J. Jones, and E. Thompson, 3–36. New York: New York University Press, 2009.

Jones, Jeffrey. "With All Due Respect: Satirizing Presidents from *Saturday Night Live* to *Lil' Bush.*" In *Satire TV,* edited by J. Gray, J. Jones, and E. Thompson, 37–63. New York: New York University Press, 2009.

Kliff, Sarah. "Wonkblog." *Washington Post,* March 9, 2012. http://www.washingtonpost.com/blogs/ezra-klein/post/the-tina-fey-effect/2012/03/09/gIQAwmj01R_blog.html (accessed September 10, 2012).

Myers, Steven Lee. "Giuliani Proposes Toughening Laws on X-Rated Shops." *New York Times,* September 11, 1994. http://www.nytimes.com/1994/09/11/nyregion/giuliani

-proposes-toughening-laws-on-x-rated-shops.html?pagewanted=all (accessed September 10, 2012).

Peyser, Marc. "Graydon Carter Proclaims the End of Irony." *Newsweek,* December 10, 2009. http://2010.newsweek.com/top-10/worst-predictions/graydon-carter.html (accessed January 18, 2012).

Purdy, Jedediah. *For Common Things: Irony, Trust, and Commitment in America Today.* New York: Knopf, 1999.

Randall, Eric. "The 'Death of Irony,' and Its Many Reincarnations." *Atlantic,* September 9, 2011. http://www.theatlanticwire.com/national/2011/09/death-irony-and-its -many-reincarnations/42298 (accessed September 10, 2012).

Rosenblatt, Roger. "The Age of Irony Comes to an End." *Time,* September 24, 2001. http://www.time.com/time/magazine/article/0,9171,1000893,00.html.

Schleifer, Ronald. "Irony, Identity and Repetition: On Kierkegaard's *The Concept of Irony.*" *SubStance* 8(25) (1979):44–54.

Spigel, Lynn. "Entertainment Wars: Television Culture after 9/11." *American Quarterly* 56(2) (2004):235–271.

Live Music: Mediating Musical Performance and Discord on *Saturday Night Live*

ALYXANDRA VESEY

In early 2012, Sleigh Bells, an indie rock act known for massive guitar riffs, propulsive beats, and breathy female vocals, was a musical guest on NBC's *Saturday Night Live.* Sleigh Bells is, above all, a loud band. Using uncommonly high volume and distortion, the musicians pummel listeners with their outsized pop sensibilities, creating an experience known for its visceral impact. Yet, slotted in between sketches on *SNL,* Sleigh Bells sounded almost tame. The band's televised performance failed to communicate the frenetic energy and sense of spontaneity it creates in concert, on recordings, and, one imagines, even for the audience in Studio 8H. Though just one example, Sleigh Bells' brief set is nonetheless indicative of *SNL*'s approach to live music over its almost four decades on NBC. Despite consistently booking acts touted for being on the cutting edge, *SNL* usually ends up making its musical guests conform to the program's aural aesthetics and advertiser-friendly atmosphere; the music flows smoothly between segments and advertisements instead of drowning them out.

Music has always been integral to *SNL,* and in this chapter I examine a number of moments from its history that highlight the show's ambivalent relationship with musical performances. On the one hand, booking certain guests has helped the program appear culturally relevant. In its earliest years, for example, *SNL* frequently introduced underground bands to a mainstream audience; punk groups like Fear and the Clash and new wave groups like DEVO and the B-52s first entered people's homes via their live performances on *SNL,* not through MTV videos. On the other hand, *SNL's* priorities (e.g., maintaining its brand identity and its advertiser-based business model) have often led producers to make choices that undercut the very edginess they want to exploit. As I will argue, an important element of this ambivalence involves the program's emphasis on liveness. As other chapters in this volume point out, *SNL* has used the appeal of liveness—the sense that anything could happen—as a way to differentiate itself. As Feuer and Couldry argue, however, celebrations of liveness often mask the fact that live programming is always constructed; producers make numerous decisions about how to set sound levels and how to frame and edit a performance, which gives them control over how viewers experience the event.[1] The event may be live, but it is not raw.

SNL has often used music to brand the show as relevant, timely, and edgy. But at the same time it has tempered the potential risks inherent in such cultural expression by making choices that help integrate a performance into the show through aesthetic uniformity and by having it conform to the show's and the network's standards and practices and to perceived mainstream audience expectations. In the rest of the chapter, I examine how *SNL* did just this through its exploitation of key genres: punk, hip-hop, alternative rock, and indie rock. I end with a more extended discussion of two infamous musical moments involving female solo artists: Sinéad O'Connor in 1992 and Lana Del Rey in 2012. The negative reactions these performances received illustrate how the disruptive possibilities of live performance are restricted and policed by television audiences, media producers, and corporate enterprises.

ALTERNATIVE TO WHAT? INDEPENDENT FROM WHOM?: ASSUMING A MUSICAL SUBCULTURAL IDENTITY

Predating cable networks' frank depictions of human sexuality and other markers of televisual edge by nearly a decade, early iterations of *SNL* emphasized adult, subversive comedic material.[2] A sense of spontaneity marked the show's early years, most famously when John Belushi sliced host Buck Henry's ear during an installment of the recurring samurai sketch. Such volatility was also evident in *SNL*'s musical performances. For example, in 1977, Elvis Costello wanted to perform "Radio Radio," an ode to anti-commercialism. Columbia Records insisted he promote what its executives believed was the more marketable single "Less than Zero." A few bars into his live performance, however, he stopped, briefly addressed the crowd, and launched into a seething performance of "Radio Radio." *SNL* did not invite Costello back until 1989, which suggests that the program's desire to maintain a subcultural image was likely trumped by its desire to maintain a working partnership with NBC and advertisers. Nonetheless, linking itself to punk helped the program construct an edge, however blunted it may have been by network television's constraints. Key figures in *SNL*'s formation, particularly Belushi, were reported to be fans of the New York, Los Angeles, and London punk scenes.[3] The program demonstrated its investment in such associations by booking artists like Patti Smith and Fear and producing comedy sketches about the chaos of the punk scene and the recording industry's cynical maneuvers to exploit it. Gilda Radner's punk poet, Candy Slice, for example, was modeled on Smith.

Over the years, *SNL* made a conscious effort to incorporate musical trends just as they began to reach mainstream prominence. However, even in pursuing new, edgier styles, *SNL* aimed to tame live performances and avoid going too far in challenging mainstream sensibilities. In October 1986, *Cosby Show* (1984–1992) actor Malcolm-Jamal Warner hosted, and the musical guest was vanguard rap trio Run-DMC, the first hip-hop act to appear on *SNL*. The show was courting a young audience, similar to that being targeted by upstart network Fox, which launched that same month. *SNL*'s popularity had been floundering since the show lost Eddie Murphy in 1984 and had failed to find a replacement.[4] Booking Run-DMC let the producers tap into hip-hop's youthful energy and to do so a few years before cable television and commercial radio fully realized the genre's market potential.[5] But hip-hop, with its roots in New York street culture, was foreign to many TV viewers. Early in their career, Run-DMC set themselves apart from their peers with minimalist production in order to foreground their rhymes. However, the group's co-producer, Rick Rubin, sampled classic rock records and convinced the trio to cover Aerosmith's "Walk This Way" for their breakthrough album,

Raising Hell. The presence of Run-DMC gave *SNL* access to a subculture on the brink of mainstream success and promised to deliver something new and unexpected within the show's well-established formula. Yet this decision minimized the danger of losing control by giving the spotlight to artists who were accessible to an audience more comfortable with rock music. The trio, of course, performed "Walk This Way," to great acclaim.

During the 1990s, *SNL* booked alternative rock acts like Nirvana, Beck, and Pearl Jam, which melded a heavy guitar sound, an ironic pop sensibility, and the slacker aesthetic[6] attributed to the work of artist Jason Rhoades, novelist Douglas Coupland, and filmmaker Richard Linklater. Again, *SNL* aimed to position itself on the cutting edge through its performance selections, but did so in a way that underscored the tension that exists between ostensibly transgressive music and mainstream television. In many ways, the grunge movement's position in American culture mirrored that of *SNL,* as it attempted to be commercial and countercultural at the same time. Many grunge artists were ambivalent about mainstream success, particularly Nirvana's Kurt Cobain, who wanted to maintain his underground status yet felt pressure to live up to the ballooning expectations of his record label and fans.[7]

SNL's own ambivalence was reflected in the direction comedy took on the show during this period. Led by the Frat Pack, a breakout group featuring Adam Sandler, Chris Farley, and David Spade, the comedy of the early 1990s mirrored the contradictions of alternative rock and borrowed from its aesthetics. They performed in a recurring sketch about bored, excitable teenage girls working at the Gap, a situation that seemed to want it both ways: to mock consumer culture while remaining complicit with it. Sandler was known for playing angry, infantile characters—hallmarks of alternative rock's angst-ridden white masculinity[8]—and for impersonating rock stars. He combined these talents with guitar-backed novelty songs like "Lunch Lady Land" and "Red Hooded Sweatshirt," which he performed opposite Chris Farley in cafeteria-server drag and on "Weekend Update" with Paul and Linda McCartney. Sandler included "Lunch Lady Land," which he co-wrote with Allen Covert, *SNL* writer Tim Herlihy, and *Mr. Show* (1995–1998) co-creator Bob Odenkirk, on *They're All Gonna Laugh at You!,* his debut album for Warner Bros. Music and comedy thus found an ideal symbiosis during this period of *SNL*'s history, with both the comedians and the musical guests engaging in a performance mode that appeared to reject the mainstream but, upon a closer look, dovetailed seamlessly with the priorities of the corporate-controlled culture industry.

During the second half of the 1990s and into the 2000s, *SNL* included female singer-songwriters like Jewel and Fiona Apple, who were marketed as edgy, confessional lyricists.[9] *SNL* also made room for female hybrid alternative acts like Björk and Luscious Jackson, which blended pop, hip-hop, and classical music. These acts tapped into the success of the Lilith Fair festival and the emergence of girl-power rhetoric following mainstream media's appropriative reframing of riot grrrls' feminist politics. Again, the music coincided with changes in *SNL's* comedy, most notably in the hiring in 1997 of Tina Fey, who became the show's first female head writer in 1999. The personal, gynocentric perspectives of musicians such as Tori Amos found comedic parallels in mock commercials for Pampers thongs.

Several performers have been pregnant during their tenure, a precedent Ana Gasteyer set in the twenty-seventh season. This was a reality the show foregrounded or overlooked as it suited the comedian or the sketch. Pregnancy came to be utilized for its spectacular potential, which Lady Gaga exploited when she donned a prosthetic stomach to perform "Born This Way" during the 2011 season finale. Gaga's performance was just one in a long series of famously bizarre fashion choices that have been so crucial to her star persona and commercial appeal. Through its blending of music and comedy, *SNL* has thus pushed certain mainstream ideas with regard to the portrayal of female corporeality. At the same time, however, these potentially transgressive moments have remained tied closely to commercially successful cultural trends.

In the twenty-first century, *SNL's* effort to balance subcultural edginess with mainstream commercial success has played out through its relationship with grunge's progeny, such as indie groups Modest Mouse and Fleet Foxes. Now, *SNL's* comedy intersects with the music business more than ever before. *SNL* cast member Fred Armisen, for example, came to the show with considerable indie credentials as a successful drummer. While at *SNL*, he has developed and starred in IFC's sketch program *Portlandia* (2011–present) with former Sleater-Kinney guitarist and music critic Carrie Brownstein. *SNL* star Andy Samberg has similar music credibility. His comedy-music hybrid group, the Lonely Island, is regularly featured in indie music publications such as *Pitchfork*. Both Samberg and Armisen thus represent the merging of an indie aesthetic in comedy and music that aims precisely at the simultaneous embrace of subcultural authenticity and mainstream commercial success.

Indie rock emerged in the late '60s through an amateurish, guitar-driven American underground that defined itself against mainstream rock by launching or signing with independent record labels. In the 1990s, many independent artists signed with major labels and were marketed as alternative rock. Indie music, like American independent cinema, is now less recognizable as a business model than as an aesthetic choice, as scholars Michael Z. Newman and Tony Grajeda note, pointing to an investment in quirkiness, nostalgia, ludic formalism, or lo-fi production.[10] Contemporary indie artists' complex relationship to popular music is defined by a general acceptance of commercial practices, particularly licensing. Newman notes that indie culture and advertising share the need to produce a sellable illusion of autonomy and authenticity. This kinship was visibly forged in the early 2000s when companies like Volkswagen aligned themselves with youth subcultures by deploying ironic and nostalgic sensibilities and licensing music by Nick Drake or the Walkmen in their advertisements.[11] This new use of previously subcultural musical trends exemplifies the porous co-optation of indie culture during the twenty-first century.[12] It thus, in many ways, represents a logic quite similar to that which I argue is present in *SNL*'s use of music.

Indie rock does little to differentiate itself from its mainstream counterpart. Both genres rely heavily on traditional rock instrumentation and tonic-based chord progressions. Indie rock often sets itself apart through lyrical content or performance styles that are less commercially palatable (i.e., purposely amateurish, highly mannered). However, indie rock artists also draw heavily upon mainstream commercial trends. Auto-Tune, an audio-processing tool that corrects vocal pitch, is used by many mainstream artists and has been co-opted by indie artists like Vampire Weekend and Bon Iver.[13] This indie music trend resembles Samberg's comedic approach on *SNL*'s highly popular parodies of music videos. In "Dick in a Box," for example, Samberg and guest star Justin Timberlake parody the '90s vocal group Color Me Badd through an ironic deployment of both R&B's black machismo and the genre's musical aesthetics. Thus, indie rock and *SNL's* appropriation of it negotiate ironic detachment with deeply felt nostalgia for maligned pop culture detritus.[14]

Alternative and indie rock acts position themselves—and are positioned by record labels and the press—as subcultural, cutting-edge, and at once forward-thinking and (often ironically) nostalgic for pop's (often imagined) past. It is thus perhaps the perfect genre to fit into *SNL's* pattern of balancing a sense of cultural relevance with commercial safety. Over the past decade or so, a symbiotic relationship has been crafted between the commercial indie rock segment of the music industry and *SNL*, which offers national exposure to indie rock acts while their presence provides access to hip, young consumers. But the pairing rarely results in a memorable performance, much less an infamous moment that fills viewers with discomfort or outrage. Indie rock's radical edge is already compromised by a host of commercial interests. Thus its emphasis on quirkiness, irony, and nostalgia are marketable to the same audience *SNL* hopes to reach.

DISRUPTIVE LIVENESS AND GENDER

While *SNL* has incorporated several musical trends over the decades, the program's history with musical guests suggests that its liveness is particularly fraught for female solo artists. With rare exceptions, male artists have not been singled out as instigators of controversial moments in the program's history. In contrast, Ashlee Simpson, Sinéad O'Connor, and Lana Del Rey all famously disrupted *SNL's* neatly choreographed approach to live performance. As those controversies reveal, female artists are disproportionately vulnerable to not meeting the program's institutional standards. The failure to meet audience and institutional expectations imposes disastrous professional consequences on musical performers and thus invites a critique of *SNL's* gender politics. In the remainder of this chapter, I analyze the 1992 appearance by O'Connor and the 2012 appearance by Del Rey. For *SNL*, I argue, these women's musical performances offered too much edge. In these examples, we can see the ways in which *SNL's* claims to liveness are belied by the ways its musical performances are constructed and managed.

Irish alternative singer-songwriter O'Connor and American indie artist Del Rey were punished for departing from televisual conventions of live performance. *SNL*'s minimal staging in these instances magnified the candor of both singers' performances and departed from how female artists were normally presented on the show. Female singer-songwriters' bodies are often protected and gendered by musical instruments like the piano. Female pop stars hide behind elaborate staging, intricate choreography, body-conscious costuming, and a phalanx of dancers and instrumentalists. O'Connor and Del Rey were subjected to ridicule for focusing instead on their distinctly female voices. O'Connor faced controversy for attempting to harness television's civic potential. Snark against Del Rey's underripe performance coalesced on smaller screens, illustrating that liveness's meaning is now shaped by up-to-the-minute online commentary.[15]

"FIGHT THE REAL ENEMY": SINÉAD O'CONNOR RIPS *SNL* TO SHREDS

O'Connor's controversial 1992 appearance was shaded by feminist politics even before she performed. In 1990, O'Connor had declined to appear on an episode hosted by Andrew Dice Clay, a comedian known for his misogynistic sensibilities.[16] In doing so, she stood with *SNL* cast member Nora Dunn, who also refused to appear on the episode. Following Dunn's protest and internal struggles with the cast,[17] executive producer Lorne Michaels fired her before the sixteenth season. O'Connor did make her *SNL* debut later in 1990, but the incident reinforced her reputation as an artist with strong political convictions. Of course the controversy surrounding Clay's performance also drew attention to *SNL*'s own gender politics.

O'Connor's now infamous appearance (the show received over 4,000 calls after it aired) took place two years later, on October 3, 1992. For her second song of the night, O'Connor did a cover of Bob Marley's "War" in a performance that was strikingly different than her first song, "Success Has Made a Failure of Our Home," which utilized a backing band. "War," in contrast, was sung a cappella. *SNL* personnel were aware of the stylistic differences beforehand. Both performances were blocked and staged during dress rehearsal. Michaels claimed the staff knew that the singer had rewritten a lyric about racism in order to protest child abuse.[18] In rehearsal, O'Connor dramatically raised a picture of a child at the end of the song, and *SNL* staff approved of this relatively tame political statement. The live performance went off just as the rehearsal save for the picture at the end, which O'Connor replaced with a photograph of Pope John Paul II. She tore the picture to pieces while singing the word "evil." The staff and audience were ill equipped for such a defiant performance from an unruly woman addressing viewers through the excess of her voice and unwavering convictions.[19] But it was perhaps disingenuous for *SNL* to play innocent. Apart from her final gesture, *SNL* knew that O'Connor's intent and delivery contrasted with the program's previous musical performances. The producers wanted a performance that was political and gave a sense of cultural relevance; they simply wanted it on their terms.

O'Connor's rendition of "War" defied the program's standards for live music. Most acts do not perform a cappella or alone, but O'Connor was the only musician on stage. Her excessive vocal power and dynamic contrast leant an air of heightened drama. She only diminished in volume when demanding that the audience "fight the real enemy" at the end of her performance. While a lack of dynamic contrast might have made the performance seem uninspired in another context, O'Connor's audiovisual austerity—particularly the singer's isolation on the stage and powerful vocals—subverted how we see and hear musicians on television. In addition, O'Connor kept a steady gaze on the camera, giving the performance an emotional intimacy rarely seen from female performers on U.S. broadcast television. The intimacy of the performance was actually heightened by the medium, bringing the viewers at home closer to O'Connor and her message than was the audience watching it in the studio.

Direct address was common in music videos at the time. The iconic clip for O'Connor's "Nothing Compares 2 U" consists mainly of long takes of the singer lip-syncing the song in close-up. Direct address is not uncommon in live musical segments for late-night television and sketch comedy programs either, though singers usually direct their gaze not only toward the television audience, but also toward the instrumentalists, the studio audience, and the crew. O'Connor rejected such televisual

Figure 6.1. Sinéad O'Connor tears a picture of Pope John Paul II during her performance on *SNL* in 1992.

norms. She did not engage with the studio audience during the broadcast performance, clearly breaking with entertainers' conventional address to the audience. Instead, she addressed an imagined TV viewing audience, treating her performance as a public service announcement instead of a commercial for her album.

O'Connor used "War" to protest child abuse occurring within the Catholic Church. Whether the public fully understood O'Connor's political motivations or not is unclear, but what is clear is that many people, including *SNL*'s producers, complained that her performance was inappropriate.[20] Michaels stated that the studio audience responded to O'Connor's performance with horrified silence as control booth personnel tried to get the camera operators to cut away from her face.[21] In the weeks following the performance, protests occurred throughout the country.[22] Many of them had a violent undercurrent, as various groups staged protests in which piles of O'Connor's records were destroyed. Two weeks after the performance, O'Connor appeared at a Bob Dylan tribute concert at Madison Square Garden and was booed off the stage. When the noise died down, she performed "War" in protest of her mistreatment before reportedly crying in musician Kris Kristofferson's arms.[23]

SNL, having failed to control the moment of live broadcast, redoubled its efforts to shape the backlash to "War." With previous controversial artists, they were able to preemptively minimize any chance of outrage or discomfort. They were unable to do so with O'Connor and instead placed themselves in opposition to her, forcing her outside of the system in the process. O'Connor's performance was excised from subsequent re-airings and she was never booked again. The singer was ridiculed in a handful of sketches and musical performances; soon after the episode aired, former cast member Jan Hooks reprised her strident impersonation of O'Connor in two sketches that upbraided the singer for the incident. Later in the season, Madonna held up a photograph of tabloid sensation Joey Buttafuoco after her performance of "Bad Girl," archly exclaimed "fight the real enemy," and tore up the picture. O'Connor never regained the mainstream success she had experienced in the early 1990s, and SNL had a hand in it, reducing another political actor to a joke.

"YOU MADE MY EYES BURN": LANA DEL REY'S NOT-READY-FOR-PRIME-TIME PERFORMANCE

Unlike O'Connor, Del Rey had no history with SNL prior to the negative reception she received for her January 2012 performance. In an unprecedented move, producer Brian Siedlecki in November 2011 convinced Michaels to book Del Rey before seeing her in concert.[24] (Siedlecki saw her a month later at a sold-out show in New York.) Most acts are booked after Michaels, the producers, or the music staff see artists perform to determine whether they can handle the forum. Del Rey had given only a few concerts by then, which may explain the nervousness several critics picked up in her SNL performance.[25] Del Rey made her name on tastemaker music sites as a viral sensation for her self-directed, retro-tinged music videos. Interscope Records signed her in October 2011 as part of a deal with independent label Stranger Records. Born to Die, her first album with Interscope, was scheduled for release on Monday, January 30.

Siedlecki believed he needed to act quickly so that *SNL* could be a platform for the buzz-worthy indie chanteuse's American network debut.[26]

The backlash surrounding Del Rey's appearance differed from the
reaction to O'Connor's performance in its indifference toward authenticity. Prior to her performance, a few music critics had dismissed Del
Rey for possessing limited vocal talent and for copying recently deceased
bad girl torch singer Amy Winehouse's style and persona. Some threaded
Del Rey's industry past into their appraisals.[27] Though Interscope promoted Del Rey as a new artist, she previously had released an EP and a
full-length album under her real name, Lizzy Grant. Those records were
not radically different from her output with Interscope. The clearest departure was the earlier recordings' indebtedness to punk, which Del Rey
traded for a sound informed by lounge, cabaret pop, R&B, and hip-hop
that she described as "gangsta Nancy Sinatra."[28] However, just as punk is
associated with delinquency, bands like Blondie and the Ramones cited
'60s (bad) girl groups like the Shangri-Las as influences.[29] So Del Rey's
early work was consistent with her reinvention, as some critics noted by
comparing Del Rey to Tori Amos, who originally signed to Atlantic in
the late 1980s as the lead singer for hair metal band Y Kant Tori Read.[30]

Following her *SNL* performance, critics admonished Del Rey for
changing her name—a nod to starlet Lana Turner and the Ford Del
Rey—and dying her hair Rita Hayworth red and obscuring one eye in a
style popularized by Veronica Lake. Some claimed she used collagen to
acquire a movie star pout.[31] The singer disputed claims about her upper
middle-class pedigree by clarifying that she was sent to boarding school
for experimenting with drugs and other delinquent behavior.[32] However,
questions about Del Rey's authenticity took root in the press prior to her
appearance on *SNL* and flowered after her debut.

Many commentators noted Del Rey's supposed lack of confidence on
SNL. In contrast to O'Connor's stoic glare, Del Rey did not train her eyes
on either the studio audience or the cameras when she performed "Video
Games" and "Blue Jeans." Instead, she stared at the floor or off in the
middle distance and slouched and swayed awkwardly. Del Rey also had
little control of her voice. Writers criticized the singer's unstable warble,
affected and mumbled delivery, indelicate leaps between pitches, and un-
predictable dynamics that often buried her voice in the mix. Del Rey was

admonished for being unprepared for the glare of network television's spotlight and dismissed as a charlatan who duped *SNL*'s producers into believing there was artistic integrity underneath the industry buzz.

Unlike O'Connor's a cappella cover of "War," Del Rey was accompanied by a drummer, bassist, and lead guitarist during her performance. A keyboardist who played programmed string arrangements and vocal samples rounded out the ensemble. Del Rey did not perform with backup singers. Many vocalists often sing with a trio or quartet of other singers who harmonize at various key moments during the artists' songs to provide compositional and emotional depth. Occasionally, backup vocalists also support artists who lack the skill or ballast to replicate studio trickery by smoothing over any technical errors they may commit during a live performance. Del Rey had no such buffer, which only exacerbated the deficiencies she demonstrated as a vocalist.

Whereas O'Connor's performance had direct bearing on her commercial success, it is too early to determine what effect Del Rey's *SNL* appearance might have on her career. Critics like *Rolling Stone*'s Rob Sheffield and *USA Today*'s Edna Gundersen critiqued her performance and resultant notoriety in their reviews of *Born to Die*, noting specifically that her "too live" performance resulted from a lack of professional experience.[33] As with the O'Connor incident, *SNL* was quick to turn the reception into a joke after the audience reacted to it in a way that was unexpected. However, at least to some extent, the negative publicity helped Del Rey, who was relatively unknown before her appearance. *Born to Die* debuted at number two on the U.S. Billboard 200 and went platinum, due largely to public curiosity following the *SNL* performance. Various critics debated her artistic merits[34] and interrogated the singer's Internet fame and gender performance in a panel discussion in the *New York Times*,[35] giving Del Rey a cultural visibility she lacked before bombing on live television.

SINGING THROUGH THE BACKLASH: CONCLUSION

SNL publicly objected to O'Connor's and Del Rey's performances. But facilitating such moments is part of the program's strategy. Unlike the show's main cast, many artists only appear once and thus may not feel obligated to abide by the program's rules. But most do not challenge the

Figure 6.2. *SNL* cast member Kristen Wiig lampoons Del Rey.

show's incorporative approach toward music, perhaps out of a desire for visibility. Though *SNL* remains an institution for live music on U.S. network television, most artists get swept up or footnoted in the show's broader institutional history, either as part of a larger narrative about the development of popular and left-of-mainstream music or as a reminder of the datedness that now shrouds their brief moment as part of the zeitgeist. As former cast member Kristen Wiig stated in a "Weekend Update" segment where she parodied Del Rey, "The music stage on *Saturday Night Live* is hallowed ground, and I failed to reach the high bar set by past guests like Bubba Sparxxx, the Baha Men, and Shaggy."[36] The joke might have been aimed at exposing the gendered double standard between male and female performers, but it also reinforced *SNL*'s institutional position by admonishing critics through self-deprecation.

SNL is a live television show that relies on performers to occasionally challenge the constructedness of its liveness through disobeying the process of mediation. *SNL* benefits when artists trespass the artifices of televisual liveness because those performances create a discursive space for the show to be debated and (re)watched by millions of viewers on television and a host of online sources. The rare moment when a performer calls attention to the show's illusory liveness through her inability to look at the camera or a commitment not to look away renews *SNL*'s relevance.

Neither singer regrets her appearance. Del Rey claimed to benefit from the attention following her poorly received performance.[37] For O'Connor, who was ill at ease with mainstream success,[38] the backlash allowed her to retreat into relative obscurity. She followed *Am I Not Your Girl?* with *Universal Mother* in 1994, toured with the Lollapalooza music festival, and still records. She remains invested in various religions, including Rastafarianism, and was ordained as a priest. She uses music as a platform to address sexism, child abuse, and racism.

O'Connor shredded the rules of televisual liveness and Del Rey mumbled around them, singing past backlashes that *SNL* framed and perpetuated. *SNL*'s producers did not regret how the singers were treated following their appearances. For O'Connor and Del Rey, infamy meant never having to apologize. Though historically *SNL* has succeeded in appropriating music's subcultural positioning and performative liveness, the show could not tame O'Connor and Del Rey. And while their appearances resulted in a backlash the program agitated, such failed performances are necessary for both *SNL*, which benefits from controversy through exposure, and the performer rebelling against or exploiting the program. These exceptions make the audience forget the restrictions of televisual liveness, if only for a moment, and confront the disruptive potential of live television.

Notes

1. Feuer, "The Concept of Live Television"; Couldry, "Media Rituals."
2. Elkins, "Michael O'Donoghue, *SNL,* and the Comedy of Cruelty."
3. Reportedly, Belushi was a Fear fan.
4. Shales and Miller, *Live from New York.*
5. BET was founded in 1980 and included music videos from black artists from its inception. However, MTV consistently outperformed it in terms of viewership throughout the decade, and would not launch *Yo! MTV Raps* until 1988.
6. Drucker, *Sweet Dreams.*
7. Klosterman, *Eating the Dinosaur.*

8. Sutton, "The Soft Boys."

9. Schilt, "A Little Too Ironic."

10. Newman, *Indie;* Grajeda, "The 'Feminization' of Rock."

11. Newman, "Indie Culture," 27–28.

12. Abebe, "The Decade in Indie."

13. Weheliye, "Feenin."

14. Vesey, "Pitchforking Andy Samberg's Hipster Appeal."

15. Baym, *Personal Connections in the Digital Age.*

16. James, "Review/Television"; Gerard, "Comic Is Protested as *Saturday Night Host*"; Zoglin and Mehta, "Saturday-Night Sizzle."

17. Shales and Miller, *Live from New York.*

18. Ibid.

19. Karlyn, *The Unruly Woman.*

20. "Tearing Up Late-Night TV"; "Sinéad's Slam Stirs Anger."

21. *Saturday Night Live: 25 Years.*

22. "Tearing Up Late-Night TV."

23. Pareles, "Pop View."

24. Jurgensen, "Music."

25. Gundersen, "Del Rey"; Sheffield, "Lana Del Rey's Tedious Torch Songs."

26. Prior to her *SNL* performance, Del Rey appeared on a Dutch television show and a tastemaker British music program, *Later . . . with Jools Holland,* without incident.

27. Johnston, "Lana Del Rey Hides in Plain Sight."

28. Lester, "New Band of the Day"; Mossman, "Far from Dusty."

29. McNeil and McCain, *Please Kill Me.*

30. Johnston, "Lana Del Rey Hides in Plain Sight"; Wolk, "Not So Fast."

31. Romano, "Lana Del Rey's Hipster Problem"; Brown, "A Star Is Born (and Scorned)."

32. Frere-Jones, "Screen Shot"; Brown, "A Star Is Born (and Scorned)."

33. Gundersen, "Del Rey"; Sheffield, "Lana Del Rey's Tedious Torch Songs."

34. Abebe, "Lurching toward Vegas"; Ewing, "Lana Del Rey Lights Up the Internet"; "Lana Del Rey: Just Another Pop Star"; Sisario, "Adele, of Course, but Watch Out for Lana."

35. Berkmann, "Pop: The Big Push"; "Recipe for a Pop Star."

36. Qtd. in Couch, "*SNL* Recap."

37. Gardner, "Singer Lana Del Rey Has Nothing to Hide."

38. Goldman, "Interview."

Works Cited

Abebe, Nitsuh. "The Decade in Indie." *Pitchfork,* February 25, 2010. http://pitchfork.com/features/articles/7704-the-decade-in-indie.

———. "Lurching toward Vegas." *Vulture,* January 25, 2012. http://www.vulture.com/m/2012/01/lana-del-rey-lurching-toward-vegas.html.

Baym, Nancy. *Personal Connections in the Digital Age.* Malden, MA: Polity, 2010.

Berkmann, Marcus. "Pop: The Big Push." *Spectator,* February 2012. http://images.spectator.co.uk/arts-and-culture/featured/7651668/the-big-push.thtml.

Brown, Jacob. "A Star Is Born (and Scorned)." *New York Times Magazine,* February 9, 2012, 177.

Couch, Aaron. "*SNL* Recap: Kristen Wiig's Lana Del Rey Addresses Backlash." *Hollywood Reporter,* February 5, 2012. http://www.hollywoodreporter.com/live-feed/snl-kristen-wiigs-lana-del-rey-channing-tatum-287145.

Couldry, Nick. *Media Rituals: A Critical Approach.* New York: Routledge, 2003.

Drucker, Johanna. *Sweet Dreams: Contemporary Art and Complicity.* Chicago: University of Chicago Press, 2006.

Elkins, Evan. "Michael O'Donoghue, *SNL,* and the Comedy of Cruelty." *FlowTV,* March 20, 2009. http://www.flowtv.org/2009/03/michael-o%e2%80%99donoghue-snl-and-the-comedy-of-cruelty-evan-elkins-university-of-texas-austin.

Ewing, Tom. "Lana Del Rey Lights Up the Internet." *Village Voice,* January 18, 2012. http://www.villagevoice.com/2012-01-18/music/lana-del-rey-lights-up-the-internet.

Feuer, Jane. "The Concept of Live Television: Ontology as Ideology." In *Regarding Television: Critical Approaches—An Anthology,* edited by E. Ann Kaplan. Los Angeles: American Film Institute, 1983.

Frere-Jones, Sasha. "Screen Shot." *New Yorker,* February 6, 2012, 68–70.

Gardner, Elysa. "Singer Lana Del Rey Has Nothing to Hide." *USA Today,* January 26, 2012, 1.

Gerard, Jeremy. "Comic Is Protested as *Saturday Night* Host."*New York Times,* May 11, 1990, 1.

Goldman, Vivien. "Interview." *Rolling Stone,* November 1997, 126–127.

Grajeda, Tony. "The 'Feminization' of Rock." In *Rock over the Edge: Transformations in Popular Music Culture,* edited by Roger Beebe, Denise Fulbrook, and Ben Saunders, 233–254. Durham, NC: Duke University Press, 2002.

Gundersen, Edna. "Del Rey: Torch without Fire." *USA Today,* January 31, 2012, 4.

James, Caryn. "Review/Television: *Saturday Night Live* with Andrew Dice Clay." *New York Times,* May 14, 1990, 16.

Johnston, Maura. "Lana Del Rey Hides in Plain Sight." *Village Voice,* December 7, 2011. http://www.villagevoice.com/2011-12-07/music/lana-del-rey-hides-in-plain-sight.

Jurgensen, John. "Music: A Chance to be a Ready-for-Prime-Time Player." *Wall Street Journal,* January 13, 2012, D4.

Karlyn, Kathleen Rowe. *The Unruly Woman: Gender and the Genres of Laughter.* Austin: University of Texas Press, 1995.

Klosterman, Chuck. *Eating the Dinosaur.* New York: Scribner, 2009.

Lester, Paul. "New Band of the Day: Lana Del Rey." *Guardian,* May 3, 2011. http://m.guardian.co.uk/music/2011/may/03/new-band-lana-del-ray?cat=music&type=article.

McNeil, Legs, and Gillan McCain. *Please Kill Me: The Uncensored Oral History of Punk.* New York: Penguin, 1996.

Mossman, Kate. "Far from Dusty." *New Statesman,* January 23, 2012, 53–54.

Newman, Michael Z. *Indie: An American Film Culture.* New York: Columbia University Press, 2010.

———. "Indie Culture: In Pursuit of the Authentic Autonomous Alternative." *Cinema Journal* 48(3) (2009):16–34.

O'Connor, Sinéad. "Being a Woman." *Ms. Magazine,* May 1992, 78–80.

Pareles, Jon. "Pop View: Why Sinéad O'Connor Hit a Nerve." *New York Times,* November 1, 1992, 27.

"Recipe for a Pop Star." *New York Times,* February 17, 2012. http://www.nytimes.com /roomfordebate/2012/02/17is-lana-del-rey-the-future-of-pop-stardom.

Romano, Tricia. "Lana Del Rey's Hipster Problem: Plastic Surgery, *SNL,* and Her Past as Lizzy Grant." *Daily Beast,* January 31, 2012. http://www.thedailybeast.com /articles/2012/01/30/lana-del-rey-s-hipster-problem-plastic-surgery-and-her-past -as-lizzy-grant.html.

Saturday Night Live: 25 Years of Music, Performances, and Sketches. Broadway Video Distribution, 2003.

Schilt, Kristen. "'A Little Too Ironic': The Appropriation and Packaging of Riot Grrrl Politics by Mainstream Female Musicians." *Popular Music and Society* 26(1) (2003):5–16.

Shales, Tom, and James Andrew Miller. *Live from New York: An Uncensored History of Saturday Night Live.* New York: Little, Brown, 2002.

Sheffield, Rob. "Lana Del Rey's Tedious Torch Songs." *Rolling Stone,* February 16, 2012, 60.

"Sinéad's Slam Stirs Anger." *Christianity Today* 36(13) (1992):51.

Sisario, Ben. "Adele, of Course, But Watch Out for Lana." *New York Times,* February 9, 2012, 2.

Sutton, Terri. "The Soft Boys: The New Man in Rock." In *Trouble Girls: The Rolling Stone Book of Women in Rock,* edited by Barbara O'Dair, 527–535. New York: Random House, 1997.

"Tearing Up Late-Night TV." *Newsweek,* October 18, 1992, 41.

Vesey, Alyxandra. "Pitchforking Andy Samberg's Hipster Appeal." *FlowTV,* March 20, 2009. http://flowtv.org/2009/03/pitchforking-andy-sambergs-hipster-appeal%C2 %A0%C2%A0alyx-vesey-independent-scholar.

Weheliye, Alexander G. "'Feenin': Posthuman Voices in Contemporary Black Popular Music." *Social Text* 20(2) (2002):21–45.

Wolk, Douglas. "Not So Fast." *Time,* February 6, 2012. http://www.time.com/time /magazine/article/0,9171,2105452,00.html.

Zoglin, Richard, and Naushaud S. Mehta. "Saturday-Night Sizzle." *Time,* May 21, 1990, 87.

Going Backstage: Network Heritage, Industrial Identities, and Reiterated Mediation of *Saturday Night Live*'s Work Worlds

DEREK JOHNSON

In the fall of 2007, the newly appointed head of NBC Entertainment, Ben Silverman, shared with *Esquire* magazine his aversion to the programming choices made by his predecessor, Kevin Reilly. While Silverman took issue with any number of strategies that had failed the struggling network, he held in particular disdain NBC's massive 2006–2007 investment in not one but two industrially self-reflexive series inspired by the backstage workplace of *Saturday Night Live*. While *30 Rock* (2006–2013) became a critical and cult darling, the more expensive *Studio 60 on the Sunset Strip* (2006–2007)—around which NBC had focused its fall 2006 marketing campaign—faced cancellation after only one season. As Silverman chastised, "How could you ever order two shows about the same subject matter and put numbers in their titles? That's so transparently flawed to me." The wrath of Silverman was not reserved for the overproduction of late-night sketch comedy themes, extending more widely to the network's overreliance on extending successful brands and multiplying production from them. "And why would you put on Martha Stewart and Donald Trump at the same time under the same brand [*The Apprentice*] twice a week?," he added. "I would never have done that."[1] Silverman took umbrage not just at the triple-dipping of *Saturday Night Live* by NBC, but also at the wider industrial logics of branding and franchising that rationalized the multiplied, reiterative production of television from previous successes.[2]

While surely Silverman posed these questions rhetorically in a bid to contrast his own expertise and strategies with the failures of the past, this chapter takes these challenges seriously and attempts to explain how and why *Saturday Night Live* became a site of heightened industrial interest and a nexus of new production in the 2006–2007 season. The simultaneous investment by NBC in the continued production of *SNL* and in *30 Rock* and *Studio 60* may have been presented as foolhardy by Silverman, but dismissive hindsight obscures the commonsense logics and negotiated challenges that would have informed this strategy in context. How and why did NBC embrace and depend upon the backstage work world of *SNL* as fodder or inspiration for multiple television productions? What was at stake, given ratings declines not just for the long-running sketch comedy series, but also for the network and the broadcast television industry as a whole? As Amanda Lotz writes, in the face of a multichannel, multiplatform television environment with expanded options for advertising, amateur production, audience measurement, and viewer control, "changes in competitive norms and operation of the industry have become too pronounced for old practices to be preserved; different industrial practices are becoming dominant and replacing those of the network era."[3] As network product in a "post-network" moment, the persistence of *SNL* thus demanded significant industrial adaptation and negotiation. Yet amid this shift, the continuous production of *SNL* since 1975 made the series a living link for NBC to what Derek Kompare calls the "television heritage"—a valorized history of television programming stretching back to golden ages worthy of attention, preservation, tribute, and commodification.[4] In this light, efforts to reiterate and reproduce *SNL* offer insight into how both NBC and network television producers negotiated the industrial meanings of network comedy in a shifting, post-network landscape.

With NBC commissioning two television series that seized upon a strategic intertextuality with *SNL,* the industrial adaptation in question here can be best understood in relation to what is often referred to as "media franchising." Elsewhere, I have discussed media franchising not just as an industrial practice in which cultural resources (intellectual property or otherwise) are shared across multiple contexts and communities of production, but also discursively as a cultural logic within the industry for imagining and assigning value to highly iterative forms of media production.[5] Put another way, media franchising both multiplies production and ascribes meaning to that reproduction. *SNL*, of course, has been reproduced and made meaningful through media franchising since the early 1980s, with sketches like "The Blues Brothers" serving as a resource with which to multiply production across the music and film industries. In the 1990s, *SNL* became even more firmly involved in this phenomenon, with film spin-offs of the "Wayne's World," "Daily Affirmation with Stuart Smalley," "It's Pat!," and "The Roxbury Guys" sketches. The release in 2010 of *MacGruber*, a film based on the eponymous *SNL* sketch character, is a more recent entry in this franchising tradition. With the rise of online video, spin-offs like the behind-the-scenes documentary series *SNL Backstage* in 2006–2007 emerged from a similar logic of franchised multiplication and branding. Since franchising need not be defined in transmedia terms, the repackaging of *SNL* for syndication and for best-of compilations might also be considered similarly reiterative television products. In linking this history of reiterative production to *30 Rock* and *Studio 60*, however, this chapter considers the franchising of *SNL* in a different respect. Even when no identifiable trademark, character, or intellectual property is legally exchanged, NBC's sketch comedy heritage serves to multiply and make sense of successive television productions—both as *SNL*'s production company, Broadway Video, expands its operation to make *30 Rock*, and as Warner Bros. Television produces another series about NBC and *SNL: Studio 60*.

Using franchising as a lens to examine the logics by which NBC, program producers, and industry analysts produced and positioned *SNL* for the post-network era, this chapter first explores the challenges *SNL* faced in that context—particularly insofar as television heritage discourses in the popular and trade press articulated the historical value of the series to obsolescence in comparison to newer, edgier, non-broadcast programming. Amid this pressure to rehabilitate and revalorize the network tradition represented by *SNL*, the development of both *30 Rock* and *Studio 60* for the 2006–2007 season can secondly be explored as a negotiation between NBC and its production partners over the meanings, identities, and values that would be brought to bear on the production of *SNL*. On the one hand, NBC's standing investment in *SNL* drove an expensive bidding war to control these similar series. On the other, the presence of both *30 Rock* and *Studio 60* on NBC's schedule generated a crisis of identity where producers differentiated themselves, competed for critical attention and network resources, and gave divergent meanings to their industrial reiterations of *SNL*. By looking at the "managed self-disclosures" by which producers and executives positioned themselves in relation to this reiteration and made claims to the production heritage of *SNL*, we can see how workers across multiple production contexts understood, identified, and valued their labor in relation to one another.[6] These self-disclosures were, in effect, attempts to further mediate the production culture and work world of *SNL*, which was already under narrative mediation by the two new series. In that sense, the reiteration and remediation of *SNL* through *30 Rock* and *Studio 60* allows us to conceptualize media franchising not as a stable set of practices and intellectual properties, as it is usually understood, but instead as a site of self-reflexivity where media workers construct meanings, identities, and values in relation to the shared institutions and reiterated cultural production to which they lay partial claim. Yet beyond this conceptual reworking of franchising, this case reveals specifically how *SNL* remained—as a network television institution—a crucial site of construction for professional identities and claims to network heritage by comedy production cultures negotiating the shift to the post-network era.[7]

AN OBSOLETE INSTITUTION

By the middle of the first decade of the twenty-first century, the viability of *SNL* as both industrial product and source of cultural satire had come into significant doubt in popular and trade commentary. In the analysis of *Maclean's*, for example, the series had lost the cutting-edge and conversation-setting qualities once associated with its storied past: compared to that legacy, "not much is working. The writing isn't pushing any boundaries and the players, albeit talented, aren't breaking out."[8] The cultural relevance and influence of *SNL*, in this critique, had withered away. This loss of status for the sketch comedy stalwart came also out of a negative comparison with a host of new upstart competitors in the satire market. As many commentators described it, *SNL* had been rendered obsolete by the comedy renaissance of the multichannel and the post-network eras.

According to the *New York Times*, for example, the 2006 elections brought the differences between *SNL* and a new breed of more provocative television satire into relief. Compared to how concurrent television comedies like Fox's *The Simpsons* (1989–present), Comedy Central's *Freak Show* (2006), and Roseanne Barr's HBO comedy special *Blonde and Bitchin'* (2006) had commented on the state of U.S. politics, the paper of record found it particularly noteworthy that *SNL* had stooped to "filling its airtime" with a Darrell Hammond retrospective on the eve of the elections.[9] Instead of providing cutting-edge political comedy, *SNL* was accused of retreating backward into Hammond's worn 1990s Bill Clinton impressions. As this critique suggests, *SNL* was suffering from its position in an old-fashioned broadcasting economy, forcing the series to have "long ago ceded cutting-edge lampoonery to smaller, nimbler cable shows."[10] As even the *Chronicle of Higher Education* recognized (despite its distance from the world of comedy), the dominant form of humor in American popular culture had become "satiric, snarky, and self-reflexive," and the "flat-lining" *SNL* faced competition on all sides from the "undergraduate news sources *The Daily Show with Jon Stewart* and *The Colbert Report,* the PC-free zone of *Chappelle's Show,* and the retro-animated oeuvre of Trey Parker and Matt Stone, creators of the equal-opportunity offender *South Park.*"[11] On cable, Comedy Central offered twenty-four hours a day the edginess and satire that *SNL* could only *hope* to offer once a week (in a fringe late-night time slot).

Adding to this sense of decline amid a wider comedy renaissance was the rise of competition in the form of web video. Thanks to new comedy portals like CollegeHumor.com in 1999, the debut of YouTube in 2005, and the dedicated comedy video website *Funny or Die* in 2007, the Internet offered fresh, attractive options for the distribution and consumption of comedy content. Of course, these new comedy offerings had not emerged completely in opposition to *SNL*. Former *SNL* icon Will Ferrell and former writer Adam McKay had founded *Funny or Die,* while "Lazy Sunday," a digital short first aired on *SNL* in 2005, featuring Andy Samberg and Chris Parnell, became a major source of traffic for the fledgling YouTube. Nevertheless, even these online successes suggested that a new model of comedy production and distribution might be required to make *SNL* relevant again. As the *Village Voice* wrote in its own analysis of *SNL*'s decline, the rise of web video had raised the stakes: "with the proliferation of digital online content over the past couple years in the form of viral video, blogs, and websites, plus stalwarts like *The Onion* (growing wildly online), there's another variable: choice."[12] Given the choice among so many cable and online outlets, these critics called into question the interest of viewers in seeking out a relic like *SNL* in a broadcasting context. Indeed, *SNL* offered a microcosm of the challenges threatening the broadcast industry and NBC in particular. *Esquire,* for example, described the Big Four broadcast networks as all "struggling to redefine their business as the captive audience they once commanded continue[s] to scatter among cable channels and the Web."[13] Yet NBC struggled the most, marked "The Biggest Loser" in *Esquire*'s popular accounting. In the trade press, *Mediaweek* described the network's programming strategies in terms of a "flopsweat" where executives were "grasping at straws."[14] NBC's 2005–2006 attempt to retrofit its broadcast strategies to an interactive age—dubbed by executives as NBCU 2.0—had failed to find a footing, and in a more defensive posture, the network moved next to cut expenses by $750 million and its workforce by 5 percent.

In this context, both *SNL* and the broadcast network that carried it had come to be devalued on a cultural level. That cultural valuation had economic consequences, of course, and the continued economic viability of the program also came into question. Between 2005 and 2006, viewing averages slipped from a 3.0 to a 2.6 rating.[15] Long-term comparisons proved even worse. While the 2006 premiere garnered 6.7 million viewers and a 3.2 rating, the average for 2001–2002 episodes— including reruns—sat slightly higher at 3.7. Furthermore, viewership for the twelve-to-seventeen-year-old demographic (a crucial audience for attaining relevance in venues like YouTube) had dropped even more precipitously from a 2.4 to a 1.1 rating. Though NBC executives insisted that the series had "kind of kept pace with general trends in television," it became a target for the cost-cutting measures now being pursued by the network.[16] Faced with the alternative of cutting episodes, executive producer Lorne Michaels elected to trim the size of the cast, dropping longtime cast members like Chris Parnell and Horatio Sanz, as well as the newly hired Finesse Mitchell. Even Parnell, one of the key players in the "Lazy Sunday" digital shorts, turned out not to be safe.

Some have hypothesized NBC's decision to order two additional television series based on *SNL's* backstage work world as a kind of Hail Mary pass—a desperate attempt to raise the economic and cultural standing of the sketch series by making it the symbolic center of the programming lineup. While this move certainly promised some cross-promotional appeal for NBC, the pursuit of synergy has typically been deployed selectively to maximize successes, rather than to rescue products that already seem to be failing. As Simone Murray explains, synergistic production requires an increase in production investment in order to circulate a single brand across multiple outlets, a requirement that was quite in opposition to the fiscal austerity facing *SNL* in 2006.[17] Though it may be impossible to know what NBC's ultimate motivation was (especially in hindsight, with figures like Ben Silverman publicly denying there ever was a logic), its decision to produce both *30 Rock* and *Studio 60* reinforced common perceptions of *SNL's* decline. When NBC announced its order of both series, *Maclean's,* for one, wondered whether the network meant to "save" the original following the loss of its edge.[18]

Whatever the motivation, the production of *Studio 60* and *30 Rock* was no mere response to the discourse of decline and irrelevance surrounding *SNL* and NBC, but rather a contributing factor to that narrative of decline. Following the premieres of the two new series, critics cited their derivative reiteration as further evidence of the obsolescence facing both the parent series and its network. For some commentators, the decision to multiply program offerings inspired by a series in cultural and economic decline just did not compute, demonstrating NBC's growing incompetence. "*SNL* is suffering through one of its periodically grueling unfunny years," *Rolling Stone* noted, "which makes it feel odder yet that NBC is currently airing two different programs set backstage at an *SNL*-like sketch-comedy show."[19] Compared to the comedy renaissance it posited, the *Chronicle of Higher Education* saw the "beleaguered" NBC as "cannibalizing itself" with the production of these series.[20] *Studio 60* and *30 Rock* evidenced a network that in its death throes had turned self-destructively on itself. Similarly, *Advertising Age* looked at the loss of former *SNL* cast members Tina Fey and Rachel Dratch to *30 Rock* (though the latter would eventually be recast) as a redistribution of resources that put increasing pressure on the cast members left behind. And in noting the network's plans for the online documentary series *SNL Backstage, Advertising Age* commented sarcastically: "Hey, maybe they can turn that into a show!"[21] The reiterated multiplication of *SNL*-themed productions read less as a creative renaissance than as evidence of broadcast irrelevance.

In critical readings of *Studio 60* in particular, this perception of the popular irrelevance of *SNL* was rearticulated. In the pilot episode's opening moments, the fictionalized counterpart of *SNL* executive producer Lorne Michaels, played by Judd Hirsch, launches into an unscripted on-air monologue about the mediocrity of his series and the complicity of the network in that cultural degradation: "This show used to be cutting-edge political and social satire, but it's gotten lobotomized by a candy-ass broadcast network hell-bent on doing nothing that might challenge their audience. We were about to do a sketch you've already seen 500 times. . . . We're all being lobotomized by the country's most influential industry. . . . So change the channel, turn off the TV." The *Chicago Defender,* for one, deployed this scene as confirmation of the popular irrelevance of both *SNL* and NBC: "Wow! Could *Studio 60 on the Sunset Strip* be taken as a tacit admission of guilt and a silent act of contrition by NBC, for hmmmmm, one transgression or another?"[22] Similarly, in reviewing an early version of the script (when the series had a slightly different title), *Maclean's* noted that "all these people who work on the show (that is, the fictional Studio 7) seem to recognize it's lost its status as the purveyor of contemporary comedy."[23]

Less impressed by the series' recognition of the failures of network broadcasting, other critics took the program to task for overstating the importance of *SNL* in the contemporary post-network moment. After firing Hirsch's character for his outburst, the fictional NBS network treats the situation as a public relations emergency and hires back the former writer and director of the fictional sketch series (played by Matthew Perry and Bradley Whitford, respectively). Yet some had difficulty buying into the believability of this public relations crisis. "Can you name even a single writer or director from *Saturday Night Live*'s entire history?," *New York* wondered. "More to the point, if Lorne Michaels ever did implode, would the public treat it like a cultural emergency? The clip would be posted on YouTube, laughed about for a weekend, and then the show's demographic would head back to CollegeHumor.com."[24] In this critique, the cultural aggrandizement of the fictional network comedy show seemed like fantasy, given the shifts in popular television culture in the post-network era.

Thus, by the 2006–2007 season, the perception of cultural irrelevance surrounding *SNL* and its broadcast context had taken on common-sense dimensions, and the multiplication of sketch-comedy-themed productions under the NBC network umbrella had worked to amplify that sense of popular devaluation. Even if, as some of these analysts suggested, the impetus behind commissioning both series was to save the original (though as discussed below, there is little evidence to confirm that), their eventual circulation had little such impact. By looking at the professional identities, hierarchies of status, and other elements of production culture surrounding both NBC and these mediations of the *SNL* work world, however, we can gain some insight into at least one of the reasons that the cannibalistic reiteration of a series in cultural and economic decline would have proceeded in the first place, and how this production multiplication held relevance and meaning at an industrial level even as the show's popular fortunes fell.

MEDIATING INDUSTRIAL IDENTITIES

By December 2005—almost a year before either *Studio 60* or *30 Rock* would debut—NBC had announced both series as forthcoming, but remained silent about how these prime-time productions would strategically coexist alongside one another or their late-night source of inspiration. Publicly, NBC disclosed no product differentiation or cross-promotional strategies to make sense of the move, leaving even television professionals affiliated with *SNL* guessing. Barbara Williams, senior programming vice president at Global Television, the Canadian distributor of *SNL*, for example, could not explain what NBC was up to, but she did have a strong sense of what it was not. In her view, NBC would not conceive these new productions as a means of providing prime-time visibility and support to prop up the image of the sketch series. "The kind of decision-making process that goes into what you think will be a prime-time hit with your core audience is a very separate decision from what you think works in late night," Williams reasoned. "If it turned out that there was some sort of synergy between the two, that would be terrific for NBC. But my instinct is, you don't play around with a primetime drama in the hopes that it might somehow influence a late-night show."[25] As understood by Williams, at least, such strategies would be at odds with the logics, practices, and ways of life of network production cultures.

However, while NBC may have been unlikely to pursue strategic promotion across its prime-time and late-night lineups, its interest in the series can be productively understood in terms of managing the marketplace for television programming and an imperative to negotiate would-be counterclaims to identity and authority in the NBC and *SNL* brands. In network television, series are developed by production companies—often in partnership with studios like NBCUniversal or Warner Bros.—that pitch those series to a number of networks that bid competitively for the right to distribute the product. Although shared corporate parentage often leads to collaboration and deal making between studios and networks, not every television series produced by NBCUniversal, for example, will end up airing on the NBC network, especially if the content is better matched to an audience targeted by a competing distributor. In this economy, programs can develop independently of network needs and interests, only later to seek out a compatible network home. Programs like *Studio 60* and *30 Rock*—despite being bound up in the mythologies of NBC and *SNL*—should therefore be understood not as productions of NBC, but as productions negotiated by NBC in the course of its competition with other networks to secure programming from a variety of suppliers. In this context, *30 Rock* was developed and produced in a partnership between the NBCUniversal studio and the production company Broadway Video under the direction of company founder and *SNL* executive producer Lorne Michaels. While these industrial relationships placed the development of *30 Rock* in closer industrial proximity to both *SNL* and NBC, the development of *Studio 60* at Warner Bros. by executive producer Aaron Sorkin represented the production of television relevant to both *SNL* and NBC in a separate institutional setting and a discrete production culture marked by different creative identities.

With that in mind, the 2005 bidding war that erupted between NBC and CBS for the license to distribute *Studio 60* can be considered as an attempt to secure greater oversight and moral authority over a series developed externally but directly relevant to NBC's interest in both *SNL* and its own network brand. Undoubtedly, the high production values, A-list cast, and quality pedigree attached to the Sorkin series made *Studio 60* an attractive prospect for both potential buyers. Yet as ultimately evidenced by its willingness to outbid CBS, NBC proved to be more motivated. As NBC president Kevin Reilly explained to *Business Week*, his network needed the prime-time hit that *Studio 60* (falsely) promised more than any competitor did, having lost 25 percent of its audience in the previous three years and recently having fallen to fourth place in the eighteen-to-thirty-four-year-old demographic, behind Fox. "We're coming off a couple of tough years," he explained, "and we saw this as the kind of entertainment that would bring folks back." At the same time, Reilly identified the specific content of the series as an additional motivating factor—beyond the promise of critical and commercial success offered by its high-gloss production and familiar talent. "If he's going to [lampoon NBC]," Reilly publicly explained of Sorkin's fictional NBS network, "it's better he does it on our air than on someone else's."[26] Thus, NBC was motivated to ensure that it won distribution rights for *Studio 60* over CBS not just because of general economic pressures, but because of specific cultural resonances and meanings activated by the series' fictionalization of *SNL*'s broadcast heritage and work worlds. In negotiations with Sorkin and his collaborator, Thomas Schlamme, NBC ultimately offered a $2 million per episode license fee, well above the average of $1.4 million reported by *Business Week*.[27] NBC also committed to a minimum thirteen-episode order (compared to the usual nine), agreed to a penalty for early cancellation, contributed a significant $10 million marketing budget, and of course promised non-interference in the creative process.

Once the show was secured by the network, however, industrial negotiation over the cultural proximity of *Studio 60* and its ability to lay claim to the identities and traditions of NBC and *SNL* did not end. The victory of NBC in the bidding war brought *Studio 60* into a more institutionally sanctioned relationship with *SNL* that was nevertheless marked by tension on the level of production culture and the professional identities of above-the-line labor. By invoking the production heritage of *SNL* in spirit if not in name, Sorkin's series not only made claims to speak for and about a tradition of broadcast television comedy long identified professionally with Lorne Michaels, but it also traded in an interpretative

Figure 7.1. *Studio 60*'s "News 60" segment—a clear reference to *SNL*'s "Weekend Update."

mediation of backstage sketch comedy production culture that could be seen as competing with Michaels's own development of *30 Rock* at and with NBC. Suddenly, the two productions found themselves aligned as part of NBC programming strategy and their shared connection to *SNL*, yet they began to compete with one another for marketing and promotional attention from the network as well as for cultural status and legitimacy. It is at this level of production culture—rather than any narrative connection to *SNL*—that these series might be considered part of an *SNL* franchise, in that producers occupying similar industrial positions and sharing a certain number of institutional affiliations and industrial resources nevertheless sought to differentiate themselves and their mobilizations of *SNL* from one another.[28] These franchised production cultures, therefore, prompted producers to self-reflexively construct oppositional identities and deploy public discourses to legitimize (and delegitimize) creative labors that appeared to make competitive claims to a heritage shared across multiple sites of cultural production.

Lorne Michaels used the venue for mediated public disclosures afforded by press interviews to claim *SNL* as his own territory and to delegitimize Aaron Sorkin's ability to authoritatively speak for or about the franchise. On the most basic level, Michaels used public self-disclosures to establish that he had the idea for an *SNL*-inspired prime-time series first, or at least independently. "The show was in development before we heard about the Aaron Sorkin show," he stressed to *USA Today*. "I was told about the Aaron Sorkin show by Kevin Reilly by phone call. They're not similar shows."[29] Paramount for Michaels in the construction of his professional identity in this context of franchised production was establishing his labor and his ability to speak for *SNL* as different from Sorkin's. In the *Village Voice*, for example, Michaels made a particular point of taking a 2006 *Studio 60* episode to task for its suggestion that racial diversity (or the lack thereof) would be a major source of tension behind the scenes at an *SNL*-like show. "No it isn't," Michaels protested. "It is in Aaron Sorkin land, but it isn't here."[30] Interestingly, by drawing upon the discourses of authorship surrounding Sorkin ("Aaron Sorkin land," "the Aaron Sorkin show"), Michaels acknowledged the creativity and personal style of his peer producer, yet did so in a way that disarticulated Sorkin from *SNL* and highlighted his inability to speak in an authentic way about its production culture. "Aaron Sorkin land" was a territory far removed from that of Michaels at *SNL* and *30 Rock*. Similarly, Michaels downplayed the heavy-handed criticisms of network television upon which Sorkin's show revolved, framing them as uninformed and anachronistic. "This is a new insight, that networks are not to be trusted?," Michaels asked incredulously in the *New Yorker*. "The reality is that the network isn't that powerful anymore—talent is."[31] Once again, Michaels made a claim to greater insider knowledge about the world of contemporary comedy (and network broadcasting in general), emphasizing the idea of talent in order to paint Sorkin's thematic emphasis on network interference and oversight as out of touch with the creative process. Promotionally, this emphasis on talent also allowed Michaels to gesture to his own thematics: early *30 Rock* episodes focused heavily on the loose-cannon personality of actor Tracy Jordan (played by *SNL* alum Tracy Morgan) and his ability to disrupt the production of a fictional sketch series. More important, however, Michaels's emphasis on the shifting power of talent framed Sorkin's perspective as the product of a bygone past, inappropriate to the changing contemporary television landscape. Michaels laid competitive claim to a professional identity not just based in a superior sense of how the world of sketch comedy works, but also one more attuned to a post-network era, when the power of the network was in question. In downplaying the power of the network, Michaels also po-

sitioned himself as much in opposition to NBC as to Sorkin, characterizing NBC's decision to order both programs as a "surprise" that "muddied
the water."[32] Ultimately, the frustrated producer "protect[ed] his turf," as
the New Yorker presented it, not only by discursively denying Sorkin access to the "real" production context of SNL, but also by physically bar-
ring him, resisting collaboration, and refusing the Studio 60 producer's
request to observe the making of SNL.[33] Through this discursive identity
work as well as his control over production space within the comedy franchise, Michaels claimed a monopoly of creative authority over the popular narrativization and mediation of SNL's work world.

Sorkin, on the other hand, proved far less interested in using public
disclosures to lay claim to franchise identity in relation to SNL. In the absence of such claims, the authorship discourses surrounding Sorkin (and
highlighted by Michaels) worked to make Studio 60 more legible as part
of an authorial oeuvre than as a co-branded content franchise. As a critic
in New York opined, the content of the dramatic series was less about
SNL than it was about Sorkin himself: "It's not a show about a comedy
franchise; it's a show about Sorkin's career." Referring to the greater parallels between Studio 60's fictional showrunner, Matt Albie, and Sorkin's
own drug abuse and ouster from The West Wing in 2003, as well as the
producer's penchant for idealized workplace families, this commentary
suggested that the connection to SNL was tenuous at best. "Much has
been made of its debt to Saturday Night Live, but they don't have much in
common unless you think Lorne Michaels is likely to interrupt his show
to damn your TV remote as 'a crack pipe.'"[34] While this dismissal suggested Michaels's complicity in the irrelevance and complacency of network comedy, it nevertheless affirmed Michaels's attempts to disarticu-
late Studio 60 from the SNL franchise.

Nevertheless, while critics and industry insiders may have perceived
this disjuncture between Sorkin's authorial identity and the production
identities of Michaels's SNL, at the level of marketing to popular audiences, the two programs continued to demand distinguishable industrial identities. For programming executives like Kevin Reilly, the co-
existence of so many SNL-themed series was not creative competition,
but merely a line of complementary products in need of some brand differentiation. According to the NBC president, each show had different
talent and its own tone and flavor: "Tina is more madcap, and Aaron

is exploring issues and character dynamics and has a real romance at the center." Yet crucially, Reilly added: "The only way we could screw it up . . . is if the audience gets confused."[35] Thus, onscreen/offscreen talent like *30 Rock*'s Tina Fey also played a role in publicly negotiating the distinctions between the different series and crafting a unique production identity for each. Echoing Reilly in *USA Today*, Fey emphasized the generic differences between her series and *Studio 60* while recognizing "at the same time, your grandma's going to be confused."[36] On the one hand, her articulation of product differentiation as a problem that would only really pertain to older, assumedly out-of-touch audiences defuses concern about the similarity between the series—in a way commensurate with her own sarcastic but neurotic image. On the other hand, commentary in the article in question frames her concern as genuine: "She worries viewers will suffer from late-night fatigue."[37] Once again, this negotiation of shared interest in the industrial meanings, identities, and traditions revolving around *SNL* suggests a franchising-like industrial relationship, in that franchise producers often balance a multiplication of spin-off productions with the fear of "franchise fatigue" in which market oversaturation causes viewer interest to flag.[38] In this regard, Fey's public presentation of a professional identity differentiated *30 Rock* from the perceived competition at *Studio 60*, but also from *SNL*. In another *USA Today* interview, for example, she emphasized that *30 Rock* was its own show and could not be directly understood as a piece of *SNL*. "None of the actual events are real, just sort of the vibe of the place," she stressed. "And the people are amalgams of people."[39] Much like her "grandma" quip, Fey again used comedy to negotiate this product differentiation dilemma, assisting in the promotion of *30 Rock* by writing a promo that directly confronted the similarities among all the *SNL*-themed series. By making a joke of the similarities—Alec Baldwin mistakenly believes he's co-starring with Amanda Peet of *Studio 60*—Fey ridiculed the notion that the series would be confused. Moreover, in the process, she made a claim to identity for both herself and her series as the "funny" one—the series whose producers could be ironic and self-deprecating, in contrast to the earnestness of Sorkin's production.

In the end, the industrial relationships between these series drove a play of identity across and between productions and practitioners working from different positions within a shared institutional structure and industrially meaningful heritage. Viewed through the lens of franchising, the multiplication of *SNL*-themed production can be said to not simply have served the cross-promotional interests of NBC, but instead created complex relations of production in which different stakeholders competed for resources and attention while also crafting professional identities and positioning themselves within industrial hierarchies. In this case, at stake was the ability to claim a production relationship to the heritage of network television, legitimacy in mediating *SNL's* production cultures, and a public presentation of creative identity in the post-network era.

CONCLUSION

In exploring the struggles of professional identity surrounding NBC's triple-dipping from the legacy of *SNL* in 2006–2007, this chapter has been only tangentially concerned with the production of the late-night sketch comedy series itself. At some level, that series became merely grist for the mill from which two new configurations of network television production sought to develop their own industrial identities under the umbrella of a shared network struggling in the post-network economy. Nevertheless, through that production, both series engaged with the cultural legacy of *SNL*—a piece of broadcast television heritage to which each production community found it advantageous to lay claim, even as those opposing claims required the articulation of differentiable production identities to stake out their unique positions within that shared tradition. While economically devalued and increasingly perceived as culturally irrelevant, *SNL* continued to have purchase as networks and producers alike sought the ability to control, articulate, and alternatively include and distance themselves from its heritage. As I have suggested, this complex network of stakeholders in the reiteration and mediation of *SNL's* work world might be considered a form of franchising in that *SNL* became a set of backstage meanings and identities shared and exchanged across heterogeneous production communities and spaces of identity in broadcast television. Whether we quibble over that "franchising" term, the point is that *SNL* had clearly become something larger than a single television series: an organizational umbrella under which both the economics and the cultural significance of NBC's programming came to be mediated and understood. Indeed, in popular reception, the different contexts of production and the competing production identities of *SNL*, *Studio 60*, and *30 Rock* often did not preclude understanding them as a shared entity. On NPR's *All Things Considered*, for example, host Robert Siegel perceived the new series as "both based on or spin-offs from *Saturday Night Live*."[40] On a definitional level, and certainly in the context of the managed public disclosures offered by talent like Michaels and Fey, this is patently false. Yet in terms of a structure of feeling, this misstatement captures the significance of the relationships among these series. In the post-network era, a perceived-to-be-obsolete *SNL* had become increasingly relevant to and persistently meaningful in the construction of production identities in network television and the mediation of network comedy work worlds.

Notes

1. Qtd. in Belloni, "It's Ten O'Clock," 194+.
2. Gitlin, *Inside Prime Time*; Johnson, *Branding Television*; Johnson, *Media Franchising*.
3. Lotz, *The Television Will Be Revolutionized*, 7–8.
4. Kompare, *Rerun Nation*, 102.
5. Johnson, *Media Franchising*; Johnson, "Devaluing and Revaluing Seriality."
6. Caldwell, *Production Culture*.
7. This chapter therefore draws its approach from the burgeoning field of production studies. Such work examines how the material organization of cultural production influences the content that is produced, as well as how that organization shapes the self-reflexive meanings, professional identities, and communities through which media workers understand that process and position themselves within work worlds. Many scholars working in production studies have rightly criticized the managed self-disclosures of media workers as hype or spin that cannot offer insight into real working conditions and practices, preferring ethnographic methods. Here, I embrace self-managed disclosure not as a means of accessing the "truth" of production, but as a rich site at which professional identities and industrial cultures are publicly constructed and articulated. For more on production cultures and professional identities, please see Caldwell, *Production Culture*; Mayer, Banks, and Caldwell, *Production Studies*; Negus, *Music Genres and Corporate Cultures*; Pratt, "The Cultural Economy"; and Santo, "*Batman* versus *The Green Hornet*."
8. Deziel, "Two New Shows Succumb."
9. Stanley, "When It Comes to Political Parody, Upstarts Outrun the Classics," E1.
10. Ibid.
11. Doherty, "Taking Humor Seriously without Being Glum," B10–B11.
12. Sklar, "That '70s Show," 16.
13. Belloni, "It's Ten O'Clock."
14. Berman, "Getting a Fix on NBC."

15. Learmonth, "Fox Drives 'Spike' into Latenight," 20.

16. Sklar, "That '70s Show," 20.

17. Murray, "Brand Loyalties."

18. Deziel, "Two New Shows Succumb."

19. Edwards, "A Dangerous Woman," 102, 104.

20. Doherty, "Taking Humor Seriously without Being Glum."

21. Atkinson, "The Water Cooler," 14.

22. Moore, "Shows-within-Shows," 16.

23. Deziel, "Two New Shows Succumb."

24. Sternbergh, "The Aaron Sorkin Show," 71.

25. Deziel, "Two New Shows Succumb."

26. Grover, "The Show within a Show at NBC."

27. Ibid.

28. Johnson, *Media Franchising.*

29. Oldenburg, "*30 Rock,*" D4.

30. Sklar, "That '70s Show," 20.

31. Friend, "Shows about Shows."

32. Sklar, "That '70s Show," 22.

33. Friend, "Shows about Shows."

34. Sternbergh, "The Aaron Sorkin Show," 71–72.

35. Friend, "Shows about Shows."

36. Freydkin, "Fey Feels Ready for Prime Time," D1.

37. Ibid.

38. Johnson, *Media Franchising.*

39. Oldenburg, "*30 Rock,*" D4.

40. "*Ugly Betty* Leads Pack of New TV Series."

Works Cited

Atkinson, Claire. "The Water Cooler." *Advertising Age* 77(41) (2006):14.

Belloni, Matthew. "It's Ten O'Clock. Do You Know Where Your Network President Is?" *Esquire,* July 27, 2009 (orig. December 2007). http://www.esquire.com/features /silverman1207.

Berman, Marc. "Getting a Fix on NBC." *Mediaweek* 16(40) (2006):30.

Caldwell, John. *Production Culture: Industrial Reflexivity and Critical Practice in Film and Television.* Durham, NC: Duke University Press, 2008.

Deziel, Shanda. "Two New Shows Succumb to Saturday Night Fever." *Maclean's* 118–119(52) (2005):44–46.

Doherty, Thomas. "Taking Humor Seriously without Being Glum." *Chronicle of Higher Education* 53(21) (2007):B10–B11.

Edwards, Gavin. "A Dangerous Woman." *Rolling Stone,* February 14, 2006, 99, 102, 104.

Freydkin, Donna. "Fey Feels Ready for Prime Time on *30 Rock.*" *USA Today,* October 9, 2006, D1.

Friend, Tad. "Shows about Shows." *New Yorker,* April 24, 2006, 48–50.

Gitlin, Todd. *Inside Prime Time.* Berkeley: University of California Press, 2000.

Grover, Ronald. "The Show within a Show at NBC." *Business Week,* July 31, 2006, 62–63.

Johnson, Catherine. *Branding Television.* London: Routledge, 2011.

Johnson, Derek. "Devaluing and Revaluing Seriality: The Gendered Discourses of Media Franchising." *Media, Culture and Society* 33(7) (2011):1077–1094.

———. *Media Franchising: Creative License and Collaboration in the Culture Industries.* New York: New York University Press, 2013.

Kompare, Derek. *Rerun Nation: How Repeats Invented American Television.* New York: Routledge, 2005.

Learmonth, Michael. "Fox Drives 'Spike' into Latenight." *Variety,* September 11–17, 2006, 20, 25.

Lotz, Amanda D. *The Television Will Be Revolutionized.* New York: New York University Press, 2007.

Mayer, Vicki, Miranda Banks, and John Caldwell, eds. *Production Studies: Cultural Studies of Media Industries.* New York: Routledge, 2009.

Moore, Frazier. "Shows-within-Shows: A Pair of NBC Fall Series Take a Look Within." *Chicago Defender* 101(25) (2006):16.

Murray, Simone. "Brand Loyalties: Rethinking Content within Global Corporate Media." *Media, Culture and Society* 27(3) (2004):415–435.

Negus, Keith. *Music Genres and Corporate Cultures.* London: Routledge, 1999.

Oldenburg, Ann. "*30 Rock:* It's Not about *SNL,* but the 'Vibe' Is There." *USA Today,* August 16, 2006, D4.

Pratt, Andy. "The Cultural Economy: A Call for Spatialized 'Production of Culture' Perspectives." *International Journal of Cultural Studies* 7(1) (2004):117–128.

Santo, Avi. "*Batman* versus *The Green Hornet:* The Merchandisable TV Text and the Paradox of Licensing in the Classical Network Era." *Cinema Journal* 49(2) (2010): 63–85.

Sklar, Rachel. "That '70s Show." *Village Voice,* November 1, 2006, 14–22.

Stanley, Alessandra. "When It Comes to Political Parody, Upstarts Outrun the Classics." *New York Times,* November 3, 2006, E1.

Sternbergh, Adam. "The Aaron Sorkin Show." *New York,* September 18, 2006, 71–72.

"*Ugly Betty* Leads Pack of New TV Series." *All Things Considered,* October 19, 2006.

PART THREE

Social Politics and Comedic Representation

Bringing the Black: Eddie Murphy and African American Humor on *Saturday Night Live*

RACQUEL GATES

In the more than thirty-five years that *Saturday Night Live* has been on the air, only fifteen African Americans have appeared as regular cast members or featured players. Many of these gifted performers were relegated to marginal roles next to their white costars or dismissed after a single season. Some, such as Tim Meadows, Chris Rock, and Damon Wayans, accused the show's writers of limiting their participation on the show and dismissing their ideas for sketches.[1] In spite of *SNL*'s well-deserved reputation as a force of social critique, the show has been erratic at best in its treatment of African American issues and cast members.

And yet, in the 1980s, an era that would become synonymous with Ronald Reagan's conservative politics, Eddie Murphy emerged as the breakout star on *Saturday Night Live*. A crossover performer who attracted both black and white audiences, Murphy was a hybrid figure who blended the brash social satire of comedians like Lenny Bruce and Richard Pryor with the more affable, safe, storytelling persona of Bill Cosby. It is this element of mainstream acceptability that has led many scholars to overlook the sociopolitical significance of Murphy's work on *SNL* and to dismiss his film and television performances as inherently apolitical, a claim that I argue is based less on Murphy's actual performances and more on the presumed incompatibility between social critique and crossover success. Referring to Murphy's film work, scholar Donald Bogle writes, "Murphy's movies paid lip service to racism (perhaps even exploited it) but took no stands at all."[2] Cultural critic Nelson George characterized Murphy in the following way: "he isn't angry or intensely political or overly socially conscious."[3] J. Fred MacDonald was less generous in his assessment of Murphy's performances on *Saturday Night Live,* dismissing Murphy's success by noting that the comedian "scored well in two minstrel favorites."[4] The use of the word "minstrel" is telling, since it references not only the form of Murphy's performances on *SNL* (in the tradition of minstrelsy and vaudeville) but also the type of humor that Murphy is presumed to be performing: stereotypical and designed for a white audience.

This chapter interrogates the assumption that Murphy sacrificed political relevance upon crossing over into mainstream film and television in the conservative 1980s. I look closely at Murphy's performances on *SNL* and argue that his work pioneered new performative strategies that straddled the line between marginalized black insider humor and mainstream white comedy. On the surface, Murphy's performances appeared to be tailored to appeal to mainstream white audiences. Many of his characters and sketches, however, contained aspects of subversive black humor that spoke to black audiences and black perspectives. I examine the complicated ways that Murphy's work in *SNL* sketches intervened in contemporaneous discourses of racial identity and racial politics, and I offer an in-depth analysis of his *SNL* short film "White Like Me," which is a particularly good example of Murphy's distinctive style.

IT'S ALL ABOUT THE CROSSOVER: RACIAL REPRESENTATION IN THE 1980S

Murphy's contributions on *Saturday Night Live* are particularly important in the context of black representation in the media during the 1980s. The era was characterized by an emphasis on carefully coded rhetoric aimed at downplaying the continued significance of racism. On the political front, the arrival of Reaganism and the New Right ushered in a wave of conservatism that permeated social and political discourses. As Jimmie L. Reeves and Richard Campbell note, conservatives exploited existing anti-welfare and anti–affirmative action sentiments and employed rhetoric about black immorality, most notably in the form of the black "welfare queen" and the "war on drugs," "to gain popular support for economic policies that favored the rich."[5] Furthermore, a new emphasis on political correctness, which often took the form of a seemingly neutral, "color-blind" rhetoric, made frank discussions of race all the more difficult. According to Reeves and Campbell: "By denying the existence of institutionalized racism, attributing black failure to lack of initiative or impoverished values, and adulating black stars as proof that racial barriers to success had evaporated, Reaganism simultaneously tapped into historically deep undercurrents of racism in American culture and absolved whites of any implication in that history."[6] Sociologist Herman Gray contends that the mainstream media were complicit in this politically problematic shift in language:

> We witnessed the formation and institutionalization of discourses, articulated by Reagan and engineered by his sophisticated spin doctors, that moved quietly but steadily from "African Americans" to "welfare," from "equal opportunity" to "preferential treatment," from "racism/discrimination" to "reverse discrimination," from "tax recipients and social entitlements" to "taxpayers and civic responsibility," from "morality" to "immorality," and from "shared public responsibility" to "private charitable giving." Through its immediacy and pervasiveness, television quietly framed these shifts, announcing the news daily in softer, shorter, more visually dramatic, and conceptually simpler bites.[7]

Television programs like *The Cosby Show* (1984–1992), with its representation of the upwardly mobile African American Huxtable family, unwittingly aided the shift from explicitly racist rhetoric to more subtle racially coded discourse. As Sut Jhally and Justin Lewis argue in their study of *Cosby*'s reception, "The Huxtables proved that black people can succeed; yet in doing so they also prove[d] the inferiority of black people in general (who have, in comparison with whites, failed)."[8] On an ideological level, therefore, *The Cosby Show* presented blackness as separate from African Americans, a state of being that one could "transcend" if one so desired.[9] In the words of Linda Williams, this effectively functioned as a form of "color-muteness" rather than the "color-blindness" it purported to be.[10] This rhetoric not only failed to recognize the continuation of racial inequalities in the 1980s, but also promoted a mythical image of U.S. political progress while covering up the fissures that continued to exist. These fissures actually grew wider as Reagan's government cut social welfare programs and reversed the gains accomplished by his more liberal predecessors.

Color-muteness created a particularly tricky position for Murphy, the lone black performer at the time on *SNL*. On the one hand, visual markers of race were evident in Murphy's skin color and in the ways in which he grounded his humor in aspects of his black identity. His *SNL* Gumby character, for example, drew its humor from the amusing contradiction between Murphy's own youthful, hip blackness and the green cartoon character's white, Jewish voice and Borscht Belt humor. On the other hand, the logic of mainstream appeal dictated that his blackness be used in service of making white audiences laugh while not alienating them.

Murphy's situation was emblematic of a larger transformation occurring in film and television at the time, which placed the emphasis on crossing over: the appeal of black performers and black cultural products to nonblack audiences and consumers. On the radio and in record stores, the term "urban" became the preferred way to refer to music by African American artists because it signified blackness in a vague sense but avoided an explicit mention of race. According to Nelson George, this shift in language was aimed at increasing sales among nonblack consumers.[11] This, in turn, meant that record companies raced to discover new artists and to redefine existing ones to fit in with this new crossover world. Whitney Houston's marketing as a pop diva, for example, rather than as a soulful R&B singer, demonstrated this trend. Michael Jackson stood at the crossroads between past and future, straddling the line between the traditional black music world of Motown (as the last of the great Motown artists) and the new era of MTV.

A combination of industrial and social forces had spurred the proliferation of blaxploitation films in the 1970s, but a new set of factors acted on television in the 1980s. In addition to a growing conservatism in U.S. politics, significant changes in the television industry were altering the landscape of racial representation in the media. Both Ken Auletta and Herman Gray note the impact that the increasing popularity of cable television had on the networks. Auletta argues that cable, with its endless options for viewers, put pressure on the networks to more actively court viewers.[12] Gray notes that the industry used blackness to achieve two goals. First, the major networks believed that putting black stars in their programming would attract African American viewers, thus making up for any viewers lost to the lure of cable programming. Second, blackness (in the form of black performers) signified "quality" and hipness, characteristics that defined cable television and that the networks desperately wanted to replicate.[13] At the same time, networks did not want to create all-black programming, for fear of alienating white viewers. Thus, crossover appeal became central to programming. In this chapter, I understand the concept of "crossover" to mean black performers' popularity with both black and white audiences (as opposed to black audiences alone). A black entertainer whose performances are consciously designed to appeal to white audiences (such as by invoking stereotypes or avoiding black-oriented humor) is one example of crossover, as is a program that incorporates African Americans into a predominantly white cast and storylines. Both of these aspects of crossover describe Eddie Murphy's work on *Saturday Night Live.*

Many scholars and critics have questioned the sociopolitical significance of black representations designed for crossover appeal, particularly given that so many occurred within the confines of lighthearted comedic fare in both film and television. Film scholar Donald Bogle, for instance, notes, "Predictable comedies . . . assured the mass audience that African Americans and whites could laugh together without fretting about social issues."[14] Yet, as author Mel Watkins argues, comedy has a long history as a tool of social criticism and catharsis among African American communities and has included "two disparate strains of humor: the often distorted *outside* presentation in mainstream media (initially by non–African Americans) and the authentic *inside* development of humor in black communities (from slave shanties and street corners to cabarets) as well as in folklore and black literature, films, and race records."[15] In other words, Watkins draws a distinction between the type of comedy that blacks performed primarily for white audiences (e.g., minstrel shows) and the type performed by blacks for black audiences (e.g., race films). While the former entertained white audiences with stereotypes, the latter offered social commentary and criticism.

Of course, the line between these two forms of humor was not always clearly drawn, and seemingly straightforward black performance tropes might include subtle barbs aimed at whites. Thus, black performances were often polysemic texts that could be read one way by white audiences while possessing an entirely different meaning for black ones. Mel Watkins traces the African American practice of using comedy to criticize social inequality back to its roots in West African cultural traditions. Marvin McAllister argues that the black penchant for parody as a way to put people and situations into a black-oriented context dates back to the theater in the years just after the American Revolution, when "New World Africans crafted complex, contradictory, and multilayered performances that celebrated, parodied, and even historicized Indian, African, and European others."[16] In the days of slavery, for instance, African Americans created the cakewalk as a means of poking fun at the airs put on by their white owners. As Watkins, McAllister, and others such as Bambi Haggins have argued, comedy—particularly parody and satire—has historically functioned as a tool for African Americans to criticize mainstream institutions and practices while operating *within* mainstream institutions and practices, a way of pointing out issues and problems while avoiding detection.[17]

I argue that Murphy's identity as a crossover star did not minimize the subversive elements of African American humor or African American critique embedded in his work. Because his performances on *Saturday Night Live* were tailored to please both black and nonblack audiences, he created sketches and characters that seamlessly combined social critique and mainstream appeal. Murphy, of course, was not the first black performer to bring black forms of humor to television. Flip Wilson's popular eponymous variety show included a number of characters from black experience such as his preacher, Reverend Leroy. And Watkins cites Richard Pryor's popularity in the 1970s (including the short-lived *Richard Pryor Show* in 1977) as bringing black comedy into the mainstream. However, although these African American performances bore some resemblance to Eddie Murphy's *SNL* sketches and characters, I argue that Murphy's performance demonstrated a new hybrid identity that would continue to influence African American performance in popular culture from the 1980s onward. I contend that this aesthetic crystallized in the characters and sketches that Murphy developed while a cast member on *SNL*. This performance style, which was the result of multiple factors—Murphy's blackness and connection to African American humor, the production and contextual issues unique to *Saturday Night Live,* the historical time period—changed the nature of African American performance in the public space of network television.

Considering comedy and variety more broadly, scholars and critics have noted the ways that the variety show has served as a tool for musings on race and race relations that might be too progressive for more straightforward genres like social realist dramas, even in the relatively liberal 1960s.[18] And, of course, African American comedians have always offered insightful, often scathing analyses of race in the darkened spaces of bars and comedy clubs.[19] Murphy, coming from a background in comedy clubs, undoubtedly brought this sensibility into his performances on *SNL*.

Mel Watkins argues that invisibility and malleability are traits that characterize African American performers and their comedy traditions. His description of African American humor as the "shadow" which haunts American concepts of race is especially instructive in analyzing Murphy's performances on *SNL:*

> African-American humor can be seen as a shadowy comic vision that satirizes and humanizes America's main body. As Pirandello suggested, it variously stretches and turns, creating grotesque apparitions or comic shades that reflect the perfidy and concealed desires of the mainstream. Sometimes, as at high noon, it may coincide perfectly with the main body, demonstrating a convergence of humor and social aspirations. But usually it veers to this side or the other, twisting wildly and ridiculing a mainstream that vainly attempts to legitimize its rigid and often absurd pretense of decorum and propriety.[20]

As a "shadow," Murphy moved throughout *SNL*, occupying multiple subjectivities. Sometimes, his performances aligned perfectly with a mainstream concept of an African American man as a nonthreatening buffoon. At other times, his performances offered glimpses of characters from African American experience and skewered white America's lingering racism.

A DIFFERENT KIND OF TOKEN BLACK GUY

Murphy's ability to infuse *Saturday Night Live* with his own African American–inflected brand of humor was enabled by the internal politics of the show. In 1980, the man responsible for *SNL's* launch and success, Lorne Michaels, left the program after serving as executive producer for five years. Although his replacement, Jean Doumanian, had been an associate producer for *SNL* under Michaels, she wanted to distinguish herself from her predecessor by reworking the show from the ground up. In addition to building new sets and hiring a new writing staff, Doumanian sought to realize her vision of the new *SNL* with a fresh cast. Unlike Michaels, who cast writer-performers primarily from improvisational troupes such as Second City, Doumanian recruited promising stand-up comedians with little to no background in improvisational comedy. This decision made it possible for Murphy, a nineteen-year-old comic, to secure a spot on the show as a featured player.[21]

Though Doumanian was more flexible than Michaels with regard to cast members from comedy backgrounds, her ideas regarding the racial composition of the cast mirrored her predecessor's. Lorne Michaels had cast Garrett Morris and then let him languish on the sidelines. Doumanian made it clear that she wanted one—and only one—black cast member on *SNL*. As Doug Hill and Jeff Weingrad note in their history of the show, Doumanian's "goal was to have three women and four men, one of them black."[22] *SNL* talent coordinator Neil Levy claims that Doumanian initially turned down Eddie Murphy because she had already cast actor Robert Townsend.[23] According to Levy, "She only wanted to hire one black actor and Townsend hadn't signed his contract yet, so she signed Eddie."[24] In other words, Doumanian was less interested in bringing a truly multicultural perspective to the show and more concerned about ensuring the appearance of diversity. This eventually became a crucial force in defining not only the nature of Murphy's involvement in the show, but also the types of characters that he would create during his *SNL* tenure.

As the "token black guy," Murphy had no doubt about the role he was expected to play on *SNL*. His job was to import the urban edge into the all-white show when called upon. Murphy's job was, clearly, to bring the black. However, if race was not the focus of a sketch, Murphy was often relegated to the background as little more than an extra. He rarely played the part of the straight man in sketches. Years later, comedian Chris Rock would experience the same marginalization, noting, "On *SNL*, I either had to play a militant or a hip-hop guy."[25] The options for black cast members were clear: bring the black or work as a glorified extra. Black cast members thus found themselves in a difficult situation. If they wanted visibility on the show, they had to actively play up their blackness in the characters and sketches that they developed. At the same time, doing so meant continued marginalization and exclusion from sketches that did not explicitly deal with race.

While this type of racial tokenism resulted in Garrett Morris's marginalization on the show in the 1970s, Murphy used it strategically to his advantage. Murphy was rarely integrated into the center of most sketches. Part of this was no doubt due to his status as a featured player, since the main parts of any sketch were written for the named cast, with supporting roles (such as that of a bartender or waiter) going to the featured players. Murphy's race, however, had an unmistakable impact on his participation. For instance, if a scenario called for a married couple, writers usually paired a white female cast member with a white male. And, if writers did occasionally make an exception, the interracial pairing became the focus of the sketch rather than the foundation. Murphy complained, "If I'm playing the husband and my wife is white, the audience is waiting for a black joke."[26] This meant that on those rare occasions when Murphy was given the spotlight, it was nearly always in a monologue-driven bit where he was segregated from the rest of the cast, such as his Raheem Abdul Muhammed character in the "Weekend Update" segment. These star-turning moments, ironically resulting from the show's implicit racial segregation, became rich opportunities for Murphy to assert his creativity and introduce an African American voice into the show.

The backstage politics of *Saturday Night Live* created a perfect environment for Murphy to get away with the type of thinly veiled criticisms that he made in his performances. Doumanian faced an uphill battle when she took over as executive producer. After Michaels and the original cast left, most of the writing staff resigned; the ones who remained harbored a deep resentment of the new executive producer. NBC executives drastically cut the show's budget from $1 million per show to $350,000. This left Doumanian with the nearly impossible task of casting, staffing, and creating a hit show in a little under three months with a reduced budget.[27] Not surprisingly, the new season got off to a shaky start and never fully recovered. Sketches failed to make audiences laugh, and the network consistently pressured Doumanian to deliver better ratings. Therefore, Doumanian was willing to take chances on Murphy and allow him creative freedom that she might not have had she been operating under less desperate circumstances. This was evident one night during Murphy's first season when the show was running short on material and

Figure 8.1. Eddie Murphy distinguishes himself from former cast member Garrett Morris during "Weekend Update."

had five minutes of airtime to fill. One of the producers suggested that Murphy take the stage and do some of his stand-up routine in order to make up the difference.[28] Doumanian agreed. As he would continue to do throughout his career on *SNL*, Murphy used the circumstances to his advantage and further distinguished himself as the show's breakout star.

Another opportunity occurred during that same first season on the show. Murphy had continually prodded Doumanian to give him a more substantial role, and he was finally given a chance in a short segment during "Weekend Update." Previously, Murphy had appeared in the background of sketches or played supporting characters, but this would be his first prolonged performance on *SNL*. Murphy played Raheem Abdul Muhammed, a high school basketball player from Ohio who offered his thoughts about a recently instituted racial quota that mandated that Cleveland high schools include a minimum of two white players on their basketball teams. As Raheem, Murphy made fun of whites' tendency to co-opt elements of African American culture and style: "In the '60s we wore platform shoes, then y'all had to wear platform shoes. In the early '70s we braided our hair, then in the late '70s y'all had to braid your hair. Now it's 1980: we're on welfare and by the end of next year y'all going to be on welfare, too."[29]

Murphy's short monologue was a hit with the studio audience, and it sent a message to both *SNL* writers and producers that Murphy was a valuable asset. More significant, Murphy's performance gave a preview of the type of hybrid comedy and complex, social satire that he would continue to bring to the show in the characters he developed. In the Raheem monologue, the welfare comment hinted at the real-life economic and educational disparity between blacks and whites, implying that whites' desire for black culture and style was inextricably connected to white privilege. For instance, the decision to implement a white racial quota on Cleveland basketball teams was an attempt by white administrators to deflect attention from the disparity of educational quality between blacks and whites in the city.[30] Placed in this real-life context of white "me-tooism," Murphy's monologue opened with silly surface humor (braids, platform shoes) and then transitioned into sociopolitical commentary (welfare), all the while maintaining a lightheartedness that never became too explicitly critical. Murphy's approach to social commentary was markedly different from Richard Pryor's, who hosted *SNL* on December 13, 1975. Pryor designed sketches that centered on explicit racial issues such as anti-black discrimination by the police and white flight, and the dialogue he wrote included a bevy of racial slurs.[31] NBC executives were so anxious about Pryor's reputation for pushing the boundaries of appropriateness that they demanded a seven-second delay in the live broadcast to catch any "obscenities."[32] Murphy's comedy, however, contained none of this kind of in-your-face humor. Instead, he wove his cultural commentary into more conventional—even stereotypical—performances.

Murphy demonstrated a unique gift for blending nonthreatening racial humor with a more caustic social critique. He lured audiences in with standard sketch comedy fare: impersonations, physical comedy, and pitch perfect comedic timing. At the same time, he gave the audience more than they bargained for by coupling the obvious jokes with subtle barbs and mordant comments. For instance, in another "Weekend Update" segment that season, Murphy appeared as himself and gave his thoughts on why he, a nineteen-year-old eligible for the draft, should not be compelled into military service: "If I get drafted, who's going to be the token black on *Saturday Night Live*, huh?" He then did spot-on impressions of singer Stevie Wonder and comedian-actor Bill Cosby, showing his impressive mimicry skills for the first time on the show. Murphy closed the monologue by suggesting former cast member Garrett Morris as his replacement in the draft, deftly adding, "Word has it he has a lot of free time right now."

Murphy accomplished three important goals in this monologue. First, he revealed some of the unique talents that had gone unnoticed and underutilized on *SNL*. Soon, writers and producers would provide ample opportunities to highlight Murphy's impressive impersonations not just of Stevie Wonder and Bill Cosby, but also of Buckwheat, James Brown, Mr. T, Jesse Jackson, and numerous others. Moreover, Murphy's ability to imitate various voices and dialects played a central role in the original characters he developed on the show, such as his Borscht Belt Gumby. Second, by taking Garrett Morris as his object of derision, Murphy used the monologue as an opportunity to define himself in direct contrast to Morris. By pointing out Morris's age and referencing his career decline, Murphy went for a very personal assault on his *SNL* predecessor in which he presented himself as a new kind of black performer who would indeed bring the black desired by *SNL* executives, but who would not tolerate the type of marginalization that had plagued Morris during his tenure on the show. Murphy's words were not simply aimed at Morris, however; they also targeted the way that *SNL* and its executives had treated the first African American cast member. Murphy hence accomplished the third goal of the monologue: he let the producers and writers know that he was fully aware of the marginalized treatment Morris had endured and made it clear that *he* expected to be treated very differently. It was as if Murphy were saying "I'm watching you" to both Doumanian and *SNL's* writers, making it known that he was a very different kind of "token" than they were accustomed to dealing with.

Murphy took advantage of these opportunities to demonstrate the distinctive African American perspective that he could bring to *SNL* and began to appear more regularly on episodes. According to Hill and Weingrad, Murphy would invent characters and scenarios and the writers would help him flesh out the details of individual sketches. In this way, Murphy was able to insert his voice and point of view into the show with characters such as Raheem Abdul Muhammed (who, after his initial appearance on "Weekend Update," became a recurring character who gave his opinion on news stories and popular culture), the white-hating Tyrone Green, and Mr. Robinson, Murphy's inner-city parody of Mr. Rogers. Midway through his first season, Murphy was promoted from featured player to the official seventh member of the cast.[33]

Once Doumanian left the show and Dick Ebersol took over the executive producing duties, *SNL* utilized Murphy's creative talents even more. In response to the negative feedback that Doumanian's season had received, Ebersol fired everyone that she had cast with the exception of Murphy and Joe Piscopo, who now took over as the unquestioned stars of the show. According to James Downey, a longtime *SNL* writer, Ebersol's strategy was to feature the most popular cast members and their characters as frequently as possible.[34] This meant that Murphy and Piscopo appeared more often than their cast mates. Ebersol knew that Murphy was central to the show's success and, as a result, he gave Murphy tremendous creative freedom and even allowed him to prerecord some of his sketches (rather than appear on the live show) in order to have more free time to pursue his burgeoning film career in Hollywood.[35] Given free rein to do nearly anything he wanted (and with writers now eager to design sketches and characters for the star), Murphy mastered the art of pleasing the audience while offering a black-oriented social critique rooted in African American cultural traditions.

"WHITE LIKE ME"

"White Like Me" is a sketch in which Murphy goes undercover as a white man to investigate the reality of racial difference. A notable example of Murphy's hybrid style, it represents the combination of crowd-pleasing humor and subtle social commentary that Murphy perfected while on *Saturday Night Live.* On the one hand, the sketch displays Murphy in comical whiteface as he finds himself in a series of absurd and entertaining scenarios. On the other hand, "White Like Me" criticizes liberal racism while simultaneously paying homage to black comedic traditions. It is the latter that I focus on here.

The polysemic nature of the sketch is evident in its title, which references multiple source texts. First, "White Like Me" is most obviously a play on the 1961 nonfiction book *Black Like Me* written by John Howard Griffin. In the book as well as the subsequent 1964 movie adaptation (starring actor James Whitmore), a white journalist goes undercover as an African American man to expose the racism of the U.S. South. The book was premised on the notion that the author—a white man—could fully comprehend the experiences of a black person and thus "prove" the existence of racism by changing his skin tone for a month. Though seemingly well intended, the book and the film reinforce the liberal racist assumption that the existence of racism in the South—a situation that African Americans had long understood, criticized, and rallied against—needed to be validated by the allegedly "objective" perspective of a white man. Moreover, the two *Black Like Me* projects suggest that one only need to don black makeup for a month in order to fully comprehend the historical, social, and cultural impact of racism, thus ignoring the systemic nature of racism in favor of interpersonal interactions.

Next, Murphy's "White Like Me" references a previous *Saturday Night Live* sketch performed by Richard Pryor. When Pryor hosted *Saturday Night Live* in 1975, he appeared in a sketch in which he played an author named Junior Griffin, who had just completed a book titled *White Like Me*, chronicling his experiences of going undercover as a white man. There is a close-up of the book in Pryor's sketch, and the audience sees a photo of Pryor in white makeup and a curly wig. By expanding Pryor's short sketch into a short film of the same title, Murphy was paying homage to one of his comedy idols.

Murphy's "White Like Me" thus puts into practice Henry Louis Gates Jr.'s concept of signifyin(g). On the most obvious level, "White Like Me" references the titles of both Griffin's *Black Like Me* and Pryor's "White Like Me" sketch: "To rename is to revise, and to revise is to Signify."[36] Murphy's short film fits Gates's description of signifyin(g) as a practice historically developed as coded communications where meaning was created and understood by African Americans while simultaneously shielded from criticism and punishment from white outsiders. The nature of this practice, Gates asserts, was twofold: it allowed for a criticism of aspects of white hegemonic structures outside the controlling gaze of whites, and it also encouraged an intertextual dialogue that privileged the recognition and theorization of black cultural texts.[37] Understood from this perspective, the sophistication of Murphy's performance becomes clear. He pokes fun at the premise of Griffin's book and its pretensions. At the same time, he honors an African American comedy legend and connects himself to Pryor's legacy. This latter point has broader significance as well. By symbolically aligning his sketch with Pryor's, Murphy also aligns himself with Pryor's reputation for doing "dangerous" black comedy. In this way, Murphy signifies on his own persona for being "safe" and nonthreatening. Finally, he manages to achieve all of this while also delivering a hilarious sketch that both black and white viewers could enjoy whether they fully understood the intertextual references or not.

"White Like Me" was made possible by Murphy's status as a crossover star. Having left the show ten months earlier to act in films full time, Murphy returned to *Saturday Night Live* as both host and Hollywood superstar.[38] By the time that "White Like Me" aired on December 12, 1984, Murphy was not only one of the biggest stars in *Saturday Night Live* history, but he had also achieved motion picture success with *48 Hrs.* (1982), *Trading Places* (1983), and *Beverly Hills Cop* (1984). It was Murphy's persona as an affable, safe comedy star—constructed by his roles in these films—that made his whiteface critique of white privilege in "White Like Me" so surprising, and thus so potent.[39] With "White Like Me," Murphy fixed his sights on white privilege, systemic racism, and the very notion of the "safe" black man that he had come to represent.

Murphy opens "White Like Me" by explaining that there are allegedly two Americas: one for whites and one for African Americans. Murphy's analysis of the differences between the two strikes at both the personal and the structural level. He tells viewers that he has decided to explore the situation for himself by going undercover as a white man. During the transformation process, Murphy's comments are mocking and point out the more laughable aspects of white behavior as seen through black eyes. In the prep room, a makeup artist applies white foundation to the actor's skin while Murphy looks at videotapes and greeting cards to get a crash course in the behavior and cultural values of white people. On the one hand, "White Like Me" reinforces a type of cartoon whiteness that viewers might easily dismiss as having no connection to real-life white people or institutions. At the same time, however, the representation of Murphy's transformation suggests the labor that goes into the construction of white identity in the first place.

The preparation focuses on Murphy suppressing his familiar black traits and substituting a performed brand of hyper-whiteness that is presented as bland, stuffy, and disingenuous. Murphy studies the soap op-

Figure 8.2. Eddie Murphy warns the audience that the white people they meet may just be African Americans in disguise.

era *Dynasty* (1981–1989) to learn how to walk with his butt "real tight." He mimics Hallmark cards to master the art of corny sentimentality. As a result, he crafts a whiteness that consists of a kind of hyper-attention to the disconnect between his black self and the theatrical whiteness that he performs. The sketch's focus on this tension effectively constructs whiteness as intrinsically false, composed of "correct" social cues and norms rather than an organic expression of individual personality and style, as Murphy's blackness is presented. This emphasis on the construction of white masculinity suggests that whiteness is difficult for Murphy to perform correctly because it *is* a performance, one with right answers and wrong ones, with rules and regulations and an entire system of organizations designed to exclude African Americans from its privileges.

Once the transformation is complete, Murphy's experience as a white man shifts from personal embodiment to observations of systemic racism and white privilege. He leaves the television studio and explores New York City as Mr. White. This shift is crucial for two reasons. First, although the tone of the film remains humorous, it moves from the initial riff on white behavior and culture to the realm of the very tangible privileges that whiteness confers in the real world. Whether it is a free newspaper, a no-questions-asked bank loan, or a party on the public bus, membership in the white race clearly has benefits. Visual artist and author Adrian Piper examines the significance of the bus party bit, arguing that the scene is "a joke, perhaps, but not entirely." According to Piper, "To look visibly black, or always to announce in advance that one is black is, I submit, never to experience this kind of camaraderie with white people, the relaxed, unguarded but respectful camaraderie that white people reserve for those whom they believe are like them: those who can be trusted, who are intrinsically worthy of value, respect and attention."[40] By exploring the notion that white people act differently when blacks are not around, Murphy goes beyond what would be a very clichéd stand-up bit about the differences between African Americans and whites and instead launches a wry look at how race and structural racism operate on numerous levels.

Second, "White Like Me" emphasizes the ways that white privilege functions in everyday life. Employed to portray white privilege in both absurd as well as disturbingly realistic scenarios, the whiteface he wears does not create privilege as much as it allows Murphy to access it. In each of the scenarios, Murphy is exposed to this secret world of opportunity only in the absence of other African Americans, and only when he himself disavows blackness. When he is given a free newspaper by a white storekeeper, the storekeeper justifies the action by saying, "There's nobody around." The swinging party on the bus can only begin once the last (recognizable) African American man departs. And finally, when Murphy attempts to get a loan at a bank with no collateral and no identification, he is initially rejected by the African American loan officer until his white colleague comes in to "save the day" by giving Mr. White a stack of money. But Murphy guarantees the intimate white camaraderie of which Piper writes by verbally renouncing the African American bank officer. "What a silly Negro!" proclaims Mr. White, and he and the white banker share a hearty laugh.

By setting up a number of scenarios in which the whiteface Murphy discovers the secret world of whites, "White Like Me" does more than just expose viewers to the concept of white privilege. It also validates the suspicions that African Americans may have felt at the time—namely, that they were still on the losing end of unfair practices and biased treatment, even though they could not always find hard evidence to point to. For African Americans, the certainty that structural racism exists is often coupled with the inability to address concretely the omnipresent specter of white privilege. What scholar Phillip Brian Harper refers to as the "evidence of felt intuition" too often gets dismissed as "playing the race card." Murphy, cloaked in whiteface as well as in his celebrity persona as a "safe" African American, gives voice and credibility to these suspicions.[41]

Murphy's whiteface character is subversive in yet another way. In his reading of "White Like Me," Marvin McAllister argues that the experiment demonstrates Murphy's, and hence other African Americans', ability to penetrate the privileged spaces typically hidden from black view.[42] Bambi Haggins counters by arguing that Murphy's final threat, "I've got a lot of friends. And we've got a lot of makeup"—accentuated by the camera's humorous reveal of various African Americans in Murphy's entourage having their white makeup applied—rests on a conservative notion of individual mobility and effort, that the transgression is limited to those with access to its means, rather than being a broad, community-wide movement. Yet I offer that the sketch's closing image of the group, rather than the individual, could be read as a vision of the black community rather than just a single person. After his sojourn into whiteness, Murphy returns to his black identity, and recruits a small army to take the journey themselves. Though the group is small, it is still significant that "White Like Me" ends with a vision of African American solidarity as opposed to individual success. The end of the sketch also carries a barely concealed aggression that is clear in the closing line: "I've got a lot of friends. And we've got a lot of makeup. So the next time you're hugging up with some really super-groovy white guy, or you meet a really great super-keen white chick, don't be too sure. They might be black."

This closing remark by Murphy, which invites whites to interrogate whiteness, is noticeably different in tone from the rest of the sketch. Whereas the absurdity of both the premise and Murphy's appearance may have provided some viewers with a distraction from the social critique up until this point, the delivery of Murphy's final statement makes it less a punch line and more of a menacing threat. The point of the sketch, it would seem, is not that Murphy has succeeded in fooling the world by posing as a white man. Instead, "White Like Me" allows a temporary journey through the world of whiteness as seen through black eyes. Neither Murphy nor the character he plays is actually discovering the world of whiteness, but rather *revealing* it to the audience via whiteface.

Like his "Weekend Update" segment where he let producers and audiences know that he was not going to be marginalized like Garrett Morris, Murphy's closing statement in "White Like Me" speaks to a larger issue than the one immediately apparent. It is a warning that the "safe" African Americans whom whites allow into their homes, see at the movies, and watch on television every Saturday night might not be the affable, agreeable individuals that they appear to be. In this regard, Murphy himself becomes the symbol of all other black figures, both mainstream and marginal. The experiment demonstrates Murphy's ability, and hence the potential of other African Americans, to penetrate the privileged spaces typically hidden from black view. The whiteface in "White Like Me," it might be said, is simply the visual representation of the ways that Murphy and other upwardly mobile African Americans slip in and out of the mainstream all the time, and an acknowledgment that such moves are, in fact, strategic rather than fully assimilationist in nature. The threat, therefore, is not just that of a lone black masquerading as white. Instead, it suggests a full-scale invasion and subversion of white spaces. And finally, Murphy's suggestion that some alleged whites might *already* be black reinforces this threat, and it pokes at deep-seated white fears of race mixing and miscegenation.[43]

LIVE FROM NEW YORK . . . IT'S THE EDDIE MURPHY SHOW!

Eddie Murphy's skillful navigation of mainstream popular culture proved that African American humor could survive and even flourish in the midst of a politically conservative time when an emphasis on crossover appeal threatened to eradicate any meaningful representation of race on American television. By taking the limitations that were meant to keep him marginalized and using them to his advantage, Murphy's professional strategy for negotiating the racial politics on *Saturday Night Live* mirrored the performative approach that he took in creating characters and comedy sketches. Instead of languishing on the sidelines like other African American performers on the show, Murphy's skillful integration of African American humor and mainstream appeal led to the creation of an inside/outside humor hybrid that allowed him to critique the media's treatment of African Americans even as he simultaneously rose to media superstardom. Though Murphy's success was made possible by the very social, political, and cultural factors that tried to marginalize him (and other African American performers), this chapter has argued that his identity as a crossover star was the conduit through which Murphy delivered some of his most pointed social critiques. Hiding his social commentary in plain sight, Eddie Murphy projected a little blackness into American homes every Saturday night. *Saturday Night Live* wanted someone who would bring the black, and the show got more than it bargained for.

Notes

1. Shales and Miller, *Live from New York*.
2. Bogle, *Toms, Coons, Mulattoes, Mammies, and Bucks*, 281.
3. George, *Post-Soul Nation*, 23.
4. MacDonald, *Blacks and White TV*, 240.
5. Reeves and Campbell, *Cracked Coverage*, 74.
6. Ibid., 53.
7. Gray, *Watching Race*, 34.
8. Jhally and Lewis, *Enlightened Racism*, 95.
9. Ibid., 97.
10. Williams, *Porn Studies*, 276. In her discussion of the depiction of race in pornographic films, Williams quotes scholar Susan Courtney and argues that one consequence of an emphasis on color-blindness is the creation of "a culture now so determined to be officially blind to racial differences that it has created a new kind of taboo around their very mention." She argues that while we ostensibly take note of racial differences, the logic of color-muteness tells us that we are not supposed to notice them.
11. George, *Post-Soul Nation*, 55.
12. Auletta, *Three Blind Mice*, 195.
13. Gray, *Watching Race*, 66–67.
14. Bogle, *Toms, Coons, Mulattoes, Mammies, and Bucks*, 268.
15. Watkins, *On the Real Side*, 41.
16. McAllister, *White People Do Not Know How to Behave*, 7.
17. Haggins, *Laughing Mad*.
18. Sutherland, *The Flip Wilson Show*.
19. Haggins, *Laughing Mad*.
20. Watkins, *On the Real Side*, 569.
21. As a featured player, Murphy's contribution to sketches was considerably lighter than those of performers in the regular cast.
22. Hill and Weingrad, *Saturday Night*, 388.
23. Townsend never signed his contract and backed out of the show in order to pursue other projects.
24. Qtd. in Shales and Miller, *Live from New York*, 200.
25. Ibid., 420.
26. Qtd. in Sanello, *Eddie Murphy*, 33.

27. Shales and Miller, *Live from New York*, 190.

28. Ibid., 201.

29. *Saturday Night Live*, season 6, ep. 3, orig. airdate: December 6, 1980.

30. Vecsey, "Sports of the Times: Quotas Wrong for School Sports."

31. Pryor's "Word Association" sketch with Chevy Chase, in which the two men volley racial epithets back and forth during a job interview, is a particularly good example.

32. Haggins, *Laughing Mad*, 58.

33. Hill and Weingrad, *Saturday Night*, 422.

34. Shales and Miller, *Live from New York*, 224.

35. Ibid., 257.

36. Gates, *The Signifying Monkey*, xxiii.

37. Gates writes, "Theirs is a meta-discourse, a discourse about itself. These admittedly complex matters are addressed, in the black tradition, in the vernacular, far away from the eyes and ears of outsiders, those who do not speak the language of tradition" (ibid., xxi).

38. February 25, 1984, was Murphy's last episode as a cast member.

39. I define whiteface as the representation of whiteness and white identity by African Americans through the use of physically transforming makeup.

40. Piper, "Passing for White, Passing for Black," 23.

41. Harper, "The Evidence of Felt Intuition," 116.

42. McAllister, *White People Do Not Know How to Behave*, 11.

43. The threat in the closing line brings to mind Piper's suggestion: "The ultimate test of a person's repudiation of racism is not what she can contemplate *doing* for or on behalf of black people, but whether she herself can contemplate calmly the likelihood of *being* black" ("Passing for White, Passing for Black," 16).

Works Cited

Auletta, Ken. *Three Blind Mice: How the TV Networks Lost Their Way.* New York: Vintage, 1992.

Bogle, Donald. *Toms, Coons, Mulattoes, Mammies, and Bucks: An Interpretive History of African Americans in American Films,* 4th ed. New York: Continuum, 2001.

Gates, Henry Louis, Jr. *The Signifying Monkey: A Theory of African-American Literary Criticism.* New York: Oxford University Press, 1988.

George, Nelson. *Post-Soul Nation: The Explosive, Contradictory, Triumphant, and Tragic 1980s as Experienced by African Americans (Previously Known as Blacks and before That Negroes).* New York: Penguin, 2005.

Gray, Herman. *Watching Race: Television and the Struggle for Blackness.* Minneapolis: University of Minnesota Press, 1995.

Haggins, Bambi. *Laughing Mad: The Black Comic Persona in Post-Soul America.* New Brunswick, NJ: Rutgers University Press, 2007.

Harper, Phillip Brian, "The Evidence of Felt Intuition: Minority Experience, Everyday Life, and Critical Speculative Knowledge." In *Black Queer Studies: A Critical Anthology,* edited by E. Patrick Johnson and Mae Henderson, 106–123. Durham, NC: Duke University Press, 2005.

Hill, Doug, and Jeff Weingrad. *Saturday Night: A Backstage History of Saturday Night Live.* New York: Beech Tree, 1986.

Jhally, Sut, and Justin Lewis. *Enlightened Racism: The Cosby Show, Audiences, and the Myth of the American Dream*. Boulder, CO: Westview, 1992.

MacDonald, J. Fred. *Blacks and White TV: Afro-Americans in Television since 1948*. Chicago: Nelson-Hall, 1983.

McAllister, Marvin. *White People Do Not Know How to Behave at Entertainments Designed for Ladies and Gentlemen of Colour: William Brown's African and American Theater*. Chapel Hill: University of North Carolina Press, 2003.

Piper, Adrian. "Passing for White, Passing for Black." In her *Out of Order, Out of Sight*. 2 vols. Cambridge, MA: MIT Press, 1996.

Reeves, Jimmie Lynn, and Richard Campbell. *Cracked Coverage: Television News, the Anti-Cocaine Crusade, and the Reagan Legacy*. Durham, NC: Duke University Press, 1994.

Sanello, Frank. *Eddie Murphy: The Life and Times of a Comic on the Edge*. Secaucus, NJ: Carol Publishing, 1997.

Shales, Tom, and James Andrew Miller. *Live from New York: An Uncensored History of Saturday Night Live*. Boston: Little, Brown, 2002.

Sutherland, Meghan. *The Flip Wilson Show*. Detroit, MI: Wayne State University Press, 2008.

Vecsey, George. "Sports of the Times: Quotas Wrong for School Sports." *New York Times*, December 3, 1980.

Watkins, Mel. *On the Real Side: Laughing, Lying, and Signifying—the Underground Tradition of African-American Humor That Transformed American Culture, from Slavery to Richard Pryor*. New York: Simon and Schuster, 1994.

Williams, Linda. *Porn Studies*. Durham, NC: Duke University Press, 2004.

"Is This the Era of the Woman?": *SNL*'s Gender Politics in the New Millennium

CARYN MURPHY

The existence of a gender divide in comedy is highlighted by media trend stories proclaiming its demise. *Bridesmaids* (2011), for instance, launched a thousand blog posts debating its merits as "proof" that women are funny.[1] In the months following its release, press coverage of the fall television season emphasized the number of new situation comedies featuring female protagonists, and the fact that some of these shows were created by women.[2] In early 2012, the comedy gatekeeper for *Late Show with David Letterman* (1993–present) was fired after a *New York Times* profile indicated that he almost never booked female comics.[3] Articles, reviews, and blog posts about these events have to acknowledge an entrenched bias against women in comedy, even if they're claiming that this bias is no longer relevant. Authors and commentators often point, either with admiration or derision, to Christopher Hitchens's 2007 *Vanity Fair* provocation, "Why Women Aren't Funny." Hitchens presented the heterosexist argument that men have to be funny in order to attract women, and that women are not biologically predisposed to create humor because men are attracted to them physically (so women do not need to be funny to attract men).[4] The article sparked a larger discussion of sexism in comedy, and many refutations pointed to *Saturday Night Live* as an American comedy institution and the recent prominence of its female cast members, including Tina Fey, Amy Poehler, Maya Rudolph, and Kristen Wiig. Even before Hitchens drew additional attention to it, the "era of the woman" at *SNL* had drawn a substantial amount of popular press attention that acknowledged the show's male-dominated history in order to proclaim the ascendance of women in its ranks.[5]

In this chapter, I analyze the gender dynamics of *SNL* as a male-dominated workplace that has historically supported a comedy taste culture that excluded and marginalized women. I examine the popular press coverage of perceived changes to the comedy institution during the period in which Tina Fey served as head writer and cast member (1999–2006, referred to here as the "Tina Fey era"). Popular press coverage of these seasons has overstated the extent to which gender equity has been achieved at *SNL* and in the production of comedy as a whole, in ways that are consistent with a dominant cultural narrative of postfeminism. I question the extent to which long-standing production practices changed during this time, and thus the extent to which this period legitimately closed the gender divide in comedy at *SNL*.

In its most general sense, "postfeminism" refers to a cultural condition after feminism. Yvonne Tasker and Diane Negra define it as "a set of assumptions, widely disseminated within popular media forms, having to do with the 'pastness' of feminism, whether what is supposedly past is merely noted, mourned or celebrated."[6] Although this is a contested term, I use it here to refer to the dominant cultural narrative that feminism is no longer relevant, desirable, or necessary because gender equity has been achieved.

Despite industry claims of progress, numerous studies have indicated that gender bias continues to affect women's employment in media production.[7] In her research on radio production in the early 1990s, Rosalind Gill used discourse analysis to argue that although gender discrimination still shaped commercial broadcasting, industry professionals denied its existence, relating the absence of women in the workplace to factors other than gender.[8] In her analysis of inequalities in new media, she defines this issue as "the increasing 'unspeakability' of structural inequalities" and terms the phenomenon "the postfeminist problem." The notion that feminism is no longer relevant or necessary has become so generally accepted that workers disavow the reality of gender disparities in hiring and promotion, even when differences are stark. In Gill's study, media professionals used discourses of postfeminism to explain that opportunities in their fields were merit-based, and they were reluctant to acknowledge the possibility of discrimination based on factors of identity.[9] In this chapter, I rely on Gill's idea of the postfeminist problem to analyze claims about changes in the gender dynamics at *SNL* in the early twenty-first century. In the next section, I offer a historical overview of the show's gendered workplace dynamics to contextualize my analysis of the popular reception of the Tina Fey era as a postfeminist phenomenon.

"A BIT OF A BOYS CLUB": *SNL*'S TRADITION OF MALE-DOMINATED COMEDY

The rigorous production schedule at *SNL,* still in use today, became entrenched in its first season. Writers pitched initial sketch ideas to the host on Mondays, and then moved forward with material that received a positive response. Cast members were not often credited (or compensated) as writers, but were typically expected to collaborate on the development of sketches. Writers worked through the night at least once a week in order to prepare material for table reads on Wednesdays, when the cast and crew gathered to assess the informal presentation of sketches. Material that received a positive response in the read-through stage moved forward for dress rehearsal on Saturday, and sketches that worked well were then performed on air. For pitches and sketches to succeed, they had to be "funny in the room," and the majority of people in the room (cast, crew, and often host) were men. In the early years, Michael O'Donoghue's aggressive verbal comedy and the physical antics of John Belushi, Chevy Chase, and Dan Aykroyd were supported by this system. Though women like Gilda Radner, Laraine Newman, and Jane Curtin were strong comic performers, they often expressed frustration with the supporting roles they played in many of the sketches that made it all the way through the process. In *Saturday Night: A Backstage History of Saturday Night Live,* Doug Hill and Jeff Weingrad claim that because of this production schedule, "a lot of the women writers' sketches weren't making it on the air, and the women performers were getting too many secretary and receptionist parts, written by the men."[10]

Accusations and denials of institutionalized sexism weave a common thread that can be traced through histories of *SNL.* Performers, writers, and producers disagree about the extent to which working conditions fomented a male-dominated environment in which women found it difficult to thrive. The consistency of the denials may be related to the show's original identity as a countercultural force in broadcast network television. In 1975, the show's content was marketed as "not ready for prime time," and its perspective was informed by oppositional politics that were aligned with the rejection of traditional values.[11] According to writer Neil Levy, "It was almost like all the leftover spirit of the sixties found its way into this show—that spirit of rebellion, of breaking through whatever boundaries were left."[12] In contrast to typically male-dominated comedy troupes, SNL's original cast was designed to feature equal numbers of men and women (a balance which was tipped with the last-minute hire of Chase). The original writing staff of eleven included three women: Rosie Shuster, Anne Beatts, and Marilyn Suzanne Miller. Although women were writing more frequently for prime-time sitcoms in the mid-1970s, the number of women on staff at SNL was unusually high.[13]

Although the cast and writers were aware of the sexual revolution and second wave feminism, advancing gender equality was not a shared goal. Histories of SNL indicate that women who worked there were aware that they were treated differently because they were women, but they could not agree to organize and demand better treatment as a group. Hill and Weingrad claim that the female writers and performers convened after two months of working on the show to discuss the difficulties involved in getting their material to air. The agreed-upon strategy of working harder as individuals is attributed to Miller, who supposedly said, "The show was no different from any other corporate environment. You either put up quality work or shut up. Organized movements got you nowhere."[14] For Miller, an experienced comedy writer, SNL was not a particularly liberated or countercultural milieu; it was a new iteration of the male-dominated comedy world, which functioned as a microcosm of the larger patriarchal society.

In *Live from New York,* Beatts relates her discovery that NBC had "accidentally" paid her as much as O'Donoghue, her then-partner and a writer who was also part of the original staff. Beatts told NBC she would not return the money they claimed to have given her in error, and she further informed them that they would have to continue paying her the equal rate.[15] Although the story she recounts is brief, it reflects her individual experience of gender-based wage discrimination. She does not offer a definitive statement of the resolution, and she gives no indication that she discussed the network's policy with the other women on staff. Anecdotes such as these indicate that at this time, female writers and performers did not work together to respond to discriminatory practices.

The most high-profile example of institutionalized misogyny at *SNL* is John Belushi's supposed, repeated claim that "women aren't funny."[16] Although some accounts state that Belushi may not have seriously believed this, he supported the statement by sabotaging female writers' material at table reads and lobbying executive producer Lorne Michaels to "fire all the women writers."[17] He also refused to appear in sketches written by women; the role of Todd in Beatts's "Nerds" sketch was originally written for him, but became a hit with Bill Murray.[18] Belushi's behavior is often qualified and excused in variations of this story, in a way that epitomizes the show's response toward charges of "boys club" exclusionary practices throughout its history.[19] Some writers, including Miller, argue that Belushi had a point, and that early material from the women on staff was not very strong.[20] This theory reveals the early emergence of a gendered burden of representation at the show; there was pressure on the few women involved in the creative process to disprove a generally accepted notion about gender and comedy, as compared with the men on the staff, who were presumably attempting to prove their own individual talent.

There are additional claims that Belushi's sexism was just part of his erratic personality, but even in recent interviews, original cast member Jane Curtin has characterized the early years of *SNL* as "primarily a misogynistic environment."[21] Aykroyd has said that he would "question whether it was a boys club," because the women in the cast were strong performers.[22] His denial appears alongside the anecdotes of fraternity house antics that liberally pepper histories of the show. Aykroyd and Belushi decorated their office walls with panties that were mailed to them by female fans;[23] writer Terry Southern taunted a network censor with hardcore pornographic material;[24] and Belushi verbally confronted Beatts with such antagonism that she burst into tears.[25] Although the entrenched system seemed to reward sexist behavior and aggressive bullying, the claim that women could nevertheless succeed in this environment by proving their individual abilities is repeated from the early years through the 1990s era in which the sophomoric humor of Adam Sandler and Chris Farley dominated the show.

When Michaels left *SNL* in 1980, Jean Doumanian was promoted from associate producer to replace him. Although she held the job for less than six months, it is often referred to as a low point for the series.[26] Doumanian did not have the support of her staff; writer Barry Blaustein recalls being invited to sign a petition to get her fired on the first day he reported to work.[27] Doumanian was supplanted by Dick Ebersol, who produced the show from 1981 to 1985, a period in which Eddie Murphy and Joe Piscopo were comedy focal points.[28] There were few women in the cast, and they often had little to do.

When Lorne Michaels returned to the show, the established gender dynamics among the performers experienced a shift. Nora Dunn joined the cast in 1985, and Victoria Jackson and Jan Hooks were added the next season. Although Jackson often played variations on a ditzy blonde stereotype, Hooks established herself as a versatile and talented character actor. After leaving *SNL* to join the predominantly female cast of *Designing Women* (1986–1993), she described the change as "jumping from a pool of testosterone into a pool of estrogen." Although she declined to criticize the male-dominated structure of *SNL,* explaining that it was no different from the world at large, she characterized her new workplace as "very nurturing, very supportive" in contrast.[29] Dunn expressed surprise at the lack of support she received from the show when she declined to appear in a 1990 episode hosted by Andrew Dice Clay.[30] Musical guest Sinéad O'Connor also chose to withdraw rather than appear alongside the shock comedian, who was notorious for material that was offensive and misogynist.[31] Hooks and Jackson performed with Clay in the season's finale, and Dunn was not invited to return for the next year. Dunn's experience seems to demonstrate that women who questioned the prevailing mentality were summarily dismissed, which belies the claim that women could establish themselves simply by working harder.

Dunn characterized *SNL* as a "frat show" prior to her exit,[32] and the juvenile male antics taking place on- and offstage only increased when Farley and Chris Rock were added to the cast, and they were soon joined by Sandler, David Spade, and Rob Schneider.[33] Janeane Garofalo was an established comedian before she joined the cast in 1994, having appeared in multiple films and in the casts of the video and sketch comedy series *The Ben Stiller Show* (MTV, 1990–1991; Fox, 1992–1993) and the late-night parody *The Larry Sanders Show* (1992–1998). Prior to starting work, Garofalo made critical statements to the press about the current emphasis on sophomoric humor. She left after less than a season and has been very direct in interviews about the amount of misery she experienced in the male-dominated environment. She has referred to the brief time she spent at *SNL* as the "year of fag-bashing and using the words 'bitch' and 'whore' in a sketch,"[34] and recalled that male writers would not develop sketches for women.[35] In her statements, she also has assumed personal responsibility for failing to deal with the pressures of the show in a healthy way,[36] but her complaints about gender bias and the overall lack of show quality received a predictably defensive response from the male writers she worked alongside. One of them, Fred Wolf, repudiated her claim that the show was a "men's club" and said her issues resulted from personal insecurities.[37] His denial stands in contrast to a scathing *New York* magazine piece on that season, the show's twentieth, which reported that Farley was making prank phone calls from the writers room during which he released flatulence into the receiver, Norm Macdonald punched a writer "in the head, knocking him to the floor," male colleagues taunted Laura Kightlinger with obscenities until she cried, and a group of male writers debated the merits of a sketch joke about *60 Minutes* commentator Andy Rooney raping his colleague Lesley Stahl.[38] The tales of men behaving badly and actively working to silence women's participation and perspective support the contention that it would have been difficult for anyone who challenged this dynamic to succeed during this time.

Histories of the show mark the twentieth season as an artistic low point. Due to network pressure and declining ratings, *SNL* began a major period of rebuilding with the twenty-first season, in 1995. Molly Shannon and Tim Meadows were among the few cast members who remained from the previous year; new hires included Will Ferrell, Cheri Oteri, and Darrell Hammond. In *Live from New York*, longtime writer Jim Downey recalls that it became "very much a performer's show" at this time, because the staff was encouraged to write sketches for recurring characters.[39] More than ten new writers were hired, including Paula Pell, who remembers that even in her first year, the show began receiving more positive press attention in response to the changes.[40] Tina Fey has joked that the show was still in flux two years later, and that she was hired because they were "looking to diversify";[41] she was one of three women on a staff of twenty-three. Fey became the head writer in 1999 and joined the cast as the co-anchor of "Weekend Update" in 2000. At this time, a fresh wave of press coverage began to report on the ascendance of women at *SNL*.

"THE CONSCIOUSNESS CHANGED": POPULAR RECEPTION OF THE TINA FEY ERA

In 2002, *Newsweek* proclaimed: "For most of its 27 years, *Saturday Night Live* has been comedy's premier boys club. But not anymore."[42] Tina Fey was often centrally implicated in this type of coverage, as in a *Television Week* profile headlined "Rewriting *SNL*'s Old-Boy Tradition," which claimed that she "helped erase *SNL*'s reputation for gender bias."[43] As ratings improved in the new millennium, journalists and reviewers correlated *SNL*'s renewed popularity with changes to the show's overall content and the increased visibility of women in the cast, which were reported as interrelated phenomena. In addition to claims about the ascension of women behind the scenes, trend stories argued that the show's humor became "feminized" in the first decade of the 2000s, as women in the cast were strong performers whose abilities were showcased more prominently than in the past.[44] While these stories celebrated the defeat of gender bias at *SNL*, they were simultaneously deeply invested in a gender divide. This coverage in national magazines and newspapers supported narrowly constructed definitions of masculine and feminine humor in order to buttress the premise that gender difference exists, but no longer works to marginalize women in comedy.

Although the show's feminization is exaggerated, there was an evident shift in the visibility of female performers that began in the late 1990s. As noted above, in prior eras, female cast members raised concerns about being consigned to supporting roles. When Paula Pell and Fey began working in the writers room, the cast included Cheri Oteri and Molly Shannon, who became associated with recurring characters that were the comedic focuses of sketches. When Fey joined the cast, Shannon, Ana Gasteyer, Rachel Dratch, and Maya Rudolph were appearing regularly, often as central characters. Shannon exited as Amy Poehler entered in 2001, and during the next few seasons, numerous sketches featured ensemble casts of women, which had been a rarity in past seasons. Although the cast changed each year, trend stories argued that the foregrounding of these talented performers was indicative of a permanent shift in *SNL*'s gender politics, one that was capable of addressing (or erasing) the significance of its male-dominated history.

Tina Fey initially drew press attention in 2000, when she joined the cast as the co-anchor of "Weekend Update," with Jimmy Fallon. The anchor post enhances performers' visibility because they use their own names and do not overtly appear to be in character; the weekly segment is a vital part of the show's appeal for much of the viewing audience. Michaels designed the Fallon-Fey pairing, the first *SNL* anchor team in nearly twenty years, as a play on opposites. Fey told an interviewer that Lorne envisioned her as the "girl who studied" and Fallon as the "charming guy who didn't really do his homework."[45] In their first show together, Fey performed a "Women's News" segment that offered comedic commentary about gendered media coverage. This became a regular segment that underscored the separation of her perspective from Fallon's. The characteristics that Fey and Fallon emphasized in their roles are not inherently gendered, but they became so through their performance as a female-male comedy team.

In popular press coverage, the divide between "smart" and "silly" that Fey and Fallon exploited with their anchor characters was extrapolated to apply to the women and men in the cast as a whole. In a 2003 review for the *New York Times,* Emily Nussbaum claimed that sketches would "alternate maddeningly between smart satire and eye-rolling frat-boy humor," and she associated the women in the cast with the former (and clearly preferable) type. She credited the women, including Dratch, Rudolph, and Poehler, with "many of the stronger character pieces, and fewer of the juvenile throwaways."[46] Critics noted that women in the cast would "regularly outshine their male colleagues," emphasizing a gender divide by proclaiming these performers' success in an imagined competition.[47]

The popular press narrative about the women's achievement was rife with contradictions, at once noting the success of comediennes at *SNL*

Figure 9.1. Tina Fey and Amy Poehler became symbols of the purportedly dramatic shift in *SNL*'s gender politics.

as a sign of gender equity and simultaneously marking women's success in comedy as unusual and potentially fleeting. Women in the cast were continually called upon to address "the gender issue" in reportage during this time period. In response to frequent inquiries about the differences between female and male writers, Fey developed a stock answer: "Women tend toward more character-based, subtle observations. Men are more amused by fighting bears, sharks, and robots," which echoed the separation between feminine and masculine comedy that press coverage emphasized at this time.[48] Amy Poehler stressed in interviews that she preferred to be evaluated on the basis of her comedy and not her gender, but the nature of the trend story made that an impossibility.[49]

In 2008, *Vanity Fair* published Alessandra Stanley's response to the Christopher Hitchens article referenced above. She profiled Tina Fey, Amy Poehler, Maya Rudolph, and Kristen Wiig, arguing that the success of these *SNL* performers was evidence of a gendered shift in comedy culture. According to Stanley: "Comedy has changed on sitcoms, in clubs, and on *Saturday Night Live*. The repertoire of women isn't limited to self-loathing or man-hating anymore; the humor's more eclectic, serene, and organic. 'The consciousness changed' is how Lorne Michaels explains the difference."[50]

Significantly, Michaels was not referencing an alteration in the mind-set of male comedy writers and performers, but in comediennes. Stanley echoed Michaels's view, suggesting that the long-standing bias against women in comedy was a result of their limited "repertoire." Her coverage incorporated several salient aspects of the reception of the Tina Fey era. It asserted that comedy itself had been transformed, not just at *SNL* but in general. It implied that the long-standing bias against women in comedy was the result of the type of humor associated with comediennes, and asserted that as women moved past that, barriers to entry and to achievement became negligible. By further inference, women in previous eras were limited by their own range, and not by institutional discrimination.

THE CRASS CEILING: WORKPLACE DYNAMICS IN THE TWENTY-FIRST CENTURY

The 2000–2001 season featured five women in a cast of thirteen, or "the most female players *SNL* has ever had": Tina Fey (who was also a head writer), Molly Shannon, Ana Gasteyer, Rachel Dratch, and Maya Rudolph.[51] Beyond the change in numbers, trend stories claimed to note a change in roles as women had moved "from saucy sidekicks to stand-alone stars,"[52] attaining a position of equality, or even dominance, at *SNL*. In the central narrative of the popular reception of the Tina Fey era, the success of women during this time demonstrated that the long-standing gender divide in comedy production had become irrelevant. But an examination of the composition of the cast and writers room undermines these claims and suggests that the show has not overcome its male bias.

Women never comprised more than one-third of the cast from 2001 to 2006. This proportion had been slightly exceeded in 2000, a situation that resulted from Michaels's last-minute addition of Fey as "Update" co-anchor, "after he already had his 'full complement' of female performers."[53] Although he has claimed that he does not have a quota, his phrasing indicates that there were a limited number of spots available for women, and this did not change in the early 2000s. When the press reported the "Update" anchor pairing of Fey and Poehler as a "first" for women in 2004, Michaels responded that he and Fey made this casting decision based on "comic chemistry, not equal opportunity."[54] His comments implied that the show was in some way gender-blind and that advancement was based on merit, but the "full complement" of women in the cast has never grown beyond five performers.

Popular press coverage consistently has overstated the significance of Fey's position as the first female head writer in *SNL's* history through errors of omission. Journalists and reviewers almost never explain what the position entails, and they rarely observe that during the majority of her tenure (1999–2006), she worked alongside a male head writer.[55] Dennis McNicholas was also a head writer from 2000 to 2004, when he was replaced by Andrew Steele.[56] Throughout the show's history, detractors have claimed that the ability of women to showcase their talent was hampered by the fact that they were outnumbered, and consequently ignored or overruled in the production process, as previously described. During the years that Fey served as head writer, the number of women on the writing staff did not significantly increase. When Fey became head writer, she was one of two women on a staff of twenty-one. Although there were four female writers in season thirty (2004–2005), this contingent made up only one-sixth of a staff of twenty-four. In an "*SNL* All-Stars" episode of *The Oprah Winfrey Show* (1986–2011) that aired in April 2011, Fey explained that the presence of a female director and stage manager contributed more support for women's talent during these years; this information notwithstanding, overarching claims about the extent of the gender shift in the Tina Fey era are contradicted by the persistence of male-dominated casts and writers rooms.

In her own writing and in interviews with journalists, Fey's comments about the show's sexist reputation are always measured, and she generally denies any serious workplace issues related to gender imbalances. Her discussions of gender relations and workplace conditions are consistent with the "postfeminist problem" that Rosalind Gill has documented in media production. Shortly after joining the cast, Fey told an interviewer that while she believed that some women "had difficulty" in the past, "the group of people that's there now are very evolved."[57] In a Writers Guild interview, she explained, "If there are mostly guys writing the show, then the material will skew a little male heavy. It's not malicious or intentional."[58] Although Fey does not go as far as some journalists in claiming female dominance at *SNL,* her stance is consistent with a post-feminist ideology in which traditional barriers to women's advancement are no longer functioning.

Even though her position as head writer involved supervising the writing staff, Fey's own accounts indicate that during her tenure it remained difficult to garner men's support when female writers developed material specific to women's experiences. In her bestselling memoir, *Bossypants,* Fey recalls her "proudest moment as one of the head writers at *SNL.*"[59] When a group of male writers and producers voted down a commercial parody about feminine hygiene products, Fey and Paula Pell (who wrote the piece) succeeded in changing the men's minds. Fey realized that the men didn't know enough about the product to understand the joke and she took it as evidence that "[t]here was no 'institutionalized sexism' at that place," but instead a lack of understanding generated by the cultural separation of gendered experiences.[60] In a 2004 interview, she told the same story but included the detail that "the producers sat on that commercial for the better part of a year," which implies that the decision makers' androcentrism was still creating a significant barrier for female comedy writers.[61] The parody aired in 2002, which indicates that although Fey was the head writer, and both Fey and Pell had been working successfully on *SNL* for many years at the time they pitched the idea, their male colleagues still did not trust their comedic sensibilities. This is a story that Fey has repeated in multiple venues, and one she interprets as a success because "we were heard."[62] Upon closer examination, however, it contradicts the popular press narrative that women were equal (or even in charge) at *SNL* during this period.

Popular press coverage detaches Fey and her success from the rest of the writers and performers at *SNL,* which elides an important shift that did occur in workplace dynamics at this time. The female cast members and writers of the Tina Fey era formed intensely collaborative relationships; the network they established is the most significant shift in the traditional workplace dynamics of *SNL,* and it mimics the function of the boys club in prior companies. Fey scripted the recurring "Sully and Denise" sketch for Dratch, and Pell co-wrote sketches with both Dratch and Fey. Fey chose Poehler to replace Jimmy Fallon as "Weekend Update" co-anchor when he left *SNL* in 2004.[63] When she wrote the hit teen comedy *Mean Girls* in 2004, Fey included roles for Gasteyer and Poehler. Dratch and Poehler co-starred in *Spring Breakdown* (2009), which Dratch co-wrote. Kristen Wiig scripted a central role for Maya Rudolph in the hit *Bridesmaids*. During the 2011 television season, Fey, Poehler, and Rudolph starred in NBC sitcoms, two of which were produced by Lorne Michaels.[64] Emily Spivey, a former *SNL* writer, created *Up All Night* (2011–present), which stars Rudolph.

Male cast members established collaborative relationships from the show's early years, as evidenced in the partnership of Aykroyd and Belushi. In the Tina Fey era, the practice has been utilized to an extent that had never been true of female creative talent in the past, and it has continued to open up opportunities for these writers and performers.

CONCLUSION

The phenomenon that Rosalind Gill terms the "postfeminist problem" can productively be utilized to analyze the contemporary landscape in which creative laborers deny the continuing relevance of sexist attitudes, policies, and practices in the workplace because of their adherence to the "commonsense" notion that gender discrimination has been vanquished. In the early twenty-first century, journalists and reviewers trumpeted the success of women at *SNL* as evidence that gender equity had been achieved in the traditionally male-dominated arena of comedy. This coverage was complicated by its deep investment in gender difference, as well as significant evidence that advances toward gender parity in the cast and writing staff have been limited. The specific emphasis on Tina Fey and her position of authority as head writer and "Weekend Update" anchor positioned her success as merit-based, a narrative that worked to deny the systemic barriers that have hampered women's advancement at *SNL* throughout its history. The talented comediennes at *SNL* have succeeded in the new millennium by working collaboratively, not only as sketch writers and performers on the show, but also in numerous films and situation comedies.

Women who write and perform comedy continue to be put forward as evidence that women are funny, which indicates that the issue is no more settled in 2012, at the time of this writing, than it was during the "era of the woman" at *SNL*. The examples I have referenced in this chapter are a testament to the ongoing nature of this discussion, which itself points to the entrenched nature of gender bias.

Notes

1. Karina Longworth notes the pressure that was put on this film, which stars *SNL* cast members Kristen Wiig and Maya Rudolph, as "a referendum on the viability of women in Hollywood comedy" (*"Bridesmaids* Gets Screwed").

2. See, for example, Nussbaum, "She-Runners."

3. Eddie Brill was profiled by Jason Zinoman in "The Comedy Gatekeeper Who Makes Letterman Laugh." The article states that only one female comic was booked on *Late Show* in 2011, and quotes Brill: "There are less female comics who are authentic." Brill's subsequent firing was reported by Dave Itzkoff, "Stand-Up Comedy Booker for *Late Show* Loses Job."

4. Hitchens, "Why Women Aren't Funny," 54.

5. Paula Pell, who wrote for the show during this time, describes the press attention as "Is this the era of the woman?" coverage in Kenneth Bowser's documentary, *Saturday Night Live in the 2000s: Time and Again* (2010).

6. Tasker and Negra, *Interrogating Postfeminism*, 1.

7. See Bielby and Bielby, "Women and Men in Film," on film writers; and Bielby and Bielby, "Cumulative versus Continuous Disadvantage," on television writers. Martha Lauzen publishes statistical analyses of women working in film and television each year, including "The Celluloid Ceiling" and "Boxed In," through the Center for the Study of Women in Television and Film (http://womenintvfilm.sdsu.edu/research.html).

8. See Gill, "Ideology, Gender and Popular Radio" and "Justifying Injustice."

9. Gill, "Life Is a Pitch," 258.

10. Hill and Weingrad, *Saturday Night*, 245.

11. The perception of the show as rebellious was shared among comedy writers, including Mitch Glazer, who called it "an experiment to see what can be done with entertainment on television, what's possible; and at its best it challenges everything that television is." Qtd. in Partridge, *Rolling Stone Visits Saturday Night Live*, 10.

12. Qtd. in Shales and Miller, *Live from New York*, 51.

13. As points of comparison in sketch comedy and variety programming, *The Smothers Brothers Comedy Hour* (1967–1969) and *Rowan & Martin's Laugh-In* (1968–1973) both aired in prime time and did not employ any women as staff writers. Executive producer Lorne Michaels worked as a staff writer at *Laugh-In*.

14. Qtd. in Hill and Weingrad, *Saturday Night*, 245–246.

15. See Shales and Miller, *Live from New York*, 34.

16. Hill and Weingrad, *Saturday Night*, 233. See also Kahn, "Women in the Locker Room," H30. Original cast member Jane Curtin recalls that Belushi and Chase used to state this directly; qtd. in Shales and Miller, *Live from New York*, 144.

17. Hill and Weingrad, *Saturday Night*, 233.

18. Michaels claims that in order to get Belushi to perform material written by Beatts or Shuster, "somebody would have to say that a guy had written it"; see Shales and Miller, *Live from New York*, 74.

19. Fey used the phrase "a bit of a boys club" to refer to *SNL*'s reputation in the sketch "Great Women Writers," which did not make it to air, but was circulated online when she hosted the show on May 7, 2011.

20. Hill and Weingrad, *Saturday Night*, 233.

21. Curtin made this statement during an episode of *The Oprah Winfrey Show* which originally aired on April 12, 2011. She appeared as part of an "*SNL* All-Star Reunion."

22. Shales and Miller, *Live from New York*, 145.

23. Robert Klein is quoted on this ibid., 160.

24. Ibid., 210.

25. Hill and Weingrad, *Saturday Night*, 233.

26. For example, Janeane Garofalo refers to it as a "low" in the show's cycle of highs and lows in Shales and Miller, *Live from New York*, 387.

27. Blaustein is quoted on this ibid., 194.

28. Ebersol and Michaels developed *SNL* together in 1975, when the former was the head of late-night programming at NBC.

29. Qtd. in Kahn, "Women in the Locker Room," H31.

30. Beers, "Dunn In," 10.

31. "Dicey Problem," 95.

32. Qtd. in Beers, "Dunn In," 10.

33. These comics dominated the early to mid-1990s at *SNL*, and NBC even marketed them as "The Bad Boys of *Saturday Night Live*" in a 1998 television special.

34. Qtd. in Shales and Miller, *Live from New York*, 389.

35. Meadows, "Ladies of the Night," 55.

36. See Shales and Miller, *Live from New York*, 389.

37. Ibid., 390.

38. Smith, "Comedy Isn't Funny," 30–41.

39. See Shales and Miller, *Live from New York*, 427–428.

40. Ibid., 429.

41. Fey, "Lessons from Late Night," 22.

42. Meadows, "Ladies of the Night."

43. Lisotta, "Rewriting *SNL*'s Old-Boy Tradition."

44. In 2002, Meadows called the show "strikingly feminized"; see "Ladies of the Night," 55.

45. Qtd. in Baldwin, "Update with Destiny."

46. Nussbaum, "It's the Revenge of the Ignorant Sluts."

47. Lisotta, "Rewriting *SNL*'s Old-Boy Tradition."

48. Qtd. in Meadows, "Ladies of the Night," 56. More recently, Fey has slightly quali-fied this, acknowledging that it is reductive; see her *Bossypants*, 136.

49. See, for example, Itzkoff, "Please Don't Tell Her She's Funny for a Girl."

50. Stanley, "Who Says Women Aren't Funny?," 190.

51. Meadows, "Ladies of the Night," 56.

52. Freydkin, "It's News to Them."

53. Meadows, "Ladies of the Night," 56.

54. Kennedy, "A First for Fake News."

55. See, for example, Witchel, "Update Anchor"; Meadows, "Ladies of the Night"; and Kennedy, "A First for Fake News."

56. At the time, Fey was aware of the tendency of journalists to overstate her position of authority at *SNL* through errors of omission. She told an interviewer in 2004, "One thing I always bring up, and it rarely gets printed, is that I share my job with a guy named Dennis McNicholas. I always say that, and people just don't print it." See Rems, "Mrs. Saturday Night," 42.

57. Qtd. in Huguenin and Chernikoff, "*Rock* Star Tina."

58. Spitznagel, "Tina Fey Update," 30.

59. Fey, *Bossypants*, 138.
60. Ibid., 140–141.
61. Qtd. in Rems, "Mrs. Saturday Night," 43.
62. Fey, *Bossypants*, 141.
63. Kennedy, "A First for Fake News."
64. Michaels produces Fey's *30 Rock* and *Up All Night*, which stars Rudolph; Poehler is also a writer and producer on *Parks and Recreation* (2009–present).

Works Cited

Baldwin, Kristen. "Update with Destiny." *Entertainment Weekly,* May 10, 2002.
Beers, D. "Dunn In." *Mother Jones,* September–October 1990.
Bielby, William, and Denise Bielby. "Cumulative versus Continuous Disadvantage in an Unstructured Labor Market." *Work and Occupations* 19(3) (November 1992):366–489.
———. "Women and Men in Film: Gender Inequality among Writers in a Culture Industry." *Gender and Society* 10(3) (June 1996):248–270.
"Dicey Problem." *Newsweek,* May 21, 1990.
Fey, Tina. *Bossypants.* New York: Little, Brown, 2011.
———. "Lessons from Late Night: What Separates the Women from the Men." *New Yorker,* May 11, 2011.
Freydkin, Donna. "It's News to Them: Female Co-Anchors Make *SNL* History." *USA Today,* November 26, 2004.
Gill, Rosalind. "Ideology, Gender and Popular Radio: A Discourse Analytic Approach." *Innovation in Social Sciences Research* 6(3) (1993):323–339.
———. "Justifying Injustice: Broadcasters' Accounts of Inequality in Radio." In *Discourse Analytic Research: Readings and Repertoires of Texts in Action,* edited by Erica Burman and Ian Parker. London: Routledge, 1993.
———. "'Life Is a Pitch': Managing the Self in New Media Work." In *Managing Media Work,* edited by Mark Deuze, 249–262. London: Sage, 2010.
Hill, Doug, and Jeff Weingrad. *Saturday Night: A Backstage History of Saturday Night Live.* New York: Beech Tree, 1986.
Hitchens, Christopher. "Why Women Aren't Funny." *Vanity Fair,* January 2007.
Huguenin, Patrick, and Leah Chernikoff. "*Rock* Star Tina: The Rise of Fey, from *SNL* Writer to Sitcom Phenom and Box-Office Draw." *New York Daily News,* September 28, 2008.
Itzkoff, Dave. "Please Don't Tell Her She's Funny for a Girl." *New York Times,* March 18, 2007.
———. "Stand-Up Comedy Booker for *Late Show* Loses Job." *New York Times,* January 18, 2012.
Kahn, Eve. "Women in the Locker Room at *Saturday Night Live*." *New York Times,* February 16, 1992, H30–H31.
Kennedy, Randy. "A First for Fake News." *New York Times,* October 12, 2004.
Lisotta, Christopher. "Rewriting *SNL*'s Old-Boy Tradition." *Television Week,* September 19, 2005.
Longworth, Karina. "*Bridesmaids* Gets Screwed." *Village Voice,* May 11, 2011.
Meadows, Susannah. "Ladies of the Night." *Newsweek,* April 8, 2002.
Nussbaum, Emily. "It's the Revenge of the Ignorant Sluts." *New York Times,* May 11, 2003.

———. "She-Runners." *New York Magazine,* August 29, 2011.

Partridge, Marianne, ed. *Rolling Stone Visits Saturday Night Live.* New York: Dolphin, 1979.

Rems, Emily. "Mrs. Saturday Night." *Bust,* April 2004, 40–47.

Rosenblum, Emily. "Rachel Rolls with It." *New York Magazine,* October 15, 2006.

Ryzik, Melissa. "Producer, Writer, Star and One Funny Mama." *New York Times,* April 17, 2011.

Shales, Tom, and James Andrew Miller. *Live from New York: An Uncensored History of Saturday Night Live.* Boston: Little, Brown, 2002.

Smith, Chris. "Comedy Isn't Funny." *New York,* March 13, 1995.

Spitznagel, Eric. "Tina Fey Update." *Written By* 8(3) (2004):26–34.

Stanley, Alessandra. "Who Says Women Aren't Funny?" *Vanity Fair,* April 2008.

Tasker, Yvonne, and Diane Negra. *Interrogating Postfeminism: Gender and the Politics of Popular Culture.* Durham, NC: Duke University Press, 2007.

Witchel, Alex. "Update Anchor: The Brains behind Herself." *New York Times,* November 25, 2001.

Zinoman, Jason. "The Comedy Gatekeeper Who Makes Letterman Laugh." *New York Times,* January 12, 2012.

SNL's "Fauxbama" Debate: Facing Off over Millennial (Mixed-)Racial Impersonation

MARY BELTRÁN

As *Saturday Night Live* sketches go, it was well mannered and seemingly innocuous. In "Democratic Debate," a sketch that aired on February 23, 2008, during the height of the presidential campaign, Fred Armisen and Amy Poehler portrayed the contenders for the Democratic nomination, Senators Barack Obama and Hillary Clinton, in a CNN-hosted debate. Poehler wore her hair in a severe hairstyle as part of her impersonation, while Armisen, in his first performance as Obama, sported close-cropped curly hair and barely perceptible, light tan makeup (later described in the media as "honeyface" after Armisen told a journalist it was called Honey).[1] The sketch lampooned Obama's growing popularity and celebrity with Americans as reaching such a height that the news anchors facilitating the debate fawned over every word of Armisen-as-Obama. Poehler's Clinton, in contrast, was forgotten, barely getting a word in edgewise.[2]

The sketch was broadcast on *Saturday Night Live*'s first show on the air after a writers strike had forced it to take a three-month hiatus; in that time Senator Obama had been gaining in the polls and in cultural prominence with the U.S. public, but *SNL* had been unable to acknowledge this through the usual impersonation sketches. "Election years are very good for us," producer Lorne Michaels had noted in a *New York Times* article regarding the comedy series' need to get back on the air as soon as possible.[3]

As Michaels's comment implies, the sketch was par for the course for *Saturday Night Live* in a number of ways. The weekly series has skewered contemporary politics and social life since its debut in 1975; presidents and other politicians, film and television stars, prominent musicians, and other public figures have long been lampooned by the Not Ready for Prime Time Players after achieving a certain level of fame. In the week that followed *SNL*'s broadcast of the "Democratic Debate" sketch, however, it briefly became a center of controversy and discussion in a manner that Michaels may not have foreseen, as a small but vocal portion of the audience panned the casting of Armisen as tantamount to "blackface" performance, although many other viewers responded more neutrally. More specifically, in news articles and blog postings with titles such as "Did *SNL* Go beyond the Pale with Fauxbama?" and "Black Face Is Ba(ra)ck?"[4] viewers, journalists, and cultural critics responded to the casting of Armisen, who is of German, Japanese, and Venezuelan descent, as Obama, who is of Kenyan and Anglo American heritage and is typically described in the mainstream media as black. As I describe in more detail below, the debate exposed multiple and often opposing views on a variety of overlapping topics, from the boundaries of propriety for cross-racial performance in television sketch comedy, to racial and ethnic impersonation by mixed-race actors, to the racial politics of casting on *SNL* more generally.

Michaels quickly defended the casting decision, first stating simply that he felt the sketch and the performers in the roles had broad appeal.[5] In later interviews he and other *SNL* representatives also indicated that several performers, including African American featured player Kenan Thompson, had auditioned for the role of Senator Obama, with Fred Armisen ultimately chosen as being the best fit for the role. The choice of Armisen to portray Obama was not remarkable in relation to *Saturday Night Live*'s racial politics of casting and performance in recent years. In the 1990s and particularly in the first decade of the twenty-first century, *Saturday Night Live* had cast Armisen and other performers of mixed heritage in a variety of cross-racial and cross-ethnic roles. *SNL* cast members who have been deployed in this manner include Rob Schneider of Jewish and Filipino descent, and Maya Rudolph, of African American and

Jewish heritage. Armisen joined the cast in 2000 and has continued ever since. Importantly, there are no clear social norms for what is considered politically correct casting for such "mixed" performers. In turn, *SNL* producers have not followed any identifiable logic in how they have utilized Schneider, Rudolph, and Armisen. Rudolph's impersonations, for example, include Oprah Winfrey, Beyonce Knowles, Lucy Liu, Jennifer Lopez, and Donatella Versace. Fred Armisen also has portrayed characters and public figures of diverse ethnic backgrounds and those considered both black and white, including President George W. Bush, musical artist Prince, former Iranian president Mahmoud Ahmadinejad, Italian American television personality Joy Behar, and David Paterson, former governor of New York. Reactions to these performances, moreover, appear to have been almost universally positive, indicative of what I consider to be a contemporary public interest in entertainment that reinforces notions that we've entered a presumed "post-racial" era.[6] The racial fluidity emphasized in such performances, I argue, is celebrated as politically correct, if sensational, fun, particularly when the performers are of mixed racial heritage and can claim partial in-group status in relation to their roles.

Given the lack of widespread criticism of Rudolph's and Armisen's earlier performances as African American public figures, it is notable that Armisen's casting as Senator Obama—one of the few mixed-race figures he has portrayed—elicited sharp complaints by some viewers that this was "blackface" performance. For instance, Daniel Holloway, writing for the *Huffington Post,* asserted that the *Saturday Night Live* producers' attitude was, "Who needs a black guy when you've got a Latino and a bucket of face paint?"[7] For these viewers, casting Armisen was disrespectful not only to Barack Obama and to African American performers who were not considered for the role, but also to African Americans more generally for blithely recreating a theatrical tradition that was demeaning to the race. Meanwhile, many others disagreed that the casting was problematic and appeared concerned only with whether the performance felt accurate or was funny. As one viewer wrote in response to a video clip of the sketch on the Hulu website: "Every so often, *SNL* has a really great sketch that people talk about, and this could be it. Maya Rudolph coming back was great, and Fred Armisen is getting a lot better as Obama (darker make-up could help though lol). I thought Kristen, Andy, and the new guy's song was really funny, and all the songs fit in perfectly. I really liked it! (Michelle W)."[8]

When Armisen and Rudolph performed in a second Obama sketch on October 25, 2008, right before the presidential election, some viewers again complained. That evening, Armisen and Rudolph, who was guest starring after leaving the show a year earlier, portrayed Barack and Michelle Obama in a triumphant moment. In the sketch, because of Senator Obama's lead in the polls, the Obamas scrap a planned televised speech about important issues for a more fun "Barack Obama Variety Half-Hour," featuring fellow Democrats and the Obamas singing for the television audience.[9] While light on political content, the sketch became a viral sensation on the Internet, and elicited both more complaints about and further defense of Michaels's casting choices. Rudolph appears to have been generally given a pass in her portrayal of Michelle Obama in these comments. This was not the case regarding the casting of Armisen, however. Some journalists, bloggers, and viewers commenting on news articles once again criticized *SNL* for not casting an African American actor in the role.

A heated debate played out among viewers in newspapers, in magazines, and particularly on the Internet over the public and critical reception to *SNL*'s Obama sketches in 2008. What can we learn from the controversy and related commentary regarding the influence of post-racial rhetoric and the resulting shifts in the boundaries of socially approved, comedic cross-racial performance in recent years? Are social taboos more flexible in relation to performances by mixed-race individuals? And how did public confusion regarding how to categorize performers (and politicians) of mixed heritage play into the controversy? These questions have guided my analysis of the "Fauxbama" discussion. To explore audience responses to the casting of Fred Armisen and, later, Dwayne Johnson as Barack Obama in *Saturday Night Live* sketches, I surveyed news articles, critical reviews, and informal comments by journalists, independent bloggers, and fans in established popular news outlets, on video-sharing sites such as Hulu and YouTube, and on personal websites. Databases such as Lexis/Nexis and Academic Universe and Internet search engines such as Google were utilized to obtain the widest possible breadth of responses. The findings I summarize here, however, illuminate the responses of only a portion of the *SNL* audience—the portion that expresses its views via

Figure 10.1. Fred Armisen in honeyface impersonates Senator Barack Obama alongside Maya Rudolph as Michelle Obama.

the Internet or other mediated forums—rather than representing an actual cross-section of *SNL* viewers.

ARMISEN'S OBAMA, SKETCH COMEDY, AND CULTURAL MEMORY OF "BLACKING UP"

As previously noted, journalists, *SNL* viewers, and critics responded in large numbers to the "Democratic Debate" and "Barack Obama Variety Half-Hour" sketches in various online forums in the weeks and months that followed their broadcast on *Saturday Night Live*. Critics of Armisen's Barack Obama typically felt that the casting and performances were offensive. More specifically, they ascribed the casting and performances to retrograde politics that, like old-school minstrelsy, perpetuated notions of African Americans as inferior to white Americans. For example, Yesha Callahan, in a posting on her blog, *[Flahy][Blak][chik]*, wrote, "Hollyweird has taken us back to the old fashioned 'black face' genre of entertainment."[10] Hannah Pool, writing for the London-based newspaper the *Guardian*, commented, "Casting a black actor wouldn't have guaranteed the quality of the sketch, but it would have made the whole thing a lot less shoddy. Let me get one thing straight. The moment anyone starts reaching for 'blackface,' they are on extremely dodgy territory."[11]

These writers make evident both that some viewers read Armisen as white and Obama as black, and that taboos regarding white actors performing in African American roles still exist for some audience members. This needs to be understood in relation to the history of minstrelsy and blackface performance, an embarrassing legacy in U.S. theater, film, and radio. For over a half century beginning in the mid-1800s, American racial politics and performance traditions dictated that African Americans be represented by white actors in dark makeup, only as caricatures and broad, presumed comedic types. Donald Bogle succinctly describes such roles in early films as "toms, coons, mulattoes, mammies, and bucks";[12] a related history in theater and radio has been documented by scholars Eric Lott, Michael Rogin (examining blackface performance in theater and early film), and Michele Hilmes, who focuses on what she terms the "black voice" in early radio, such as that of the popular duo Amos 'n' Andy.[13] As these scholars document, such caricatures devalued African Americans and reinforced notions of their inferiority to whites. African Americans also were required to "black up" to perform (literally and figuratively: donning pitch-black makeup and performing minstrelsy in their acts), while in later decades the roles in which they might be cast were severely limited to demeaned characterizations inspired by previous minstrel types.

As the entertainment media have attempted to rectify the historical distortion of African American images, they have typically demonstrated a great desire to avoid casting choices and performances that might remind viewers of this history. Among other things, this has translated to strong taboos against performers darkening their skin to portray African American characters, particularly in dramatic roles. The producers of *Saturday Night Live,* for instance, have presumably taken at least some care over the years to avoid blackface performance and to be responsive to viewers' complaints regarding what they found offensive. (There have, however, been a few instances of white performers portraying African American figures on *SNL* in the past, as I detail below.) Importantly, in relation to actors donning makeup to portray African Americans today, the passage of time has resulted in a lessening of knowledge of the history of minstrelsy in American performance, film, and radio. Public definitions of and reactions to what is viewed as an actor "blacking up" thus entail more complicated dynamics.

While this history has become more distant and definitions of and reactions against what is viewed as blackface performance continue to shift, generic conventions also have shifted in film and television. In particular, shifts in popular comedy content and style have begun to complicate social understandings of and reception to cross-racial performance in comedy. Comedians such as Sarah Silverman, Dave Chappelle, and Louis C.K. and television sketch comedy series such as *Saturday Night Live* and *MADtv* (1995–2009) have led the trend for comedy that showcases an ironic spin on notions of race, gender, and religion and that emphasizes ethnic and racial performativity in a manner that crosses the former boundaries of propriety. As a result, the borders of political correctness are becoming blurred, as noted by scholars of contemporary television comedy such as Amanda Lotz.[14] Potential social confusion regarding standards of acceptability resulting from these trends of postmodern comedy style is compounded, moreover, by the growing tendency of some Americans to embrace the utopic notion that the United States now operates in a color-blind or "post-racial" fashion.[15]

Given these cultural shifts, it comes as no surprise that responses to Armisen's casting reflected contrasting stances on and definitions of cross-racial performance in media culture. These can in part be traced to the divergences in cultural memory described above, which appear to coincide with age and race. Writers who linked Armisen's casting to the history of minstrelsy in the United States appeared to be older than the defenders of the casting. Many Fauxbama critics also self-identified as African American or mixed-race. Defenders of the casting choice, in contrast, wrote in language and forums that marked them as young and most likely white. Characterizing the debate as a skirmish over passé norms of political correctness, some of these writers acknowledged having almost no knowledge of the history of minstrel performance. For example, college student Joe Mancino, writing in the *Georgetown Independent* about the debate over Armisen's casting, copped to his own lack of awareness of the history of blackface prior to being schooled on the topic by his older sister.[16] He noted that he had even unthinkingly planned a Halloween costume that would have involved blacking up to portray an African American public figure. "Before this, I had only a vague idea of the history of 'blackface' and its offensive nature," Mancino added.[17] This sort of disconnect with cultural memory prevailed among some of the writers who felt the critique of Armisen's casting was too harsh. For example, Joshua Alston, writing for *Newsweek*, expressed the opinion that the history of blackface performance was simply no longer an issue: "If watching Armisen play Obama makes people uncomfortable, it's because watching a white actor with his skin darkened calls to mind a painful chapter in America's history. But minstrelsy, at least white minstrelsy, doesn't exist anymore."[18] In other words, younger, white writers were least likely to view the legacy of minstrelsy as a relevant concern to contemporary media representation. This pattern parallels what Cherise Smith describes as the present "post-racial and postidentity discursive environment,"[19] in which contemporary performances of racial boundary crossing may be viewed by many Americans as simply celebratory and as disconnected from dynamics of power or privilege.

In reactions to contemporary cross-racial performances, choices made regarding how makeup is used also arguably are key to what is viewed as socially acceptable. Heavily satirical instances of blackface performance aside (such as when *It's Always Sunny in Philadelphia*'s [2005–present] Mac donned dark brown makeup to pose as Murtaugh in *Lethal Weapon* [1987] in another example of his clueless absurdity),[20] actors substantially darkening their skin for a performance meant to be realistic has been viewed as taboo in film and television comedy for over a half century. With this in mind, it's unsurprising that *SNL*'s producers emphasized that "honeyface," or light tan rather than darker makeup, was used to help Armisen portray Barack Obama. We can see a similar impulse at work in the light tan makeup Darrell Hammond donned to portray the Reverend Jesse Jackson on the show in recent years—in stark contrast to the dark makeup Billy Crystal wore to portray Sammy Davis Jr. in *SNL* sketches during the 1980s. In sum, ensuring that Armisen was not seen as blacking up was imperative to defending the performance as politically neutral.

Understanding the specific media or theatrical context in which cross-racial performance is situated can additionally illuminate how the American public might respond. In discussing cross-racial performance in live theater, Dorrine Kondo has expounded on the pleasures inherent to performances for which racial transformation is central: "There is something thought-provoking about seeing a person of one race or gender 'don' the characteristics of so many who are 'others' along so many different axes. The spectacular display of acting virtuosity and quick-change artistry are sources of amazement and audience pleasure."[21]

Kondo and Smith examine such dynamics in theatrical performances and artwork, respectively, that are centered on racial and ethnic transformation.[22] Both ultimately highlight how such performances and art illuminate ambivalences and contradictions in contemporary U.S. racial politics. In contrast to the *Saturday Night Live* sketches, however, these are performances set in theatrical spaces and with audiences well aware of the politicized intentions of the artists. While similar pleasures may be experienced in relation to televised sketch comedy, it is set in a less overtly politicized performance space and typically viewed in audience members' own homes. With its brief format, minimal sets and costumes, and reutilization of actors in a variety of roles, the trappings of sketch comedy arguably heighten attention to its performative nature and to distinctions between actors and their roles; this spectacle of self-conscious, incongruous impersonation is arguably one of the major pleasures for sketch comedy viewers. It may in this respect offer leeway for racial impersonation that pushes social boundaries without prompting offense. Fred Armisen's Obama is not the first example of perceived cross-racial performance on *Saturday Night Live*. As previously mentioned, examples of white actors playing African Americans on *SNL* include Billy Crystal's Sammy Davis Jr., dark makeup included, and Darrell Hammond's portrayal of the Reverend Jesse Jackson.

The wide breadth of voices that commented in public arenas on Armisen's Barack Obama in comparison to those that responded to Hammond's and Crystal's impersonations is important to interrogate. With respect to individuals' ability to participate in a public sphere of discussion on popular culture, the Fauxbama debate (and my ability to trace it) were greatly enabled by developments in new media and Internet-based authorship. For one, the Obama sketches could be viewed on YouTube, Hulu, and other video-sharing sites—impossible during the first years of *SNL*—while Internet-based tools and forums increased the possibility for diverse and at times opposing voices to enter public discussions regarding the casting choice and cross-racial impersonation more generally.[23]

Meanwhile, the importance of Barack Obama as the first president of mixed-race descent, combined with confusion over both Obama's and Armisen's racial status, arguably fueled the intense schisms noted in viewers' interpretations of *SNL*'s Fauxbama casting. Confusion over mixed-race performance arguably hasn't lessened with the rise in mixed-race visibility in popular culture in the twenty-first century. In the following section I home in on the unique performance and reception dynamics associated with what I term "mixed racial impersonation" and how Fred Armisen's Barack Obama served as a litmus test of popular standards regarding such cross-racial performance.

RACIALLY FLUID FUNNY?: MIXED RACE
AND RACIAL IMPERSONATION

As previously noted, the contradictory reactions to Fred Armisen's casting were compounded by confusion regarding the racial identity of President Obama, who self-identifies as both black and biracial, and regarding Armisen's own mixed heritage. Clearly, a performer of mixed heritage complicates the politics of casting with respect to cross-racial or politically correct performance, as does impersonating a public figure or performing as a character of mixed heritage. Does mixed-racial or mixed-ethnic status provide a figurative, all-encompassing fluidity in which no performative stretch is too far, given that such performances are viewed by society as uncategorizable in relation to race? While Fred Armisen's and Maya Rudolph's prior casting and performances on *SNL* would appear to confirm this, the Fauxbama controversy underscores that some limits do exist even to the freedom often afforded to mixed-race performers in this regard.

Importantly, attitudes about the acceptability of cross-racial performance by mixed-race performers are informed by viewers' readings of these actors; Hollywood paradigms of racial categorization have a major influence in this regard. I have noted elsewhere how Latina stars of mixed heritage typically are cast and promoted as fitting into one racial category (as white or nonwhite) despite self-identification as multiracial.[24] The media industries and U.S. audiences, well trained by our consumption of Hollywood media products, place mixed-race performers in color-coded racial categories that influence their traversing of racial borders. Rudolph and Armisen, for instance, prior to the Obama sketches were afforded great ethnic and racial fluidity on *Saturday Night Live,* presumably based on their ethnically ambiguous looks, assimilability to whiteness, and public knowledge of their mixed heritage. Even so, Rudolph and Armisen may be read idiosyncratically by some, resulting in differing definitions of the political valence of their impersonations. Given the complexity of these dynamics, public perception ranges widely regarding mixed-racial impersonation, or perceived cross-racial performance by a performer of mixed heritage. For example, viewers expressed widely differing opinions and attitudes regarding whether Armisen's portrayal of Obama was made politically correct by the performer's own mixed heritage. While some critics felt it fully excused his casting, others did not. For example, viewer and blogger Claire Light described Armisen as "extremely multiracial" (and was one of the few writers who also emphasized that Obama himself is half white).[25] While Light appeared satisfied with Armisen's casting, other writers were troubled that he was not at least half black. Callahan noted that Armisen was "a white guy, not a black man or even a bi-racial man."[26] Moreover, many viewers also displayed confusion about Armisen's specific ethnic identity. His racial and ethnic background often was inaccurately described (as in the Callahan quotation), with some writers aware of but emphasizing only one or two elements of his heritage. Robert W. Armijo was completely off the mark in describing Armisen as Filipino on *The Spoof!* website, for instance, while other writers defined Armisen as simply "white and Asian."[27] Such comments illustrate the confusion many Americans have about mixed-race performers and how this can compound uncertainty or create a desire to forgo all former social standards about cross-racial performance when performers can claim mixed racial status.

An imagined color line still is consistently policed by some viewers, however. As the Fauxbama debate illustrates, a mixed-race performer's perceived relationship to blackness and the perception of the blackness of the individual being impersonated are both integral to notions of politically inoffensive performance. Popular and critical response to a third *SNL* Obama sketch aptly illustrates how such dynamics play out. On *Saturday Night Live* on March 7, 2009, a spoof of President Obama uniquely utilized two different performers to portray the president. In "The Rock Obama," President Obama was portrayed first by Fred Armisen. In the sketch's scenario in the Oval Office, the president is told by White House chief of staff Rahm Emanuel (Andy Samberg) that he has a meeting with

Republican senators McCain, Hutchison, and Coburn, all responsible for blocking his spending bill. He is urged by Emanuel to "get angry" with them, but he insists he will maintain his cool and instead will "kill them with kindness." As the meeting wears on, however, he begins to be pushed to his limits of frustration. His anger builds and builds, until suddenly he can hold himself back no longer and is transformed. Not only has his affable and conciliatory demeanor been replaced by angry resolve; he also has grown physically, splitting his clothes like the Incredible Hulk, becoming "The Rock" Obama. Armisen was at this time replaced by actor Dwayne Johnson (also known as "The Rock," his moniker from his professional wrestling days). The Rock Obama now speaks in Tarzan film pidgin English and clearly is afraid of no one. No longer interested in negotiating with the senators, he simply throws them out of a White House window. When insurance giant AIG calls, asking for an extra $40 billion for its budget, he responds by hanging up the phone with such force that it breaks into pieces. Later, however, President Obama, once again played by Armisen, startles Emanuel awake; we learn that Emanuel has dreamed the whole scene. The sketch ends with Emanuel repeatedly urging Obama, "Will you please get angry?" Armisen-as-Obama cheerfully responds each time, "Nope!"[28]

Notably, there was great disparity in how *SNL*'s two Obamas were received by viewers and the entertainment news media after their introduction to the American public. In the week that followed the debut of The Rock Obama, there were no complaints about casting found in searches of the broadcast and Internet-based news media and popular culture blogs, in reviews, or in other mentions of Johnson's performance. Instead, the video of the sketch was passed around the blogosphere as particularly funny and as evidence of Johnson's comedic chops. In appearances on daytime talk shows, clips were shown, and Johnson was praised for the performance. As one viewer commented, "Last night Dwayne 'The Rock' Johnson played Obama, was apparently quite funny, and the audience didn't have to feel guilty about it if they laughed. Bonus!"[29] Johnson has since been brought back for other performances as The Rock Obama. The pointed panning of Armisen's Obama in the first two Obama skits and the subsequent praise of Johnson's portrayal illuminate the complicated dynamics of mixed-racial impersonation in contemporary media culture. Notably, Johnson, like Armisen, is of mixed heritage; he is of black Nova Scotian (Canadian) and Samoan descent.

Figure 10.2. Obama "gets angry," transforming into The Rock Obama, played by Dwayne "The Rock" Johnson.

Presumably, he is viewed as "black enough" to play Obama without disturbing the sleeping giant that is the cultural memory of minstrelsy. In contrast, the criticism by some viewers of Armisen's casting illustrates the continuing power and importance of perceived whiteness and blackness in popular responses to mixed-racial impersonation.

Along the same lines, an important element of the Fauxbama debate was an omission: the lack of attention to President Obama's own mixed-race status. Surprisingly, there was negligible focus in the discussion on Obama's distinctive racial heritage and ambiguous positioning vis-à-vis American notions of race. Obama's brown skin has apparently been more influential in this regard than his extensive sharing of information about his white mother and grandparents, highlighting the continued power of appearance and of the former "one-drop rule" to the construction of racial identities.[30] The impersonation of a mixed-race public figure raises new questions and possibilities for disagreement or debate, moreover, on what is still viewed as socially taboo with respect to impersonation comedy. In this instance, where do standards for politically correct impersonations of President Obama fall on the continuum between complete racial flexibility (i.e., anything goes), on one end, and "perfect" racial representation (only Kenyan and white American need apply), on the other? While some writers defending the casting of Armisen brought up that both Obama and Armisen were mixed, none addressed how taboos regarding blackface performance might apply in the portrayal of a mixed-race figure or questioned why President Obama is generally construed by Americans as simply black despite widespread knowledge of his European American (white) heritage.

FINAL THOUGHTS ON FAUXBAMA AND
SNL'S RACIAL POLITICS OF CASTING

The divergent reactions of viewers and critics in response to *SNL*'s Barack Obama sketches in 2008 and early 2009 highlight how fading cultural memory and confusion over how to read mixed-racial heritage are influencing norms of racial impersonation in sketch comedy forums such as *Saturday Night Live*. In the debate over Armisen's casting as Barack Obama, viewers expressed varied opinions on what they perceive as cross-racial performance by a mixed-race actor and whether they feel such performances are politically offensive or neutral. Such heterogeneity of responses naturally results from the multiple, varied subject positions of viewers of *SNL* with respect to age and race. Compounding these dynamics, a wish to embrace post-racial rhetoric also has resulted in what I see as a desire by some viewers to witness racial boundary crossing by mixed-race performers—cross-racial performances that can be enjoyed by American audiences without guilt.

Many of the writers commenting on *SNL*'s casting of Armisen also foregrounded the issue of employment equity on *Saturday Night Live*. To share some of these comments: Maureen Ryan wrote in the *Chicago Tribune:* "They couldn't find an African-American performer who was funny enough to play the junior senator from Illinois? They couldn't find one in New York? Not anywhere in the country? *Really?*"[31] In a similar argument, Hannah Pool posited in the *Guardian:* "And didn't anyone at *SNL* think that this might be a good time to increase the show's number of black cast members from one (Keenan [*sic*] Thompson) to, oh, I don't know, two?"[32] And Joel Keller, writing for *AOL TV,* noted, "What this whole story does point out is that the staff is very under-staffed as far as African-Americans are concerned."[33]

The points made by these writers underscore a broader issue embedded in the Fauxbama debate. The demographic makeup of the Not Ready for Prime Time Players has political implications that extend beyond the trend for casting actors of mixed heritage in a variety of ethnic roles or the specific casting choices for political sketches. While *Saturday Night Live*'s ability to satirize people of all ethnicities and genders appears vital, the Not Ready for Prime Time Players have consistently been mostly white and mostly male. Meanwhile, as ethnic demographics continue to shift in the United States, a diverse cast would not only provide employment and exposure to a wider group of actors but also would allow the show to include impersonations of a broader range of public figures in the U.S. and global landscape. Phillip Lamarr Cunningham rightly critiques *SNL* for its paucity of nonwhite and female actors and especially actresses of color in its ensemble casts over the decades.[34] In my research I found that only fifteen African American actors and actresses were included among the more than 300 who served as ensemble and featured players on *SNL* over its first thirty-eight years. These actors are Garrett Morris, Eddie Murphy, Damon Wayans, Chris Rock, Tim Meadows, Jerry Minor, Dean Edwards, Tracy Morgan, Finesse Mitchell, Kenan Thompson, and Jay Pharoah, while the actresses with African American heritage are Ellen Cleghorne, Yvonne Hudson, Danitra Vance, and Maya Rudolph.[35] Asian American, Latina/o, and Native American cast members have been even more scarce. Thus there have been very few *SNL* actors of color to help portray nonwhite public figures, and even fewer to portray women of color. As several individuals who weighed in on the debate over Armisen's Obama sketches noted, almost all of the African American actors in the *SNL* casts have performed in drag with some regularity as a result, far more often than has been the case in the portrayal of white female public figures. This is just an illustration of greater imbalances, however. More broadly, it is important to consider how the casting of the Not Ready for Prime Time Players limits who can be skewered as a subject of comedy and how, and the impact of such casting on notions of who is worthy of our attention as we tune in to *SNL* each Saturday night to laugh at and with the celebrities, movers, and shakers of our times.

Notes

I would like to thank Ron Becker, Nick Marx, Matt Sienkiewicz, and the anonymous reviewer of this volume for their insightful and extremely helpful revision suggestions for earlier versions of this chapter. I also thank Tom Hackett for his cogent and inspirational feedback.

1. Marcus, "Fred Armisen Performs in Honeyface."

2. "Democratic Debate" can be viewed on the Hulu website, http://www.hulu.com
/watch/10231/saturday-night-live-democratic-debate. As of September SNL archives
will be moved to Yahoo! TV, www.tv.yahoo.com.

3. Carter, "SNL Ready to Make Up for Lost Time."

4. Farhi, "Did SNL Go beyond the Pale with Fauxbama?"; Callahan, "Black Face Is
Ba(ra)ck?"

5. Farhi, "Did SNL Go beyond the Pale with Fauxbama?"

6. See Beltrán, "What's at Stake in Claims of Post-Racial Media?" The term "post-
racial," ironically, began to be utilized widely by journalists and some politicians as a de-
scriptor for supposed shifts in U.S. race relations after Barack Obama's presidential campaign and election to office in 2008. While "post-racial America" is a utopic rather than
factual trope, given that racial inequities still have grave impacts in the United States,
belief in such shifts has had a substantial impact on political policy and public opinion.
See Bonilla-Silva, Racism without Racists, for further information about the history and
impact of "color-blind" politics in the United States.

7. Holloway, "Note to SNL."

8. Michelle W., review, "Obama Address." Originally broadcast during Saturday
Night Live's season 34, ep. 6.

9. The sketch, "Solid as Barack," can be viewed at http://www.nbc.com/saturday
-night-live/video/obama-address/787181.

10. Callahan, "Black Face Is Ba(ra)ck?"

11. Pool, "Blacked Up Obama Is a Pretty Weak Joke."

12. This phrase is taken directly from the title of Bogle's book Toms, Coons, Mulattoes,
Mammies, and Bucks, which surveys early film images of African Americans in relation
to tropes established in minstrel theater in the United States.

13. Lott, Love and Theft; Rogin, Blackface, White Noise; Hilmes, Radio Voices.

14. Lotz, "Imagining Post-PC Humor"; Beltrán, "The Racial Politics of Spectacular
Post-Racial Satire."

15. This phenomenon has been explored by scholars Bonilla-Silva, Racism without
Racists; Gallagher, "Color Blind Privilege"; and Joseph, "Tyra Banks Is Fat."

16. Mancino, "The Blackface Backlash."

17. Ibid.

18. Alston, "The Dark Side of Corking Up."

19. Smith, Enacting Others, 231.

20. "Dee Reynolds: Shaping America's Youth," It's Always Sunny in Philadelphia.
Originally broadcast on FX on November 10, 2010.

21. Kondo, "(Re)Visions of Race," 82.

22. Among their case studies are the one-woman performances of Anna Deveare
Smith (analyzed by Kondo) and the performance-focused photography of Nikki S. Lee
(a focus of Smith's study). Kondo, "(Re)Visions of Race"; Smith, Enacting Others.

23. Participation in this discussion was also presumably filtered, however, by class
and race with respect to computer ownership, Internet access, and so on.

24. Beltrán, "Mixed Race in Latinowood."

25. Light, "SNL's Fauxbama Blackface Thing."

26. Callahan, "Black Face Is Ba(ra)ck."

27. Armijo, "SNL's Obama Role Goes to Fred Armisen"; Alston, "The Dark Side of
Corking Up." Slippage in U.S. racial categories adds to this confusion, moreover. Alston

and others who defined Armisen as half white may have been thinking of the U.S. government's definition of "Hispanic/Latino" as an ethnicity rather than a race and of most Latinos as racially white.

28. This first appearance of Johnson as The Rock Obama can be viewed on the NBC website, http://www.nbc.com/saturday-night-live/video/the-rock-obama/1056126.

29. Jabberin' Wookie, "SNL Finally Realizes Black Face Isn't All That Funny after All."

30. The one-drop rule of racialization by hypodescent dictated in the past that Americans with even one-thirty-second or "one drop" of African American ancestry would be designated nonwhite rather than white, as legal scholar Ian Haney Lopez documents in White by Law.

31. Ryan's "Should Obama Be Played by an African American on Saturday Night Live?" was posted online with reader comments.

32. Pool, "Blacked Up Obama Is a Pretty Weak Joke."

33. Keller, "SNL's Michaels Defends Choice of Armisen as Obama."

34. Cunningham, "Who's Going to Play Michelle Obama?"

35. Several of these performers are not even mentioned in books on the history of Saturday Night Live, highlighting their underutilization on the comedy series. Former cast member Chris Rock addresses this subject in Shales and Miller's Live from New York.

Works Cited

Alston, Joshua. "The Dark Side of Corking Up." Newsweek, March 14, 2008.

Armijo, Robert W. "SNL's Obama Role Goes to Fred Armisen; NAACP Withdraws Darrell Hammond's Image Award Nomination for Most Positive Blackface Role Still on TV in Protest." The Spoof!, February 26, 2008, http://www.thespoof.com/news/spoof.cfm?headline=s41310s4.

Beltrán, Mary. "Mixed Race in Latinowood: Latina Stardom and Ethnic Ambiguity in the Era of Dark Angels." In Mixed Race Hollywood, edited by Mary Beltrán and Camilla Fojas, 248–268. New York: New York University Press, 2008.

———. "The Racial Politics of Spectacular Post-Racial Satire: Ugly Betty and Glee." Presentation at Console-ing Passions, Eugene, Oregon, April 2010.

———. "What's at Stake in Claims of Post-Racial Media?" FlowTV, June 2010, http://flowtv.org/2010/06/whats-at-stake-in-claims-of-post-racial-media.

Bennett, Marcus. "Fred Armisen Performs in 'Honeyface.'" New York, March 13, 2008.

Bogle, Donald. Toms, Coons, Mulattoes, Mammies, and Bucks: An Interpretive History of Blacks in American Films. New York: Viking, 1973.

Bonilla-Silva, Eduardo. Racism without Racists: Color-Blind Racism and the Persistence of Racial Inequality in the United States. Lanham, MD: Rowman and Littlefield, 2003.

Callahan, Yesha. "Black Face Is Ba(ra)ck?" [Flahy][Blak][chik]: Culture, Entertainment, and the Absurdities of My Life, February 24, 2008. http://www.flyblackchick.com/2008/02/24/black-face-is-barack (accessed October 16, 2011).

Carter, Bill. "SNL Ready to Make Up for Lost Time." New York Times, February 21, 2008, http://www.nytimes.com/ 2008/02/21/arts/ television/21snl.html.

Cunningham, Phillip Lamarr. "Who's Going to Play Michelle Obama?: Saturday Night Live and Its Lack of Women of Color." FlowTV, March 20, 2009, http://flowtv.org/2009/03/who%E2%80%99s-going-to-play-michelle-obama-saturday-night

-live-and-its-lack-of-women-of-colorphillip-lamarr-cunningham-bowling-green
-state-university.

Farhi, Paul. "Did *SNL* Go beyond the Pale with Fauxbama?" *Washington Post,* February
29, 2008, http://www.washingtonpost.com/wp-dyn/content/article/2008/02/28
/AR2008022803988.html?nav=emailpage.

Gallagher, Charles A. "Color Blind Privilege: The Social and Political Functions of Eras-
ing the Color Line in Post-Race America." In *Rethinking the Color Line: Readings in
Race and Ethnicity,* 3rd ed., edited by Charles A. Gallagher, 130–142. Boston: McGraw-
Hill, 2007.

Haney Lopez, Ian. *White by Law: The Legal Construction of Race.* New York: New York
University Press, 1997.

Hilmes, Michele. *Radio Voices: American Broadcasting, 1922–1952.* Minneapolis: University of Minnesota Press, 1997.

Holloway, Daniel. "Note to *SNL:* Black People Are Funny, Too." *Huffington Post,* February 25, 2008, http://www.huffingtonpost.com/daniel-holloway/note-to-snl-black
-people-_b_88351.html.

Jabberin' Wookie. "*SNL* Finally Realizes Black Face Isn't All That Funny after All." *Jabberin' Wookie,* March 9, 2009, http://www.jabberinwookie.wordpress.com/2009/03
/09/snl-finally-realizes-blackface-isnt-as-funny-as-it-used-to-be.

Joseph, Ralina L. "Tyra Banks Is Fat: Reading (Post-)Racism and (Post-)Feminism in
the New Millennium." *Critical Studies in Media Communication* 26(3) (Fall 2009):
237–254.

Kearns, Burt. "*SNL* Avoids the Obama Blackface Issue." *Tabloidbaby,* February 24, 2008,
http://tabloidbaby.blogspot.com/2008/02/ saturday-night-live-avoids-blackface.html.

Keller, Joel. "*SNL's* Michaels Defends Choice of Armisen as Obama." *AOL TV,* February
29, 2008, http://www.aoltv.com/2008/02/09/snl-michaels-defends-choice-of
-armisen-as-obama.

Kondo, Dorrine. "(Re)Visions of Race: Contemporary Race Theory and the Cultural
Politics of Racial Crossover in Documentary Theatre." *Theatre Journal* 52 (2000):
81–107.

Light, Claire. "*SNL's* Fauxbama Blackface Thing." *Claire Light,* March 2, 2008, http://
clairelight.typepad.com/seelight/2008/03/snls-fauxbama-b.html.

Lott, Eric. *Love and Theft: Blackface Minstrelsy and the American Working Class.* New
York: Oxford University Press, 1993.

Lotz, Amanda. "Imagining Post-PC Humor." Presentation at the Television Comedy
Conference, Madison, Wisconsin, October 2011.

Mancino, Joe. "The Blackface Backlash." *Georgetown Independent,* December 5, 2010,
http://www.thegeorgetown independent.com/commentary/the-blackface-backlash
-1.2422061#.ToX_FuYeg2M (accessed October 20, 2011).

Marcus, Bennett. "Fred Armisen Performs in Honeyface." *New York Magazine,* March
13, 2008, http://nymag.com/daily/intel/2008/03/fred_armisen_does_not_wear
_bla.htm.

NIA Online. "A Real Black Man: Good Enough to Lead the Nation but Not for *Saturday
Night Live?" NIA Online,* November 7, 2008. http://www.niaonline.com/ggmsblog
/?m=200811&paged=2.

Pool, Hannah. "Blacked Up Obama Is a Pretty Weak Joke." *Guardian,* February 26,
2008, http://www.guardian.co.uk/culture/tvandradioblog/2008/feb/26
/blackedupobamaisaprettyweak.

Rogin, Michael. *Blackface, White Noise: Jewish Immigrants in the Hollywood Melting Pot.* Berkeley: University of California Press, 1996.

Ryan, Maureen. "Should Obama Be Played by an African American on *Saturday Night Live*?" *Chicago Tribune,* February 24, 2008, http://featuresblogs.chicagotribune.com /entertainment_tv/2008/02/should-obama-be.html.

Shales, Tom, and James Andrew Miller. *Live from New York: An Uncensored History of Saturday Night Live.* Boston: Little, Brown, 2002.

Smith, Cherise. *Enacting Others: Politics of Identity in Eleanor Antin, Nikki S. Lee, Adrian Piper, and Anna Deveare Smith.* Durham, NC: Duke University Press, 2011.

PART FOUR

Beyond Saturday Night, Beyond Television

Skits Strung Together: Performance, Narrative, and the Sketch Comedy Aesthetic in *SNL* Films

NICK MARX

Popular press coverage of *Saturday Night Live* commonly refers to the program as the "graduate school" of comedy.[1] Performers such as Chevy Chase, John Belushi, Bill Murray, Eddie Murphy, Mike Myers, David Spade, Adam Sandler, Chris Farley, Tina Fey, Will Ferrell, Amy Poehler, and Kristen Wiig have all honed their skills in comedic performance and developed their star personas on *SNL* before moving on to the higher-profile platform of feature films. While the show has produced some of the top box office draws of the last thirty years, some film critics tend to see the influence of *SNL* as a nuisance on the big screen. They lament the tendency of *SNL* alumni to play "the same character[s] seen on *SNL*,"[2] or question whether this performative mode can "carry a whole movie."[3] Others see an ill fit between *SNL*'s short-form comedic sensibility and the structural demands of feature-length film narratives. Reviewers noted of Ferrell's *Anchorman* (2004), for example, that it felt "like an extended skit stretched and stretched"[4] or like "loosely strung-together *SNL* skits";[5] of Fey and Poehler's *Baby Mama* (2008) that it "plays out like a very long and very mediocre sketch on *SNL*";[6] and of Sandler's *Jack and Jill* (2011) that the actor appears "caught in an abysmal *Saturday Night Live* sketch."[7]

Saturday Night Live, according to many critics, has no business being in the movie business, a sentiment bolstered by universally panned flops like *It's Pat* (1994), *Stuart Saves His Family* (1995), *Blues Brothers 2000* (1998), *Superstar* (1999), and *MacGruber* (2010). Though these movies were spun off directly from *SNL* sketches in a relatively transparent effort to capitalize on their fleeting popularity, they also highlight the same critique leveled at the films mentioned above: former *SNL* stars are too closely tied to their television personas, which disrupt conventionally representational film performances and goal-driven film narratives. Chase's smug gadabout in *Fletch* (1985) was therefore too much like the anchor he played on *SNL*'s "Weekend Update" segments. Myers buried his own personality in his characters in *So I Married an Axe Murderer* (1993), the *Austin Powers* franchise (1997, 1999, 2002), and *The Love Guru* (2008), the same way he did in portraying Dieter, Linda Richman, and Simon on *SNL*. These extrafictional comedic personas, according to critics, become the focus—often at the expense of the film's narrative. This is illustrated when *Anchorman,* for example, pauses for a silly street fight in which Ferrell can spout his characteristically absurdist non sequiturs, and when *Tommy Boy* (1995) provides Farley time to perform a song-and-dance in which he ruins a tiny sport coat with his famously fat frame. Although this type of relationship between TV stardom and film performance is not unique in the history of popular comedy,[8] it has been particularly notable in reviews, publicity materials, and fan activity surrounding *SNL* performers as they move from the small to the big screen. However, popular and critical commentaries rarely account for how the small screen aesthetics of *SNL* and the aesthetics of feature film comedy can interact to provide pleasures unavailable in each medium by itself.

This chapter examines several key *SNL* stars' transition to film, arguing that their film performances are reflective of an industrial context in which comedic stardom operates intertextually and across media. I read against the critical trope of presentational comedic performances as incompatible with film narrative and suggest that they might actually be complementary to and integrated with film narrative. My analyses are based on Philip Drake's argument that contemporary comedic performance invokes "multiple semantic frames—of fictional character, of star persona, and of generic codes and conventions."[9] This chapter thus explores the textual possibilities of contemporary comedic performance and suggests probable interpretations of its many frames by viewers. *SNL* stars' performance can certainly be read as disruptive to conventional film narrative, yet it is one of many possible layers of intertextual meaning for many viewers. As Drake notes, we may also enter into moments of more or less recognition of any one layer of meaning without detracting from our overall ability to comprehend their interactions in the aggregate.

Drake's conception of comedic performance is a useful updating of "comedian comedy," Steve Seidman's term for the film subgenre in which comedians like Charlie Chaplin and Jerry Lewis systematically undermined the representational strategies of classical Hollywood narrative with a presentational style—not unlike that of many *SNL* alumni—that "parades the specialty performer *as* a performer rather than subjugating his or her presentation to the demands of character construction."[10] Seidman suggests that this tension also plays out at the thematic level of comedian comedy films, whose stories often develop around the eccentric comedian's rejection of or acquiescence to some normative environment.[11] Indeed, one can easily map this generic convention onto any number of films starring *SNL* alumni. John "Bluto" Blutarsky (Belushi) and his cohort overrun the institutional powers-that-be in *Animal House* (1978), for example, while Billy Madison (Sandler) must abandon much of his immature behavior and accept some responsibility in order to graduate in *Billy Madison* (1995). Yet the tension between performance and narrative is not always clear-cut in constructing this theme, as each film speaks to a different sociohistorical and industrial context. Jim Whalley has demonstrated how generational conflicts inform the film performances of Belushi and Sandler, among others.[12] Henry Jenkins similarly characterizes comedian comedy as assigning static meaning to comedic performance modes that vary greatly across decades, and he suggests more proximate causes—such as the influence of vaudeville and Hollywood's shift to sound—as guiding aesthetic forces in classical comedies.[13] Although theories about comedian comedy provide a good starting point for considering the films of *SNL* alumni historically, I take Jenkins's cue and place these films' patterns of textual similarities into dialogue with the contemporary material conditions of their production and reception. In doing so, I hope to illustrate more clearly how comedic performance instructs audiences to read intertextually and across media.

For much of its history, *SNL* has foregrounded individual cast members as stars, and much of the above-mentioned critical discourse about their films bears this out. Chase, Belushi, and Sandler, among others, distinguished themselves from the *SNL* ensemble by aggressively inscribing their own personalities onto the characters they played across sketches, a dynamic at least partially born of Lorne Michaels's efforts to distinguish the program itself from contemporaneous television comedies. As I elaborate below, Michaels's strategy catalyzed the varyingly successful film careers of a number of male cast members across the 1970s–1990s at the same time that it marginalized female performers. But as *SNL* has adapted to television's contemporary "post-network" era, so too has its preferred method of star-making shifted.

Today, the overwhelming majority of *SNL* cast members hail from training grounds like the Groundlings, Second City, and the Upright Citizens Brigade, where group writing and performing skills are emphasized. Their impulses for communal performance often conflict with established notions of individual expression on *SNL,* a dilemma further exacerbated by the show's tradition of privileging solo stardom as the way to break free from television and make it in film. Contemporary cast members, as a result, have not entirely shied away from star-making performances, but have increasingly used them as complements to more dialogic, group-based modes. This dynamic is driven by *SNL* stars' increasing exposure across ever-proliferating media outlets, an environment amenable more to flexible articulations of comedic stardom than to the fixed identities of performers who merely "play themselves" all the time. The comedic personas of former cast members like Tina Fey and Will Ferrell, for example, equally accommodate the dialogic aesthetics of group performance *and* individual identities that develop from collaboration. This shift in *SNL* stars' formation requires reframing the critical discourse about their films away from a medium-specific notion of performance and toward one that acknowledges the many frames through which former *SNL* players encode meaning and audiences decode it. Today, the graduate-school metaphor no longer speaks to a singular performance mode placing individual *SNL* stars on a linear trajectory from television to film. It might be better used to describe how *SNL* performers hone the flexibility needed to accommodate the myriad cultural and industrial contexts of many media simultaneously.

SATURDAY NIGHT LIVE AND SOLO
STARDOM BEYOND STUDIO 8H

From the moment the show premiered in the fall of 1975, Lorne Michaels sought to distinguish *SNL* (then *NBC's Saturday Night*) from the vaudeville-influenced formats that had dominated many variety shows before it: "We wanted to redefine comedy the way the Beatles redefined what being a pop star was. That required not pandering, and it also required removing neediness, the need to please. It was like, we're only going to please those people who are like us. The presumption was there were a lot of people like us. And that turned out to be so."[14]

His desire to "redefine comedy" indicated a rejection of the faux sincerity and pandering characteristic of the Borscht Belt comedians that populated those programs. His Not Ready for Prime Time Players would eschew the style of Henny Youngman's "Take my wife, please" one-liners for a bolder sensibility that played to the baby boomer generation's desire for self-definition and distinction from its elders. The new comedy aesthetic advanced by early *SNL* cast members had an overtly egotistical, often aggressive style, one that has evolved as performers have adapted to the transmedial environment of the post-network era. The early style, though, was embodied most prominently in *SNL*'s first season by Chevy Chase. Tall and good-looking with an arrogant swagger that alienated his cast mates, Chase quickly became the face of the show by consciously positioning himself as its star. "I'm Chevy Chase, and you're not" was Chase's greeting in the fake news "Weekend Update" segments, which functioned as a tacit acknowledgment of Michaels's mission to set the show apart from its generic brethren. As a wheelchair-bound character in the opening sketch on October 25, 1975, Chase drew laughter after taking a hard fall. In the opening sketch the next week, Chase took an identical tumble in his bumbling impression of President Gerald Ford. Without makeup that would allow him to better approximate Ford physically, the resultant impersonation accommodated a dual reading of both presidential parody and star performance: it lampooned Ford's clumsiness at the same time that it foregrounded Chase's comedic persona. Soon thereafter, a *New York* cover story called Chase "TV's Hottest New Comedy Star,"[15] and Chase would continue to play an exaggerated version of himself in subsequent sketches that year, his only on the show.

Chase was not lacking for offers from Hollywood after his departure from *SNL*. Producers of the frat-house comedy *Animal House* crafted the lead role of Otter for Chase, a move that director John Landis adamantly opposed. Landis convinced Chase to opt instead for the lead in the romantic comedy *Foul Play* (1978), explaining to him: "Chevy, if you take *Foul Play*, you're then like Cary Grant; you're opposite Goldie Hawn, a major sex star, you're like Cary Grant. But if you take *Animal House*, you're a top banana in an ensemble, like *SNL*."[16] The expectation was for Chase to continue playing himself in much the same way he had on *SNL*, but the move would get Chase's film career off to a sputtering start. To be sure, Chase starring "as himself" would not necessarily guarantee the film's success, but it fit with industrial discourses that embraced his *SNL* star persona at the same time that those discourses attempted to distance him from it. Aggressive individuation distinguished Chase from the *SNL* ensemble on television and, at the very least, provided him with enough familiarity among audiences to attempt the next step in film. For *SNL* cast members interested in a shot at film stardom, it quickly became clear that Chase's model was the most direct route to notoriety and subsequent capitalization on the cultural cachet of the show.

Many *SNL* cast members have followed Chase on the path to a film career, but the trend warrants additional consideration in the context of the program's early climate of institutionalized sexism. Caryn Murphy's chapter in this collection notes that although *SNL* was born of countercultural impulses, ones that manifested in a comedic voice distinct from others on television, "advancing gender equality was not a shared goal." Female writers, performers, and producers early in the show's run were subjected to a range of maltreatment at the hands of male personnel. The generally hostile environment toward women meant less meaningful screen time for them and that their comedic personas factored into the program less than those of their male counterparts, creating, as Murphy writes, "pressure on the few women involved in the creative process to disprove a generally accepted notion about gender and comedy, as compared with the men on the staff, who were presumably attempting to prove their own individual talent." Although popular histories of the show highlight the more egregious instances of sexism (such as Belushi's infamous proclamation that "women aren't funny"),[17] the environment clearly influenced the softer forms of power wielded by above-the-line personnel like Michaels, too. According to original cast member Laraine Newman:

> Lorne urged me to repeat characters. I refused to do it because I wanted to, you know, dazzle everybody with my versatility. And that kept me anonymous. That was the same pitfall for Danny [Aykroyd]. He was much more comfortable doing characters, and I think that it made him less recognizable than John, who was always John even when he was the Samurai. And Billy [Murray] was always Billy. He did Todd in the Nerds but basically he was Billy. So even though I loved the kind of work that I did, and still do—I love the character work—I think it keeps you more anonymous than people who play themselves.[18]

Newman's comments speak directly to the central contradiction of performance modes on *SNL* in its early seasons. Effacement of one's personality via recurring character work meant more screen time, but without the individuation that could lead to opportunities beyond *SNL*. Performers who only "played themselves," conversely, minimized their chances to appear often in varied roles on the show in the hope that their comedic personas would click with writers, cast mates, and audiences. Clearly, the divide between the two is not absolute, but Newman's comments suggest a gendered bias toward men in the latter mode.

The original female cast member that most approximated Chase's individual style was Gilda Radner, yet even her case highlights many of the biases that marginalized women and propelled male cast members into film stardom. Radner thrived in recurring character work in her five-year tenure on the show, creating such memorable roles as Roseanne Roseannadanna, the crotchety "Weekend Update" commentator Emily Litella, and the Barbara Walters parody, Baba Wawa. She often appeared in monologues and backstage segments as herself, too, a tendency that Whalley notes was a major component of the original cast's efforts to form a rapport with its boomer audience and invite them in on the joke of television's constructedness and artificiality.[19] But while Chase imbued these segments with an aloofness that maintained distance between himself and audiences (and thus implicitly positioned himself above them as a star), Radner formed an intimate bond with viewers on their level in ways that reinforced the program's gendered hierarchy. In a bit from *SNL*'s fourth episode, Radner chats onstage with host Candice Bergen about everything from the stresses of dating to the proposed Equal

Rights Amendment. In a monologue entitled "What Gilda Ate" from the program's third episode, Radner playfully rattles off a lengthy list of her day's diet before host Rob Reiner cuts her off. While they lightheartedly lampoon some of the problems faced by many American women, these sketches take on additional significance in light of Radner's struggles with her self-image and bulimia at the time. Her vulnerability in them humanizes her and offers a point of identification for viewers, particularly female ones. Yet the fact that her femininity provides the basis for this identification and figures so prominently in her comedic persona closes the gap between Gilda and "Gilda." The blueprint laid out by Chase for TV-to-film stardom required this gap, allowing audiences to get close to him, yet keeping them far enough away so that he could position himself as a star.

Over the course of SNL's first twenty years, the cast members following this blueprint from SNL into movies—Chase, Belushi, Murray, Sandler, Farley—were overwhelmingly male performers who more or less played themselves. Evidence of the SNL boys club persists well into the 1990s, as comedians like Janeane Garofalo found cast mates Sandler, Spade, and Farley to be guilty of many of the same abuses suffered by Newman, Radner, and Jane Curtin in the original cast. And while the hiring of Fey, Poehler, Wiig, and other female cast members in the late 1990s and early 2000s did not suddenly usher in gender equality on SNL, as Caryn Murphy notes, their presence did provoke a substantive change in the popular perception—if not the actual power relations—of how SNL women could self-position as stars in moving from the program into film.

Significantly, the "Tina Fey era" coincided with a number of shifts in the entertainment media industries that fostered more polysemic forms of comedic performance in film. Broadly conceived, the changes across the 1990s and in the first decade of the twenty-first century largely moved primary control over the production, distribution, and exhibition of television out of the hands of a few broadcast networks like NBC and into a more flexible matrix of relationships among content producers, providers, and consumers.[20] The path to stardom today, then, is not the same seemingly linear trajectory—from SNL on the small screen to big screen feature film—that it was for many early performers. Although SNL might still be the primary incubator for any given cast member to test and develop his/her comedic persona, that persona is increasingly articulated across media platforms and informed by voices from a range of domains—popular culture, politics, sports, advertising, fashion— interacting more intensely and at a much more accelerated rate than in the past.

FEY, FERRELL, AND CONTEMPORARY COMEDIC STARDOM

Will Ferrell and Tina Fey have been arguably the two biggest stars to "graduate" from *SNL* in the twenty-first century and move on to multi-media careers beyond the show. They have not followed precisely the same path, but the respective comedic personas they developed along the way are emblematic of the same contemporary industrial context in which comedic stardom operates intertextually and across media. Their myriad appearances—in public forums and Internet comedy shorts as themselves; on television and Broadway as political figures like Sarah Palin and George W. Bush; and in a number of film roles—have utilized both presentational and representational performative modes, variously "playing themselves" and subsuming their personalities to character con-struction. Given their backgrounds in improvisational troupes and their overlapping time together at *SNL,* the major factors shaping their per-formances have accordingly been collaborative, dialogic, and therefore amenable to the contemporary transmedial climate. Critiques insist-ing that their films too often invoke the aesthetics of other media, then, risk overlooking the extent to which media can and often do interact in complex and complementary ways. By offering analyses of the films *Date Night* (2010), *Anchorman* (2004), and *Step Brothers* (2008), I offer strate-gies for reading Fey's and Ferrell's films with the same flexibility that al-ready frames their performances everywhere else.

In 1997 Fey joined the *SNL* writing staff, headed at the time by fre-quent Ferrell collaborator Adam McKay. Whereas Ferrell was one of the program's most popular onscreen presences for much of his tenure, Fey only occasionally appeared in sketches as a supporting player, fo-cusing much of her creative output on writing. As a result, Fey cannot be said to have had the same fully formed comedic persona as full-time cast members did, at least not until she joined Jimmy Fallon as co-anchor of

"Weekend Update" in 2000. She thrived there for six seasons, contrasting her witty charm with Fallon's impish antics and, after Fallon's departure, Poehler's volatile energy. It was during the first decade of the twenty-first century, alongside Poehler on "Update," writing for female cast members like Maya Rudolph, Rachel Dratch, and Kristen Wiig, and making guest appearances as vice presidential nominee Sarah Palin that publicity discourses made Fey the focal point of a newly ascendant female voice on *SNL*, despite it not being entirely clear what Fey's own voice was as a performer.

Though she has returned to portray Palin and to serve as host, Fey left *SNL* in 2006 to create NBC's mock-*SNL* sitcom, *30 Rock*. Her character, Liz, a thinly veiled version of herself, is the hardscrabble showrunner for *The Girlie Show*, a fictional late-night sketch comedy program on NBC. In the 2007 episode "Jack Gets in the Game," vain and neurotic cast member Jenna (played by Jane Krakowski), seeing her popularity on the show decline, begins a new season of *The Girlie Show* grossly overweight. Audiences react favorably to her new "character," and offers pour in to Jenna for movie and merchandising deals. Instead of leaving the show for greener pastures, Jenna loses weight and stays, not out of loyalty to *The Girlie Show*, but because she does not want to be typecast as "the fat girl." Through the character of Jenna, Fey expresses ambivalence about explicitly articulating a star persona as many of the (mostly male) *SNL* alumni before her did. Positioning *SNL*—by way of *The Girlie Show*—as a punch line in *30 Rock* has allowed Fey both to acknowledge the importance of *SNL* in defining her comedic persona and to ensure it is not *the* defining characteristic.

Fey has often expressed this tension through the character of Jenna. In the 2012 episode "The Ballad of Kenneth Parcell," Liz attempts to bring Jenna back down to earth by reminding her of a pact they made while they were struggling improv actors together in Chicago. "Liz, if I become famous, will you tell me if I start acting weird?," Jenna asks, to which Liz replies, "Definitely, and will you do the same for me?" Jenna bursts into laughter at the thought of Liz/Fey becoming famous. *SNL*-made fame, for Fey, is absurd, particularly when it is based on the type of antiquated, aggressively selfish mode of individuation represented by Jenna. Yet *SNL* persists as a star-making forum nonetheless, and Fey's critique of *SNL* suggests that this contradiction is a key aspect to the comedic personas of the show's alumni. Her performances on *30 Rock* vary between directly presentational moments that acknowledge the television audience with fourth-wall-breaking comments and vaguely representational scenes as the character of Liz. Indeed, Fey is quite often simply playing herself on *30 Rock,* but her performance dialogues with others on the show that offer a broader critique of *SNL.* By exposing the trappings of *SNL* stardom, as well as the comedically seedy underbelly of corporate-controlled network television comedy, Fey/Liz and *30 Rock* offer multiple points for considering how performance need not be circumscribed by any given text or medium.

Fey's film performances contain obvious overlaps with her television work, particularly in their tendency to deemphasize her individual comedic star persona. Instead of Fey as a conventional, solo film "star," her persona is more often integrated among coterminous layers of performance, narrative, and the variable amounts of extrafictional knowledge brought by audiences to the moment of viewing. This layered interaction has been inflected not only broadly by practices of transmedial production, distribution, and consumption, but also specifically by performance modes amenable to those practices. The skills for improvisation and character work that many *SNL* cast members bring with them to the show, and then take into feature films, are ideally suited for a contemporary mediascape that requires performers to wear many hats across many media. These skills also manifest in film narratives that, in Drake's terminology, enact "multiple semantic frames," allowing viewers to see both the extrafictional component parts of comedic performance and how they function as a whole within the film's reality.

In *Date Night* with Fey and fellow Second City alumnus Steve Carell, for instance, the actors play out a scene that simultaneously invokes their theater training, their respective star personas, and the generic tropes that seek to integrate both into the film's narrative. Early in the film, their characters, a bored married couple out to dinner, scan the restaurant and see a young couple on a date. In an effort to entertain one another, Phil Foster (Carell) prompts his wife, Claire (Fey), to invent the couple's backstory. They decide the couple is having an unsuccessful third date and proceed to improvise their conversation from afar. Phil affects a groggy monotone for the man, and Claire adopts the personality of a vapid ditz, responding that she's going to go home and "fart into a shoebox." After they chuckle to one another, Claire mutters to herself, "That's not . . . that doesn't make sense." The scene mimics any number of improvisation games—in which actors on one side of the stage provide commentary for the pantomimes of actors on the other—that Carell and Fey might have practiced in their time at Second City. It also invokes the dialogic rapport Fey developed with her "Update" co-anchors at SNL, punctuated by her "breaking" or acknowledging the presentational performance to herself in the scene's final beat. Importantly, though, neither frame necessarily distracts from the scene's place in the narrative. Drake suggests that such self-contained moments function as motivated narrative "enclosures,"[21] accommodating presentational performance without disrupting the verisimilitude of the film's diegetic world. Indeed, Phil and Claire—bored married couple—are performing for one another just as much as Carell and Fey—comedy stars—are performing for the film's audience.

Reviews of the film frame these layers of performative signification as complementary, too, suggesting that audiences look for—and take pleasure in—such scenes of seeming distraction. The dinner scene and others like it "create hilarious but accurate verbal portraits of contemporary types, while saying a great deal about the unsatisfactory lives that the Fosters themselves are living."[22] Another review advises audiences: "Stay for the outtakes—they're improv delights,"[23] and "funnier than screenwriter Josh Klausner's lines."[24] In addition to suggesting that improvisations invoking Fey's and Carell's comedic star personas "work" within the narrative, the reviews also point viewers beyond that narrative to material providing additional pleasures. The practice of tacking outtakes onto films' ending credits is not an uncommon one, particularly for contemporary comedies. Yet their inclusion and emphasis across a number of reviews highlights the multiple sites of meaning creation both within the film and in its ancillary material. Jonathan Gray has identified such paratexual material—reviews, film trailers, DVD extras, and merchandise—not simply as extensions of a primary text, but as "filters through which we must pass on our way to the film or program, our first and formative encounters with the text."[25] Audiences likely arrive at comedies like Date Night with some sense of how a potentially disruptive performance mode like improvisation will affect their viewing experience, as well as how that mode has been used in paratexts to character-

Figure 11.1. Tina Fey and Steve Carell perform for each other and for the audience in *Date Night*.

ize the film's stars. Audience interaction with paratextual material, then, additionally informs layered constructions of comedic star performance and catalyzes their movement across platforms. And few *SNL*-alumni-turned-film-stars have thrived in this transmedial environment as Will Ferrell has.

Ferrell has undoubtedly been the most notable Hollywood personality to embrace—and become identified with—new media comedy practices. After leaving *SNL* in 2002 for starring film roles in *Elf* (2003), *Kicking and Screaming* (2005), and *Stranger than Fiction* (2006), he co-founded with McKay the popular comedy website *Funny or Die* in 2007. With the instantly viral success of the site's first short, "The Landlord," Ferrell established a middle ground between the aesthetics of user-generated content and Hollywood prestige that the industry has been attempting to replicate since then.[26] His film career has continued to be successful, yet he has often veered from conventional paths that would clearly position him as a star. Ferrell often shows up in friends' projects and co-productions like *Eastbound and Down* (2009–present), *The Goods: Live Hard, Sell Hard* (2009), and *Tim and Eric's Billion Dollar Movie* (2012) buried deep in the persona of some bizarre character. Over the course of 2011–2012, he and McKay made several television advertisements for Old Milwaukee beer that aired only in local markets in the upper Midwest (one ran during the 2012 Super Bowl), but were shared across social networking sites the following weeks. The ads' lo-fi aesthetic and Ferrell's bumbling, faux sincere demeanor work just as much to position him just outside of the Hollywood mainstream as they do to expand the boundaries of what's included in that mainstream. Because Ferrell's comedic persona is spread so widely across roles and media, identifying a singular articulation of it within and among his films detracts from the many intertextual pleasures such variability offers.

In his seven-year tenure at *SNL*, Ferrell's comedic star persona was similarly scattered, anchored on the one hand in versions of himself as a "straight man" and on the other in erratic, volatile characters with a tendency for the absurd. No sketch better encapsulates this duality than his very first on *SNL* in the fall of 1995. Gazing over the heads of the audience while he unassumingly flips burgers on a grill, Ferrell as a plainly dressed suburban dad serenely and familiarly makes small talk with neighbors. He intermittently interrupts the polite banter to gently implore his off-screen children to stop their horseplay atop the family's shed and then returns to his conversation with the neighbor. Suddenly, his tiny eyes narrow, and his gaze shifts back to the children: "Hey! There's gonna be a meeting between your ass and the palm of my hand, if you don't get off the shed! Now, get off the shed!" Without a beat, he continues his conversation with the neighbors, who are aghast at his treatment of the children.

Ferrell honed this delicate balance between the familiar everyman and violent, impulsive surrealism in many characters and impersonations over the years. As Neil Diamond, he gently cooed to his audience before inserting non sequiturs like "I'll smack you in the mouth, I'm Neil Diamond!" and as a drunken businessman, he told tall tales of a recently deceased co-worker: "He once scissor-kicked Angela Lansbury!" The abrupt and tangential aggression in Ferrell's comedic persona hewed closely to that of Chase and Murray before him, but with Ferrell, this aggression was purely performative and rarely part of some broader process of individual distinction. Instead, it more often functioned as the initial step in a dialogic give-and-take with a fellow performer, turning what might appear initially as a tangent into another performative layer. Ferrell then translated this aesthetic—like Fey did after him—into many of his film roles, some of which have been accused of being disruptive and meandering by critics, but, as I discuss below, the films were built around this very disruptiveness.

Early in *Anchorman*, Ferrell, as the eponymous news anchor Ron Burgundy, warms up for the evening newscast by spouting comedic non sequiturs masquerading as preparatory vocal exercises, such as "The arsonist has oddly shaped feet." When the newscast begins, he looks into the camera and directly addresses the filmic audience, but only via the mediation of the fictional television audience to which he broadcasts, suggesting the same sort of dual registers of reality necessary for a narrative enclosure. This winking knowingness doubly frames both the Burgundy character performing for his studio/television audience and Ferrell's comedic performance of him, which invokes his *SNL* persona.

A similar dynamic plays out in several subsequent scenes. The day after sleeping with love interest Veronica Corningstone (Christina Applegate), Ron recounts his conquest to his news team. After each poses his idealized version of love to Ron only to have it questioned, they collectively pause to ponder what an idealized version of love would look like. Suddenly, they break out into a minute-long rendition of Starland Vocal Band's "Afternoon Delight," replete with harmonizing and mimicry of the instruments. The sequence might be dismissed as yet another "extended skit stretched and stretched" were it not for the many cues indicating it as one of many semantic frames through which we might process the scene. Ron sings the first line of the song alone, then is joined by his compatriots. Upon finishing, sports anchor Champ Kind (David Koechner) claims that the model of love they have collectively expressed "sounds kinda dumb." This explicit acknowledgment of the performance serves to maintain it as integrated within the film's diegesis: nondiegetic scoring does not cue its beginning, a character's lead-in does; and characters do not simply cordon off the musical number from their respective narrative roles, they acknowledge its relevance to them, performing simultaneously for one another and for the presumed audience of the film.

The improvisation-heavy film *Step Brothers* also provides a number of narrative enclosures that accommodate a layered comedic performance by Ferrell. After several failed job interviews, forty-something halfwits Brennan (Ferrell) and Dale (John C. Reilly) solicit investments from family and friends for their entertainment company, Prestige Worldwide. Their pitch includes upbeat techno music, an amateurish slideshow, and Brennan frantically dancing and ad-libbing over Dale's composed recitation of talking points. The assembled audience is initially amused by the duo's promises of music, event planning, and management until the presentation climaxes with a music video depicting Brennan and Dale's fantasy life of "Boats 'n Hoes." Here again the film establishes a narrative

Figure 11.2. Will Ferrell and John C. Reilly in the "Boats 'n Hoes" music video from *Step Brothers.*

enclosure that motivates the extended music video sequence, as Brennan and Dale perform for their potential investors just as Ferrell and Reilly perform for the film's audience. The layered frames for the scene take on extra significance in the context of the film's publicity campaign, which circulated "Boats 'n Hoes" virally alongside similarly scatological shorts like "Green Team" produced by Ferrell, Reilly, and director Adam McKay for *Funny or Die.* In the case of *Step Brothers,* then, seemingly disruptive narrative elements work within the context of the film and provide avenues of additional pleasure beyond it.

CONCLUSION

The *Step Brothers* scene, as well as ones like it in the films of a number of recent *SNL* alumni, indicates the need for a mode of evaluation "where terms conventionally associated with realist performance—such as 'authenticity' and 'sincerity'—have very little explanatory force."[27] That is to say, the complaint that many contemporary comedies' meandering, sketch-like narratives and ostentatious, presentational performances violate some prescribed "norm" misses the point. Given the abundance of extratextual information about *SNL* stars, their respective performance backgrounds, and their work across media, audiences likely enter the moment of viewing their films with that norm as one of many available frames for decoding. Many of the most salient comedic moments—the ones so often bemoaned by critics as "sketch-like" or *SNL*-esque in their characterization—provide ample justification for their place both within the world of the film and in the many media platforms beyond it. Indeed, one can easily find on YouTube a sampling of scenes lifted from the films of *SNL* alumni that work just as well on their own as they do in the context of the movies. Not coincidentally, these scenes often exist in the same web-based flow as sketches pulled from broadcasts of *SNL*. We can better understand these newly formed flows of comedy by acknowledging their interconnectedness from the start.

This chapter has attempted to illuminate that interconnectedness by tracing the performance styles of *SNL* stars from their time on the show to projects beyond it. I have outlined a roughly historical arc of the preferred performance mode for *SNL* alumni as shifting from individualized modes to collaborative ones, yet this shift is not uniform in all cases. Nor does Drake's reading of layered comedic performance apply only in the contemporary moment. Indeed, one can view someone like Bill Murray as performing in several ways: as sardonic Peter Venkman in *Ghostbusters* (1984); as former *SNL* star Bill Murray, whose similarly acerbic portrayal of characters like Nick the lounge singer frame our readings of him elsewhere; and as an ostensible film protagonist, whose actions can propel the narrative at the same time that they evoke associations with other supernatural comedies like *Teen Wolf* (1985) and *Beetlejuice* (1988).

SNL cast members have always utilized some mixture of performance modes on the show and in film, and they continue to do so today. This ongoing negotiation might be most usefully seen in comparing the sensibilities of Radner and Fey. Both performers share similarly idiosyncratic and brazen takes on femininity, but Radner's were more circumscribed by the internal politics of *SNL* at the time. Fey, by contrast, works in a moment with myriad outlets for her humor, inspiring a range of performances that are at the same time anchored in the comedic persona she developed on *SNL*. The contemporary transmedial moment, which makes performers available to viewers on their terms much more than in the past, has allowed for multiple and simultaneous articulations of the comedic personas of Fey, Ferrell, and other *SNL* alumni beyond the boundaries of any one text or medium. To be sure, stars—particularly outside of comedy—continue to forge personas around a personal brand, seeking to unify their identity in the public eye. But sketch comedians, with their natural inclinations for atomistic jokes and malleable, in-the-moment performances, must flexibly complement their personal brands if for no other reason than to keep working. Up-and-coming comedians regularly need to generate new content for online video sites and podcasts, hoping to catch the eyes of producers that can lead them to bigger and better opportunities. Established comedians turn to new media outlets to satiate audience demand for content, work around television and film production lead times, and latch on to the hip sensibilities of emergent comedy practices. *SNL,* after being little more than the "launching pad ... which leads to making bad movies," as Buck Henry described it,[28] is now positioned as a nexus between the two talent pools.

Notes

1. See, among others, Connelly, "'Comedy at the Edge' Looks at '70s Standup Explosion"; and Poniewozik, "All-Time 100 TV Shows."
2. Silver, "YouTube HOF: Great Moments in Selling Out."
3. Dominus, "Can Kristen Wiig Turn On the Charm?"
4. LaSalle, "Flip the Channel on *Anchorman.*"
5. Travers, "*Anchorman: The Legend of Ron Burgundy.*"
6. Times-Dispatch Staff, "*Baby Mama* Seems Like a Long, Bad *SNL* Sketch."
7. Setoodeh, "Movie Review: Adam Sandler's *Jack and Jill* Is the Worst Movie Ever Made."
8. See Murray, *Hitch Your Antenna to the Stars,* for a rich analysis of comedians negotiating the opposite trajectory—from feature films into the intimate, live aesthetic of early television.
9. Drake, "Low Blows?," 188.
10. Krutnik, "General Introduction," 7.
11. Seidman, *Comedian Comedy,* 143–146.
12. Whalley, *Saturday Night Live.*
13. Jenkins, *What Made Pistachio Nuts?*
14. Qtd. in Shales and Miller, *Live from New York,* 69.
15. Ibid., 59.
16. Qtd. in Shales and Miller, *Live from New York,* 90.
17. Hill and Weingrad, *Saturday Night,* 233.
18. Qtd. in Shales and Miller, *Live from New York,* 124.

19. Whalley, *Saturday Night Live,* 35–39.

20. See Curtin, "Matrix Media"; and Lotz, *The Television Will Be Revolutionized.*

21. Drake, "Low Blows?," 190–192.

22. Bogle, "*Date Night* and *City Island.*"

23. Travers, "*Date Night.*"

24. Phillips, "Steve Carell, Tina Fey Deserve a Better *Date Night.*"

25. Gray, *Show Sold Separately,* 3.

26. See Marx, "The Missing Link Moment."

27. Drake, "Low Blows?," 192.

28. Qtd. in Shales and Miller, *Live from New York,* 168.

Works Cited

Bogle, Charles. "*Date Night* and *City Island:* One Comedy That Knows Where It's Going, Another That Can't Seem to Decide." *World Socialist,* June 10, 2010, http://www.wsws.org/articles/2010/jun2010/date-j10.shtml (accessed February 1, 2012).

Connelly, Sherryl. "'Comedy at the Edge' Looks at '70s Standup Explosion." *New York Daily News,* January 13, 2008, http://www.nydailynews.com/entertainment/music-arts/comedy-edge-70s-standup-explosion-article-1.345455 (accessed February 1, 2012).

Curtin, Michael. "Matrix Media." In *Television after "TV": Understanding Television in the Post-Broadcast Era,* edited by Graeme Turner. London: Routledge, 2009.

Dominus, Susan. "Can Kristen Wiig Turn On the Charm?" *New York Times,* April 28, 2011, http://www.nytimes.com/2011/05/01/magazine/mag-01wiig-t.html?_r=2&pagewanted=1 (accessed February 1, 2012).

Drake, Philip. "Low Blows?: Theorizing Performance in Post-Classical Comedian Comedy." In *Hollywood Comedians: The Film Reader,* edited by Frank Krutnik. London: Routledge, 2003.

Gray, Jonathan. *Show Sold Separately: Promos, Spoilers, and Other Media Paratexts.* New York: New York University Press, 2010.

Hill, Doug, and Jeff Weingrad *Saturday Night: A Backstage History of Saturday Night Live.* New York: Beech Tree, 1986.

Jenkins, Henry. *What Made Pistachio Nuts?: Early Sound Comedy and the Vaudeville Aesthetic.* New York: Columbia University Press, 1992.

Krutnik, Frank. "General Introduction." In *Hollywood Comedians: The Film Reader,* edited by Frank Krutnik. London: Routledge, 2003.

LaSalle, Mick. "Flip the Channel on *Anchorman,* a Comedy Sketch Stretched Too Far." *San Francisco Chronicle,* July 9, 2004, http://www.sfgate.com/cgi-bin/article.cgi?file=/chronicle/archive/2004/07/09/DDGSL7I07A1.DTL (accessed February 1, 2012).

Lotz, Amanda. *The Television Will Be Revolutionized.* New York: New York University Press, 2007.

Marx, Nick. "The Missing Link Moment: Web Comedy in New Media Industries." *Velvet Light Trap* 68 (Fall 2011):14–23.

Murray, Susan *Hitch Your Antenna to the Stars: Early Television and Broadcast Stardom.* New York: Routledge, 2005.

Phillips, Michael. "Steve Carell, Tina Fey Deserve a Better *Date Night.*" *Chicago Tribune,* April 8, 2010, http://articles.chicagotribune.com/2010-04-08/entertainment

/chi-100406-date-night-review_1_carell-and-fey-date-night-tina-fey (accessed February 1, 2012).

Poniewozik, James. "All-Time 100 TV Shows." *Time,* September 6, 2007, http://entertainment.time.com/2007/09/06/the-100-best-tv-shows-of-all-time/slide/saturday-night-live/#saturday-night-live (accessed February 1, 2012).

Seidman, Steve. *Comedian Comedy: A Tradition in Hollywood Film.* Ann Arbor, MI: UMI Research Press, 1981.

Setoodeh, Ramin. "Movie Review: Adam Sandler's *Jack and Jill* Is the Worst Movie Ever Made." *Daily Beast,* November 11, 2011, http://www.thedailybeast.com/articles/2011/11/11/movie-review-adam-sandler-s-jack-and-jill-is-the-worst-movie-ever-made.html (accessed February 1, 2012).

Shales, Tom, and James Andrew Miller. *Live from New York: An Uncensored History of Saturday Night Live.* Boston: Little, Brown, 2002.

Silver, Dan. "YouTube HOF: Great Moments in Selling Out." *Grantland,* February 1, 2012, http://www.grantland.com/blog/hollywood-prospectus/post/_/id/42559/youtube-hof-great-moments-in-selling-out (accessed February 1, 2012).

Times-Dispatch Staff. "*Baby Mama* Seems Like a Long, Bad *SNL* Sketch." *Richmond Times-Dispatch,* April 26, 2008, http://www2.timesdispatch.com/entertainment/2008/apr/26/-rtd_2008_04_26_0068-ar-135182 (accessed February 1, 2012).

Travers, Peter. "*Anchorman: The Legend of Ron Burgundy.*" *Rolling Stone,* July 14, 2004, http://www.rollingstone.com/movies/reviews/anchorman-the-legend-of-ron-burgundy-20040709 (accessed February 1, 2012).

———. "*Date Night.*" *Rolling Stone,* April 8, 2010, http://www.rollingstone.com/movies/reviews/date-night-20100408 (accessed February 1, 2012).

Whalley, Jim. *Saturday Night Live, Hollywood Comedy, and American Culture.* London: Palgrave Macmillan, 2010.

Andy Samberg's Digital Success Story and Other Myths of the Internet Comedy Club

ETHAN THOMPSON AND ETHAN TUSSEY

In the heady but not quite dot-com-bubble days between the sale of YouTube for $1.65 billion in 2006 and the financial meltdown of 2008, a flurry of excessive valuations of Internet properties prompted *Advertising Age* columnist Simon Dumenco to speculate that *Saturday Night Live* cast member Andy Samberg was worth $342 million. Never mind that Samberg hadn't established a single character that could be spun off into a film, or proved himself a bankable star like Will Ferrell, or secured his own sitcom like Tina Fey. Nor could one directly credit him with a boost in *SNL*'s Nielsen ratings. "Unlike his *SNL* forebears," explained Dumenco, "who used to distribute their comedy mostly through (pathetically enough) broadcast TV, his comedy tends to get most of its distribution in digital form, in packets of 1s and 0s, which automatically makes it waaaaaay more valuable."[1] In other words, what made Samberg so astronomically valuable was the special math used to calculate the worth of new media properties and the fact that Samberg was the star of at least two bona fide YouTube megahits, the hip-hop parody videos "Lazy Sunday" and "Dick in a Box."

Dumenco's column was firmly tongue-in-cheek, but singling out Samberg as an example of a TV personality whose value was rooted in his ability to cross boundaries between old and new media was no joke. Even by 2007, Samberg had proven his worth not just as a fresh young face, but by bringing a stylistic and comic sensibility to *Saturday Night Live* that broke from the show's norm and bridged Lorne Michaels's vertically integrated comedy empire with the emerging online viewing habits of audiences. In addition to freshening up the *SNL* brand, the success of Samberg and collaborators Akiva Schaffer and Jorma Taccone (collectively known as the Lonely Island) launched a symbolically powerful model for those looking to make a career in comedy. The trio had first showcased their videos online, and now they seemed to be doing pretty much the same thing on *SNL*—living the wannabe TV comedian's dream. The success of the Lonely Island on *SNL* suggested that one could now ride the information superhighway, via YouTube, right into the heart of the television industry. Just make a funny video with your friends, and you could end up on TV, or at least with a development deal. Importantly, this narrative resonates with descriptions of Internet upward mobility espoused by a variety of new media scholars. Yochai Benkler, for example, argues that a "network information economy" means "individuals can reach and inform or edify millions around the world," allowing "greater freedom to participate in tugging and pulling at the cultural creations of others ... making the culture they occupy more their own than was possible with mass-media culture. In these senses, we can say the culture is becoming more democratic: self-reflective and participatory."[2] The success of Samberg seems to confirm the romanticized ideal of the Internet as a frontier where anything goes, where individuals are free to create and perform—a more democratic space where the public, not industry gatekeepers, decide what is funny. Just as the faces of Google's Sergey Brin or Facebook's Mark Zuckerberg signify Internet-entrepreneur-as-capitalist-dreamboat, Andy Samberg's goofy visage has come to evoke a fantasy about a successful career in comedy in the convergence era.

The view for Internet comedians at the beginning of the road into the television industry is a lot less utopian, since the road is paved by the networks' desire to maintain the hegemony of their corporate parents. That is, the television industry embraces the democratic appeal of digital technology by identifying "digital talent" and using digital platforms to cultivate television producers. Entertainment studios ask up-and-coming talent to create digital content that simultaneously matches the experimental spirit of YouTube and proves that they are worthy of working in television. These "digital minor leagues" are a new production identity in the media industries, a response to the threat of an alternative creative industry, one represented by user-generated content on YouTube and other digital platforms. The seeking out of diversity, both in skill and in background, has been a popular strategy for entertainment studios throughout the corporate conglomerate era. As Vicki Mayer and John T. Caldwell have argued, the celebration of "diversity hires" is a way for corporations to demonstrate their dedication to multiple viewpoints and a way to target important niche demographics.[3] While Mayer and Caldwell write in reference to identity markers such as gender and race, we would suggest that the Lonely Island was a different kind of "diversity hire" for NBC, one meant to signify that the network was attuned to the growing importance of digital humor, while at the same time working to shape the future of such comedy, whether on or off TV.

Still, the success of Samberg and his cohorts on *SNL* and beyond, and the extent to which their popularity has been tied to online distribution, is a powerful narrative that resonates with broader promises that the Internet can usher in a more democratic era of cultural production. That narrative obscures the ways the entertainment industry is using online content to create a corporate-controlled farm system, or in this case, an "Internet comedy club." Instead of providing a wide-open path to success for unconventional talent, the Internet comedy club tends to evaluate success by traditional benchmarks of marketability and industry savvy, operating as a talent filtration system, which helps TV's gatekeepers find talent with a track record of appealing to the types of audiences they wanted all along.

In order to better understand how that system functions and how it has evolved since the success of "Lazy Sunday," it is productive to consider another case at NBC. While Samberg represents the discovery of digital talent, Mindy Kaling exemplifies the myth of digital upward mobility within the conglomerate, as she was discovered on the stage, but gained notoriety by demonstrating her showrunning chops in a web series for *The Office* (2005–2013). As a woman of Indian descent, Kaling stands out from the majority white male members of the comedy writers room. Her difference is an asset to NBC Comcast, because as Mayer puts it, "for network television producers, diversity and inclusion in production connotes the introduction of a racialized body to above-the-line work groups, even though the team as a whole must preserve the normative status of whiteness as the most desirable audience."[4] In this sense, Kaling's digital success is less about equal opportunity and more about bringing the technology in line with the commercial concerns of the media industries.

Even the academic literature on convergence culture that is largely optimistic about paths to success on digital platforms recognizes that commercial forces will inevitably favor particular types of content over others. In describing this inequality, Henry Jenkins notes that the industry is more likely to promote digital parody over fan fiction because the latter raises legal concerns over copyright protection and plagiarism.[5] He points out that fan fiction has traditionally been produced by women while parody videos are more often produced by men, meaning that the entertainment industries' involvement in digital production limits the types of talent that can be successful on digital platforms. In her digital work, Kaling adapts her comedic sensibility to the more industry-friendly arena of parody in order to take on the identity of a digital comedian. One of her most notable series of webisodes for *The Office*, "Subtle Sexuality," is a send-up of rap video culture, like Samberg's "Lazy Sunday." Another example of this tactic is Comedy Central's sitcom *Workaholics* (2011–present), whose writer-stars garnered attention for the online videos they made as Mail Order Comedy.[6] Those videos included not just the webisode precursor to the series, but parodic hip-hop videos as well. In short, what has emerged since 2005 is a talent filtration system focused on economic viability on television and an aesthetic that uses parody and lo-fi tactics to speak to middle-class male sensibilities. These tastes have become established, in terms of both what the audience expects from digital culture and what the industry is encouraging to cross over.

FROM INTERNET TO NBC AND BACK AGAIN

Although *SNL* had been on the air for thirty years before Samberg joined the cast in 2005, his almost immediate success through the viral spread of "Lazy Sunday" signaled to younger viewers that this was not their parents' *SNL*. The circulation and popularity of "Lazy Sunday" online showed that *SNL* could move from old to new platforms. The comic sensibility of the video suggested an adjustment to the parodic and absurd comedy that *SNL* had once shepherded into the world with the likes of

Andy Kaufman but now seemed to accumulate online or in the new cable fringe of Adult Swim. *SNL* resides on what had once been the outer-most fringe of the television schedule, which to a great extent allowed the boundary pushing that went on its 1970s glory days.[7] While those earliest years were noted for their rawness and spontaneity (thus, its cast members were "not ready for prime time"), *SNL* had long ago become professionalized into a comedy industry machine. *SNL* has always drawn upon talent from comedy and improvisation groups like Second City and the Groundlings, and performers gravitate to those groups for training and connections, not to mention the chance that they might be plucked from obscurity into the cast of *SNL*. The machine extends beyond *SNL*, too, as the show spins off movies based on characters and television shows featuring former *SNL* performers (and Lorne Michaels is often involved in producing for both media platforms).

The look, feel, and sound of "Lazy Sunday" flew in the face of an industrialized approach to comedy. "Lazy Sunday" looked like something different, something more like the weird, cheap stuff online, something that, happily for NBC, suggested that *SNL* really did have a future with convergence era audiences after all. That is, network television could still deliver the kind of referential comedy that audiences wanted, and in the new places and new ways they wanted it. Most important, it showed that *SNL* could generate a viral success, something that is increasingly coveted in the ever more fractured mediascape. The eager incorporation of the Lonely Island's "Digital Shorts" series into *SNL* by Michaels and their promotion by NBC executives was a symbolic move for a network seeking to revitalize itself for the convergence era.

A closer look at Samberg's trajectory from independent web videos to *SNL* "Digital Shorts" reveals a more traditional path than the myth of the Internet comedy club suggests. Samberg himself has pointed out the mythic twisting of the Lonely Island's origin story: "We definitely used the Internet in the beginning, but we didn't become known for using the Internet until after we were on a network television show. . . . We needed a national venue before people put us back on the Internet. Then people paid attention."[8] The Lonely Island's history dates back to when Samberg, Taccone, and Schaffer met in middle school in Berkeley, California. They went their separate ways after high school, but regrouped after college and moved to Los Angeles in 2000. Their success is not a case of the trio quickly being plucked from obscurity and placed into the highest echelons of television comedy. Rather, they put themselves in the heart of the mainstream entertainment industry and learned the culture of above-the-line labor: writers, producers, actors, directors, and other creative talent. It was there, while working as industry assistants, that they began producing their own videos.[9] In the days before YouTube, the team posted the videos on their own site (thelonelyisland.com). Those earliest videos, such as "Ka-Blamo!" and "Stork Patrol," reflect the same aesthetic that would later prove so successful in "Lazy Sunday." For instance, in "Stork Patrol," while a cheaply made stork puppet lies on a bed behind him, Samberg scowls into the camera and raps lasciviously. The video exhibits what would become the trademark Lonely Island blend of original hip-hop beats and rhymes that articulate the mundane and the absurd in a way that, when combined with the visual layer of assorted hip-hop video clichés, constitutes an ironic pastiche of masculine posturing.

While videos such as "Stork Patrol" and those that followed collected online views, remuneration was lacking. The Lonely Island made further inroads into the Hollywood comedy scene when episodes of *The 'Bu*, their parody of the then-popular teen drama *The O.C.* (2003–2007), were seen on Channel 101, the showcase for online comedy that screenwriters Dan Harmon and Rob Schrab founded after becoming disillusioned trying to produce a sitcom for Fox. Harmon and Schrab began producing digital shorts for their comedian friends, and this developed into a short film contest in which aspiring comedians could share their amateur work and vote on a winner. They found the process a refreshing alternative to the entertainment industry, and opened the contests to all on the Internet.[10] The Lonely Island's success on Channel 101 proved to television executives that the comedians were popular among an influential audience of tastemakers and young people.

In addition to proving marketability to a desirable demographic, *The 'Bu* demonstrated to executives that Lonely Island could adapt the conventions of mainstream Hollywood to create a parody of the popular nighttime soap genre. The comedians lampooned the conventions of the genre by mocking the acting styles, storylines, angst, and network marketing strategies that characterize these soaps. Barbara Klinger points out that parody has been an important trope of amateur "calling card" content because it demonstrates to industry executives that the comedians are familiar with the production standards and storytelling techniques of the mainstream industry. Klinger argues that these films put amateur filmmakers in the special class of the "apprenticeship ranks, not simply by showing command of the narrative and visual language of mainstream film, but by trumping this language through a winking knowledge of its conceits and assumptions."[11] Lonely Island's send-up of teen soaps acknowledged industry conventions without threatening to appropriate them in ways that would infringe on copyright.

Samberg's producer-boss at *Spin City* (1996–2002) certainly believed in the group's commercial appeal and industry savvy, and he passed along his assistant's demo tape to the United Talent Agency, and the Lonely Island ended up with a deal to produce the sketch comedy pilot *Awesometown*. Fox, Comedy Central, and MTV all passed, but the trio had created sufficient comedy buzz that they were hired to write for Jimmy Fallon when he hosted the MTV movie awards in 2005.[12] Fallon's praise got them their *SNL* auditions. Although they write their pieces together, Samberg is the acknowledged actor of the group and it was he who was put in the cast, while Taccone and Schaffer were hired as writers to create material for him.[13]

"Lazy Sunday" was the third "Digital Short" they produced in their first season, and the second to get on the air. While that video was the first hip-hop short they had produced for *SNL*, it was very similar to the earlier "Stork Patrol," with the significant distinction that they teamed with long-established *SNL* cast member Chris Parnell. Parnell was a natural choice as a collaborator because he had performed several raps on "Weekend Update" in tribute to hosts like Britney Spears, Kirsten Dunst, and Jennifer Garner.[14] The four reportedly wrote the song together and recorded it the following night in the Lonely Island's office at *SNL* using a laptop Taccone had bought on Craigslist.[15] They shot it as a four-man team, guerrilla-style.

"Lazy Sunday," like its online precursor "Stork Patrol" and its successor "Dick in a Box," is a parody not in the sense that it makes fun of hip-hop or R&B, but because it uses hip-hop as a mode of comic address, deriving humor from the incongruity between the earnest, macho style of the rapping and the silliness of the lyrics. In contrast to Parnell's previous hip-hop paeans, Parnell and Samberg rap about all the mundane things

Figure 12.1. Andy Samberg and Chris Parnell in "Lazy Sunday."

they do en route to seeing *The Chronicles of Narnia: The Lion, the Witch, and the Wardrobe* (2005). They eat cupcakes, discuss the relative merits of Yahoo Maps, Mapquest, and Google Maps, and stop at a deli to stock up on candy for the show, where instead of spending "Benjamins" ($100 bills) they drop "Hamiltons" ($10). As similar as "Lazy Sunday" might sound to "real hip-hop," the immediate popularity of the short must be understood not as the result of Samberg's lyrical flow or the dopeness of the beats, but by the pervasive irony of the visual and lyrical content. The aggressive nerdiness of "Lazy Sunday" doesn't free hip-hop from racial signifiers, but explicitly articulates them with whiteness instead. The chorus repeats: "It's the Chronic-WHAT-cles of Narnia," referencing a euphemism for marijuana and the title of a classic hip-hop album produced by Dr. Dre (*The Chronic,* 1992), thereby paying tribute to hip-hop culture. But tweaking that into "Chronicles of Narnia" moves beyond reference into a disavowal of authenticity, eschewing white simulation of black masculinity by refraining from references to, say, "Gin and Juice" or *The Warriors* (1979), and instead embracing *The Chronicles of Narnia,* family-friendly entertainment created by a long-dead British author (and featuring exceptionally pale human characters). All the mundane activities described, while not necessarily racially charged in and of themselves, fall within the overarching narrative of two boring white guys rapping like they live the ultra-masculine fantasy lives of (black) rappers. Although an in-depth consideration of the cultural politics of hip-hop parody is outside the scope of this chapter, it is worth noting the pleasures associated with such crossing of boundaries between black culture and white culture for audiences who have grown up with hip-hop dominating popular music, and who are also aware of the cultural politics of appropriation as represented by artists like Vanilla Ice. "Lazy Sunday" encourages guilt-free enjoyment of this appropriation by suggesting that hip-hop—via parody and irony—can exist free from identity politics.

Like the new math employed by Dumenco that placed Samberg's worth at $342 million, reports of the popularity of Lonely Island clips are so wildly divergent that it's difficult to know which to cite to express the short's meteoric popularity. Ten days after "Lazy Sunday" was originally broadcast, the *New York Times* reported it had been viewed more than 1.2 million times on YouTube.[16] It was viewed 5 million times before NBC pulled the plug and demanded all its content be taken down from the site.[17] Circulation of "Lazy Sunday" is even credited with driving many people to YouTube for the first time, as the site's traffic jumped 83 percent in the weeks following the posting of the video.[18]

More video successes followed in that first season, starting with a hip-hop video starring Natalie Portman that transformed her from low-key *Star Wars* princess and vegan movie star into a Lil' Kim-esque rapping badass. Samberg's biggest success resulted from teaming up with pop star Justin Timberlake and slightly altering the parodic formula by turning to the smooth, 1990s style R&B of acts such as Color Me Badd. Just as "Lazy Sunday" closely mimicked the visual style of hip-hop videos filtered through an amateur aesthetic, "Dick in a Box" mimicked that group's videos like "I Wanna Sex You Up" and "I Adore Mi Amor."

Having decided to control their content on YouTube rather than just demand it be kept off the site, NBC posted an uncensored version of "Dick in a Box" there, and it was viewed by over 2 million people in less than a week. "In the process," wrote Jacques Steinberg, "*Saturday Night Live* appears to have become the first scripted comedy on a broadcast network to use the Web to make an end-run around the prying eyes of both its internal censors and those of the Federal Communications Commission, whose jurisdiction over *Saturday Night Live* effectively ends at the Web frontier."[19] *SNL* producers had requested that an uncensored version be posted online, and NBC was very calculated about choosing how to do so. The executive in charge of late-night programming, Rick Ludwin, only saw the video eight hours before it was scheduled to air on Saturday. After consulting with a representative from NBC's legal department, the president of NBC Entertainment, and even Jeff Zucker (the chief executive of NBCUniversal Television Group) to make sure the move was good, not bad, for the NBC brand, they gave the go-ahead. Ludwin described the network's thinking like this: "Obviously there are some people who will be offended. Those people are probably unlikely to go searching for it on the Internet."[20] By 2009, the Samberg-Timberlake collaboration had been viewed more than 60 million times on video-sharing sites.[21] That success suggests that the Lonely Island's parodic formula has staying power, and the care with which NBC handled the uncensored version reveals a highly considered approach to placing comedy online.

Since 2005, it has become clear that online videos can work as a loss leader for *SNL*, attracting viewers who wouldn't normally tune in to the show. The 2010 prime-time NBC special *Saturday Night Live in the 2000s: Time and Again,* for instance, devotes a significant amount of airtime to the "Digital Shorts" and the value of their viral spread. In the special, producer Michael Shoemaker calls them a "gateway drug" and a "way in for a lot of people to the show." Lorne Michaels is heard acknowledging this as well: "People who hadn't seen the show had seen that [digital short] then that brings them to the show." Whether Michaels is talking about the Saturday night broadcast or the franchise is unclear—and beside the point. Because they are housed alongside other videos from *SNL's* vast comedy archives, the "Digital Shorts" drive viewers to the back catalog on sites such as NBC's own, Hulu, or Yahoo, where the clips air following commercials. Thus, Samberg's new media comedy has the potential to increase the value of the old media products of the franchise since 1975, introducing new audiences to iconic sketches and forgotten material, simultaneously creating new revenue streams and reaffirming the show's cultural significance.

The fact that the Lonely Island immediately got two of its first three videos on the air at *SNL* is impressive and meaningful. The selection process for segments has always been notoriously rigorous, with performers fighting for attention from writers, and writers fighting to get their sketches on the air. Sketches are routinely cut just prior to broadcast following Saturday's dress rehearsal before a live audience. The success of "Lazy Sunday" presumably encouraged Michaels to give the team plenty of leeway to do their thing. The trio no longer pitches ideas for films to Lorne Michaels: they just make them and if Michaels doesn't like them, they don't get on the show. Perhaps this is in exchange for the "new value" the *SNL* "Digital Shorts" bring to the franchise, or perhaps it is just an unspoken recognition that Michaels is out of sync with the new media audience. Says Samberg, "We pitched to him a few times, and he's like, 'Uh, okay . . .' and when it turned out that people liked them, he's like, 'You know what? Just don't tell me, 'cause I'd rather just see it in action.'"[22]

Perhaps this loosening of Michaels's editorial control—at least when it comes to the "Digital Shorts"—is a minor return to how he had initially conceptualized the program: as breaking from "normal" TV and clearing away all the layers that tended to get in between performers and the comedy they were allowed to put on the air. Back in 1976, Michaels told *Rolling Stone,* "I envisioned this show in which all these individual styles were gotten across as purely as possible, with me clearing away the network and technological barricades. This is why *Saturday Night* must stay a *live* show, I've fought for that, to keep it *theater,* a pure communication between writers, players and audience."[23] As the *SNL* empire expanded and became more rigid over the years, Michaels's tastes became a more significant barricade to innovation than were the network's standards and practices.

A key difference from those earlier performances, of course, was that Samberg's chosen method of communication wasn't live, but the filmed, produced, and edited video. Still, the Lonely Island's prerecorded shorts weren't *SNL*'s first. The first season included seven shorts made by comedian Albert Brooks, until he departed following creative disputes with Michaels. In that first season, *SNL* also solicited short films from fans— assuring them they would not be returned and they would not be paid! This resulted in the famous "Mr. Bill" films and a number of other stop-action animations, as the consumer technology of the time largely precluded synced sound. Nonetheless, *SNL* deserves credit for this incorporation of user-generated content, long before that term existed. The lo-fi aesthetic of amateur video apparent in those Super 8 films soon gave way to more polished fare. Over the years, most shorts have been ad parodies, or one-off mock documentaries such as Eddie Murphy's "White Like Me" and the Christopher Guest–directed film starring Martin Short and Harry Shearer as an aspiring (if not inspiring) synchronized swim team. Most shorts aim for the professionalism of serious commercials, documentaries, or other television programs. Thus, in the contemporary context of the show itself, the amateur aesthetic of the Lonely Island makes the *SNL* "Digital Shorts" seem like something new on TV, despite the similarities to what might be online or what *SNL* itself might have screened decades ago.

Aside from the comic sensibility and lo-fi aesthetic of the shorts, *SNL* went to great lengths to establish that Samberg wasn't just a new face, but also a fresh comic voice for the show. He was often paired with fellow new recruit Bill Hader, whose route to the show had been fairly typical, coming up from Second City's LA contingent. Though at first glance both appeared to be the latest boyish imps in the style of Jimmy Fallon and Adam Sandler, their comic sensibilities played off one another on a "Weekend Update" installment in which they competed in an "impression-off." Introduced as new additions to the cast by anchor Amy Poehler, both comedians look young and bright-eyed, sporting shaggy haircuts and track jackets. But when the impression-off begins, a clear distinction is drawn between Hader, who mimics Peter Falk and James Mason, and Samberg, who barely attempts an imitation at all, goofily saying, "Hey, how's it going? I'm Jack Nicholson. Whaaaaatt'sss uuuupp?" Rather than the studied approach to comedy and depth of cultural capital that Hader's impressions suggest, Samberg's cultural knowledge is barely knee deep—played-out beer slogans rather than dead (or at least old) actors. Even if audiences didn't know that Hader came up through the traditional channel of Second City, the joke is that his humor is steeped in entertainment history, while Samberg is the sloppy, new media type, quickly grabbing something from pop culture—not unlike Peter Griffin on *Family Guy* (1999–present).

Despite this, or because of it, the duo has repeatedly appeared together, notably in the Lonely Island's "Laser Cats" sketches, which also play up the generational divide between Samberg's humor and that of *SNL* overlord Michaels. The sketches feature Hader and Samberg wielding cats that have evolved to shoot lasers out of their mouths as futuristic weapons. Despite their enthusiasm, the production values (the skits are

shot in and around the *SNL* offices), props, and special effects fall terrifi-
cally short, as if they were produced by the duo in their spare time. Of
course, this is precisely the point. The shorts are book-ended with presentations to Michaels, who is repeatedly disgusted by their lousy production values and dismisses the two. Their deviation from the *SNL* norm
and from Michaels's taste is thus made the joke. Since Samberg's debut
in 2005, the production values of *SNL* "Digital Shorts" have in many
cases improved dramatically. However, with each installment of a short
with "Laser Cats"-like aesthetics, the myth that nothing material separates the comedy that can be made at home and posted on YouTube from
the comedy that can be put on *SNL* is reintroduced and reaffirmed—all
the more so when we also see that Michaels does not "get" that kind of
comedy.

PIPELINE TO THE MAJORS, OR
PERMANENT MINOR LEAGUE?

Samberg's YouTube popularity promotes the idea that a star can be born
from a digital platform. Though the Internet is heralded as a place without
traditional barriers to entry, it is not a pure meritocracy; comedians must
cultivate certain attributes to distinguish themselves from the crowd.
Whereas traditional comedic venues, comedy clubs, and sketch groups
filter talent based on stage availability and the politics of the stand-up
circuit, the Internet obscures talent with its sheer volume of content.
Breaking through to *SNL* means proving one's worth to entertainment
executives in a variety of ways; cultivating a social network presence;
developing commercial partnerships; and gathering a marketable niche
following. The Internet was originally used as a place for comedians to
test out material and create a calling card with a viral video hit, but increasingly, online comedy is part of a structured talent cultivation system with particular benchmarks that determine if a comedian is ready
for prime time.

While it is true that big-time talent agencies like Creative Artists
and Endeavor are looking for the next Lonely Island, they are also looking for something more than just laughs. In particular, they are looking for comedians who have a marketable fan base. Before the Internet,
amateur filmmakers pinned their hopes of breaking into the industry on

delivering their calling-card short film to the right person and hoping it resonated with him or her.[24] A calling-card video may capture the interest of a producer, but a comedian can strengthen his/her case by demonstrating a marketable following. Alex Lasky, the president of the digital production company Lasky Media, calls the Internet "the new way to package programming" and explains, "With the instant returns from working online, the ability to see results so quickly from the testimonials you get from your fans, the core base of fans and loyalists, you are not just coming in with a pitch, a half-hour pilot. For a fraction of the cost, you produce a steady flow of content, and when you are packaging it, you are walking in with hard results."[25] Industry executives are increasingly expecting these hard results from Internet comedians because these data are compelling indicators of a comedian's market potential.

Proving an understanding of industry conventions and attracting a marketable demographic may not be enough to convince television executives that a given comedian is ready for an *SNL* tryout, however. Aspiring talent must further solidify their reputation as a worthy investment by proving that their work can be revenue generating. The dominant revenue-generating model in the digital space is corporate sponsorship, and the comedians who successfully collaborate with sponsors prove to studios that they understand the importance of industry business models. Jordan Levin, the former chair of the WB network and the current CEO of the multimedia production company and talent agency Generate, specifically searches the Internet for comedic talent that can be married to corporate brands.[26] Levin encourages Generate talent to leverage their personal brands and create "brand relationships" in authentic and organic ways.[27] This description of brand integration is similar to an argument made by Henry Jenkins that the future of advertising is "product integration" and "affective economics," where corporate sponsorships become a part of entertainment content.[28] Levin concedes that not all comedians are comfortable with the idea of corporate sponsorship despite the fact that it is the dominant revenue-generating Internet business model. Those who welcome corporate sponsorship provide talent scouts with the reassurance that they are willing to accept the marriage of art and commerce that is necessary in show business.

The Lonely Island graduated from web series to *SNL* before social networking became a significant outlet for Internet comedy and a popular venue for discovering talent. While it is rare that Twitter feeds become the basis for television sitcoms (though the Twitter feed "Shit My Dad Says" was turned into a short-lived CBS sitcom starring William Shatner from 2010 to 2011), talent agencies have asked comedians to translate their social networking skills to mainstream industry jobs.[29] Comedian Patton Oswalt, for example, fully embraces Twitter because it gives him greater control over his personal brand, and he claims to know several comedy writers who have received industry jobs because television producers followed their Twitter feeds and said to themselves, "[this person] posts eight times a day and it is hilarious every time. . . . Why don't we just hire them because they are meeting the quota that we are not getting from the people we hired?"[30] Oswalt's description of using Twitter to enter the industry sounds remarkably similar to the mythology around online video. Both digital venues represent alternative paths to success that do not require comedians to develop a stand-up act or earn an invitation to do a five-minute routine on a late-night show.[31] Comedians have embraced social media because it offers a different path to stardom while also providing a space for trying out new material and measuring themselves against other members of the comedy community.

It is tempting to believe that digital venues are ushering in a new era of democratic comedy, but this would ignore the ways the industry is standardizing the Internet comedy club. When Lonely Island and other comedians began to use the Internet as a stepping-stone to the mainstream industry, digital production was still in its infancy and was primarily dominated by user-generated content. But even then the entertainment industry was shaping Internet platforms into talent pipelines. Jenkins and Klinger have described the way Lucasfilm and iFilm used Internet video contests to discover talent and to discipline the creativity of their movie fans.[32] Since 2005, the media industries have increased efforts to cultivate their own digital venues, and in the process they have created a system for training up-and-coming talent. Digital production units represent the most prominent form of these minor leagues. Nick Marx points out that Disney, Time Warner, and NBCUniversal launched digital production units to create their own online content, but in the face of competition from YouTube and the worldwide recession, "scaled back their efforts, reshifted focus, or sought to foster talent with an already-formidable following online."[33] The talent assigned to work with the digital production

Figure 12.2. Mindy Kaling and Ellie Kemper in a "Subtle Sexuality" web short.

units are writers with a web presence. The lessons these comedians learn are the same ones that have helped undiscovered talent break into the industry from user-generated websites like Channel 101. They learn to attract marketable demographics, demonstrate an understanding of industry conventions, integrate corporate sponsorship, and manage a social networking presence.

Kaling's success at NBC is an example of the way the Internet comedy club operates within a media conglomerate. Samberg had experimented on the Internet before being discovered; Kaling was asked to make webisodes after establishing a career in the industry. Kaling first made headlines when she and comedian-actor Brenda Withers wrote a two-woman play, *Matt and Ben,* based on the friendship of Matt Damon and Ben Affleck, which was named one of *Time*'s top ten theatrical events of the year. Later, the two comedians were brought to Hollywood to develop a sitcom that never aired. Kaling was then offered a writing job with *The Office* in 2005. As she became more popular on the show, NBC signed her to a larger contract and offered her a television pilot, but before beginning this project, they gave her the opportunity to hone her talent as a showrunner by producing the web series "Subtle Sexuality." *The Office* had done several web series in the past as a way of bridging the gap between seasons and keeping the audience entertained during the summer months. Advertisements from NBC.com's corporate sponsors ran before each episode of the web series, and Kaling promoted the content on her popular Twitter feed. Certainly, there are other shows where established showrunners tweet, run advertisements, parody industry conventions, and appeal to attractive demographics, but it is significant that most web series are not produced by these showrunners. Instead, this digital labor is given to emerging talent, as it is an inexpensive way of testing a comedian's ability to reflect industry production standards. "Subtle Sexuality" became an Internet success and has subsequently earned Kaling the opportunity to direct another web series, broadcast episodes of *The Office*, and her own sitcom on Fox, *The Mindy Project* (2012–present). Kaling's commercial appeal on the digital platform (a social network presence, a loyal fan base, sponsor supported, and generically literate) made her success possible.

CONCLUSION

It is interesting that Kaling's career began with her impersonating a self-made superstar, given the way the Internet comedy club pushes comedians to tap into their inner entrepreneur. Kaling's online presence, via Twitter and other digital projects, has helped her cultivate a brand similar to the auteur status once reserved for the masculine sphere of creative labor. Kaling has parlayed her brand into a national advertising campaign for Healthy Choice and a bestselling book. In the new creative industries, the barriers to entry are not as determined by gender and race, at least not in the same manner as in the previous gatekeeping system, but are dependent on one's mastery of self-promotion, ratings acceptance, and the politics of corporate culture. Kaling and Samberg both learned industry culture through entry-level jobs and demonstrated their understanding of this culture through the low-stakes venue of digital technology. Their success is more of a testament to their understanding of the industry (and NBC's talent cultivation practices) than to the democratic potential of new media.

In May 2011, *Wired* put Samberg on its cover with the bold proclamation "How the Internet Saved Comedy." The interview and associated articles inside were scant, however, falling far short of actually demonstrating how Samberg or the Internet had "saved" comedy. Mostly, Samberg's presence on the cover evidenced that his overdetermined face was expected to appeal to the targeted tech-geek audience, signifying both contemporary, hip comedy and an Internet-trenches-to-Rockefeller-Center success story. To his credit, Samberg played down his own myth of Internet success and the transformative power of the Internet comedy club: "I don't think that the actual quality of content has changed. It's just that now there's another way for you to find it. . . . One of the common misconceptions about the Lonely Island is that we were discovered on the Internet. We actually weren't. A hand-off of a VHS tape is how we got agents, and working on the *MTV Movie Awards* with Jimmy Fallon and producers Mike Shoemaker and Steve Higgins is how we got recommended to *SNL*."[34] In September 2011, Kaling was similarly featured in a *New York Times Magazine* article that spent as much time on her tweets as it did on her role behind the scenes of *The Office*. Kaling's book was coming out, and she had gone from being the only woman on the writing staff to executive producer, and from renting a one-bedroom apartment in an undesirable area of West Hollywood to one of the well-known prizes of TV comedy, the "sitcom house."[35] Both pieces held up their respective TV comedy stars as examples of digital triumphs without talking about how they failed to make much money doing that digital work.

Kaling and Samberg deserve recognition for their ability to transition from digital platforms to mainstream television, but their successes are also evidence of the ways the entertainment industry is taming the wild west of Internet comedy. Those comedians who resonate with a particularly marketable demographic and reflect comedic conventions are most likely to cross over. The promotion of the most commercial comedic talent is shaping the practices and standards of digital labor, creating a blueprint for entering the industry, while at the same time positioning Internet comedy as a support system for traditional media industries. Kaling described the situation perfectly in this tweet: "You got talent, kid. Self-finance a webisode, then we'll shoot a 15 minute mini-sode so we can pitch a live pilot presentation. #hollywood."[36] The Internet and social media may together constitute the most high-profile comedy club ever. But while you don't need to grease a bouncer for stage time or shill for the drink specials, you still have to pay your dues, show industry savvy, and prove you have a certain kind of talent that meets the sweet spot of advertisers—white men with disposable income—and the conventions of television humor.

Notes

1. Dumenco, "What's That Hot Web Property Worth?"
2. Benkler, *The Wealth of Networks,* 4–15.
3. Mayer, *Below the Line,* 20; Caldwell, *Production Culture.*
4. Ibid.
5. Jenkins, *Convergence Culture,* 154–155.
6. "Comedy Central Greenlights *Workaholics.*"
7. For a critical overview of that early boundary pushing (real and imagined), see Day and Thompson, "Live from New York."
8. Vognar, "Web Videos."
9. D'Alessandro, "10 Comics to Watch."
10. Raftery, "With TV Fame Elusive," 14.
11. Klinger, *Beyond the Multiplex,* 233.
12. Sternbergh, "Three Easy Steps to Comedy Stardom."
13. Ibid.
14. Itzkoff, "Nerds in the Hood."
15. Ibid.
16. Ibid.
17. "Privates Joke."
18. Sternbergh, "Three Easy Steps to Comedy Stardom."
19. Steinberg, "Censored *SNL* Sketch."
20. Qtd. ibid.
21. Strauss, "Andy Samberg."
22. Qtd. in Heisler, "The Lonely Island."
23. Burke, "Laughing, Scratching, Mocking," 34.
24. Zimmermann, *Reel Families.*
25. Parpis, "Why the Web Is Not Enough."
26. Jasper Redd and American Eagle Outfitters were connected by Generate to produce the American Eagle Outfitters Campus Challenge, a comedy tour that visits college campuses. http://www.aecomedy.com/blog.
27. Jordan Levin, interview by Media Industries Project, Carsey Wolf Center (part of research for an anthology on digital distribution), Santa Monica, California, May 23, 2011. Transcript in possession of Media Industries Project.
28. Jenkins, *Convergence Culture,* 63.
29. Andreeva, "Twitter User."
30. Simmons, "Patton Oswalt."
31. Ibid.
32. Jenkins, *Convergence Culture,* 154; Klinger, *Beyond the Multiplex,* 198.
33. Marx, "The Missing Link Moment," 14.
34. Hardwick, "Pillow Talk," 150.
35. Sittenfeld, "A Long Day."
36. Mindy Kaling, Twitter post, May 5, 2011, http://twitter.com/MindyKaling.

Works Cited

Andreeva, Nellie. "Twitter User 'Shit My Dad Says' Gets CBS Deal." *Hollywood Reporter,* November 30, 2010, http://www.thrfeed.com/blogs/live-feed/twitter-user-shit -dad-cbs-52537.

Benkler, Yochai. *The Wealth of Networks: How Social Production Transforms Markets and Freedom.* New Haven, CT: Yale University Press, 2006.

Burke, Tom. "Laughing, Scratching, Mocking, Smirking, Stumbling, Bumbling and Pratfalling into the Twisted Hearts and Minds of America . . . Live, from New York . . . It's NBC's . . . *Saturday Night!" Rolling Stone,* July 15, 1976.

Caldwell, John Thornton. *Production Culture: Industrial Reflexivity and Critical Practice in Film and Television.* Durham, NC: Duke University Press, 2008.

"Comedy Central Greenlights *Workaholics* from Avalon Television and Gigapix Studios." March 2, 2010, http://www.comedycentral.com/press/press_releases/2010 /030210_workaholics-greenlight.jhtml.

D'Alessandro, Anthony. "10 Comics to Watch." *Variety,* July 17, 2006, http://www.variety .com/article/VR1117946844.

Day, Amber, and Ethan Thompson. "Live from New York, It's the Fake News!: *Saturday Night Live* and the (Non)Politics of Parody." *Popular Communication: The International Journal of Media and Culture* 10(1–2) (2012):170–182.

Dumenco, Simon. "What's That Hot Web Property Worth?" *Advertising Age,* November 5, 2007, 32.

Hardwick, Chris. "Pillow Talk with Andy Samberg." *Wired,* May 2011.

Heisler, Steve. "The Lonely Island." *A.V. Club,* May 24, 2011, http://www.avclub.com /articles/the-lonely-island,56484.

Itzkoff, Dave. "Nerds in the Hood, Stars on the Web." *New York Times,* December 27, 2005.

Jenkins, Henry. *Convergence Culture: Where Old and New Media Collide.* New York: New York University Press, 2006.

Klinger, Barbara. *Beyond the Multiplex: Cinema, New Technologies, and the Home.* Berkeley: University of California Press, 2006.

Marx, Nick. "The Missing Link Moment: Web Comedy in New Media Industries." *Velvet Light Trap* 68 (Fall 2011):14–23.

Mayer, Vicki. *Below the Line: Producers and Production Studies in the New Television Economy.* Durham, NC: Duke University Press, 2011.

Parpis, Eleftheria. "Why the Web Is Not Enough." *Adweek,* February 4, 2008.

"Privates Joke." *EW,* February 2, 2007, http://www.ew.com/ew/article/0,,20010569,00 .html.

Raftery, Brian. "With TV Fame Elusive, Video-Series Creators Seek Success Online." *New York Times,* March 26, 2005.

Simmons, Bill. "Patton Oswalt." *The B.S. Report with Bill Simmons,* January 18, 2011, http://espn.go.com/espnradio/play?id=6038679.

Sittenfeld, Curtis. "A Long Day at *The Office* with Mindy Kaling." *New York Times Magazine,* September 23, 2011.

Steinberg, Jacques. "Censored *SNL* Sketch Jumps Bleepless onto the Internet." *New York Times,* December 21, 2006.

Sternbergh, Adam. "Three Easy Steps to Comedy Stardom." *New York*, July 15, 2007, http://nymag.com/news/features/34738.

Strauss, Gary. "Andy Samberg Keeps His Comedy Short in *SNL* Videos." *USA Today*, May 15, 2009.

Vognar, Chris. "Web Videos Helped Samberg Snag *Hot Rod*." *Dallas Morning News*, August 3, 2007.

Zimmermann, Patricia. *Reel Families: A Social History of the Amateur Film*. Bloomington: Indiana University Press, 1995.

Sketches Gone Viral: From Watercooler Talk to Participatory Comedy

DAVID GURNEY

Saturday Night Live's thirty-first season started like most others in the prior decade with no major overhauls of the cast, losing only one member from season thirty and adding three relative unknowns. While two of those new faces, Kristen Wiig and Bill Hader, had the typical background of improv/sketch comedians well attuned to the demands of live performance and protean characterizations, the third was a bit of an outlier. Along with his collaborators Jorma Taccone and Akiva Schaffer as writing staff, Andy Samberg was hired based on his proficiency as a writer and as a maker of short-form comedy productions, which had largely found audiences through early use of Internet streaming video. Calling themselves the Lonely Island, the three had built a career in the fluid space of Channel 101's participatory comedy platform and their own dedicated website while concurrently pursuing writing jobs in the television industry.[1] Initially, Samberg, like many new cast members, was a fairly infrequent onscreen presence, but that began to change with the airing of the December 17 episode.

Having only appeared once before, on December 3, a title card announcing "An *SNL* Digital Short" introduced a video about cupcakes, Google Maps, the first *Chronicles of Narnia* film (2005), and other bits of pop culture referentiality, speaking to the habitus of a white middle-class Manhattanite and filtered rather cheekily through a rap song projecting hardcore swagger. Laughter and applause evidenced that "Lazy Sunday" was a hit with the studio audience, but the extent of the clip's and its accompanying song's success truly became clear in the following days when an enterprising fan posted a recording of it on YouTube.[2] Conceived of and created by the Lonely Island and set apart by its "*SNL* Digital Short" designation, "Lazy Sunday" served as a breakout performance for Samberg and a rather novel one at that. While *SNL* has a long history of including prerecorded films and videos from even its earliest days between 1975 and 1977 as *NBC's Saturday Night*,[3] for a cast member and two staff writers to generate such content on their own was largely not done. It was also a first as a moment of digital transmedial popularity for the program. Furthermore, while YouTube had gained a modest level of public recognition in its first year of existence, "Lazy Sunday" was one of the first clips to achieve a great deal of its popularity via a posting (and various mirror postings) on the website and, in turn, the short amplified the public profile of the soon-to-be-ubiquitous video-sharing website.

From its inception, *SNL* has been a potent generator of catchy bits of comic culture or, in popular Internet parlance, "memes."[4] One of the earliest examples of this is the line "Generalissimo Francisco Franco is still dead," used by Chevy Chase repeatedly throughout the "Weekend Update" segments of the first season. As a parody of the repetitious coverage of the dictator's impending death, the line continues to be used as a shorthand jab at the predictable cycles of coverage that often follow news stories long after they have been sufficiently reported. Doing a quick Internet search for the phrase will reveal its continued cachet, as it is still used frequently in news blogs and television news broadcasts alike.[5] In the years since, there have been numerous other catchphrases that have become part of the popular lexicon. They are often associated with particular recurring characters, for instance the Coneheads (Dan Aykroyd, Jane Curtin, and Laraine Newman) announcing their intention to "Consume mass quantities," or Matt Foley's (Chris Farley) repeated warning, "You'll be living in a van down by the river." *SNL* fans repeat, reuse, and recontextualize these expressions in their daily lives. Such acts of participatory amateur comedy have long aided the expansion of the program's influence beyond just those viewers who watch the initial live broadcasts. Correspondingly, many of the most quotable or imitable characters have been used as conduits for *SNL* performers, writers, and producers to move into film. Mike Myers's Wayne Campbell and Dan Aykroyd and John Belushi's Blues Brothers may be the most successful cases of this, but even more obscure characters like Al Franken's Stuart Smalley and Julia Sweeney's Pat found their way to cinema screens. Much of what made such transmedial leaps seem financially viable were the apparent public embrace and reenactment of sketches and characters, which marked them as comic material with cultural traction.

This speaks to SNL having, throughout its history, repeatedly touched off cascading assemblages of viewer engagement, which have long made its pop culture presence more pervasive than its ratings alone have indicated. While the ratings for the Saturday night broadcasts may have permanently dipped in the post-network era,[6] one clear indicator that SNL is maintaining a rhizomatic relevance is the vibrant second life (no outdated pun intended) it enjoys online. Beyond the posting of previously aired clips on NBC's official website, Hulu, and Yahoo, numerous sketches spawn tributes, adaptations, and remixes in the era of video sharing. This is especially the case with the ongoing "Digital Shorts" series. This chapter will explore some of the instances in which viewer engagement with SNL has become more apparent and dynamic online as well as the sometimes precarious relationship that SNL's producers have maintained with that engagement, especially in the earliest phase of streaming video's popularization. In many ways, SNL's introduction of its "Digital Shorts" series serves as a clear example of the growing pains of television comedy, and television content more generally, as it has been forced to come to terms with a more transmedial and publicly visible form of participatory popular culture.

LAZY PARTICIPATION, CONTENT LOCKDOWN

Fan appropriation of SNL material, or any other television sketch comedy material for that matter, has been underappreciated by media scholars, and these programs rarely attract attention in the way that many science fiction and fantasy-based media texts do. As sketch comedy often lacks any cohesive and expansive diegetic universe, this makes some sense. However, the predilection for quotation and mimicry of characters and skits from SNL and other similar segmented comedy programs, such as Monty Python's Flying Circus (1969–1974), Rowan & Martin's Laugh-In

(1968–1973), and *Second City Television* (1976–1984), is readily apparent. Just to focus on "classic" *SNL* for a moment, the Blues Brothers, the Festrunk Brothers, Judy Miller, and Father Guido Sarducci[7] have remained cultural touchstones for many fans, who use them as bases for costumes, amateur skits, and general buffoonery. Clearly, mediated comedy, especially character based and short form, has long enjoyed a hardy, if analytically ignored, participatory fan culture.

Of course, in the past, much of this activity was locally contained and mostly ephemeral. However, "Lazy Sunday" appeared at the precipice of a moment where the characteristics of networked media were quite pronouncedly coming into the hands of audiences. No longer did a clever (or terrible) imitation have to stay confined to one's close circle of friends.[8] Through the relatively accessible technologies of digital video and the Internet, even the most isolated recreation could be captured and uploaded for nearly unlimited sharing or broadcast. In other words, what once might have been a Church Lady imitation done for the audience at a high school talent show could now be made available to almost anyone with an Internet connection. Of course, there is no quality filter or content arbiter involved either. Still, the operations of video virality have a way of parsing the good (or so bad it's good) from the bad.

The participatory element is a rather strong component of cultural virality in general. But it is somewhat misleading to treat virality and participation as new phenomena when describing contemporary cultural activity. As others have noted, the circulation of memes is not really something new, but rather something old reemerging. Raymond Williams proposes that any given cultural moment should not simply be seen as dominated by particular forms of expression, but rather as a dynamic field of dominant, residual, and emerging cultural forms in flux, and through this framework, we can see the participatory and viral elements of contemporary popular culture as residual practices partially misread as emergent through their alignment with new technologies.[9] As much as a digital mash-up artist may seem to be creating in a new mode, musical rhythms and melodies have long been transferred and transposed within and across folk and high culture settings of the past. While cultural transmission in the twentieth century was often characterized by the expansive, global reach of content through various mass media, it was just as marked by a perversely artificial lockdown of the content.

Lawrence Lessig makes this argument cogently through his discussion of read-only and read-write cultures.[10] Cultural expression had always been read-write, where an audience member could remake or work with any material she experienced. The emergence of a lucrative mass market for culture beyond live performance was only achieved when recording technologies allowed such things to be locked down by commercial media industries. Consequently, to speak of participation and viral (user-to-user[s]) spread as something novel is inaccurate, even if not intentionally so. In fact, they are evidence of a resurgence of aspects of popular/folk culture that were, for a relatively short time, suppressed.

With that said, virality is a useful metaphor for describing the mechanisms of cultural transmission. I have elaborated these reasons elsewhere, but here I will synopsize that the biological virus points us to both the mode of user-to-user(s) spread and the recombinant qualities of culture, particularly through modes of comedy.[11] Thus, after "Lazy Sunday" was broadcast, it found its way to an audience beyond the size of that initial Saturday night airing by being posted on YouTube, emailed from friend to friend, and eventually touted by several other outposts of Internet culture, including *Boing Boing* and *Slate* magazine.[12] Described as a web phenomenon with the potential to breathe new life into *SNL* by attracting younger viewers, the clip's virality moved beyond a static spread where users simply forwarded the link to one another and became something more mutable and recombinant in nature when users began creating other versions of the material. Such mutation and recombination is a key to the success of the virus, whether one is discussing biology or culture. One of the first notable variations on "Lazy Sunday" came in the form of "Lazy Monday," a video crafted as a direct "West Coast response" by two aspiring filmmakers, Sam Friedlander and Adam Stein, and their production partner, actor Mark Feuerstein. Opening by calling out Samberg and Parnell for posturing as though their *SNL* bona fides make them "bad," the song and video closely follow the original's template with Stein and Feuerstein bragging about mundane aspects of their LA-based days, including painting their own pottery, ordering fancy coffee drinks, and listening to NPR while stuck in traffic. Though it uses a different backing track, its relationship is clear through the callout and the juxtaposition of menacing (if measured) rapping and slight lyrical content recounting a daily routine.

Figure 13.1. "Lazy Ramadi," the "Lazy Sunday" takeoff made by two U.S. soldiers stationed in Iraq in 2006.

Posted a month after "Lazy Sunday," "Lazy Monday" was featured by other web destinations, including the *CollegeHumor* website and *USA Today*'s Pop Candy blog, and on television via G4's *Attack of the Show!* (2005–2012) and VH1's short-lived *Web Junk* (2006). It was only the beginning of a series of even less industry-connected spoofs and responses coming from a diverse array of sources, including improv comedy troupes ("Lazy Muncie"), business school students ("Crazy Monday"), and precocious tweens (another "Lazy Monday" based in Chicago rather than LA). One of the most popular and notable of these parodic rap responses is "Lazy Ramadi," an entry made by two staff sergeants, Matt Wright and Josh Dobbs, both Muncie, Indiana, natives who were stationed in Iraq in the winter of 2006 and who had enjoyed the playful online exchange between *SNL* and some of their hometown's talent. After being circulated online, Wright and Dobbs's short found further exposure through mentions and interviews on Fox News, MSNBC, ABC's *20/20* (1978–present), and NBC's *The Tonight Show with Jay Leno* (1992–present). Making light of the enlisted soldiers' vacillation between boredom bred of isolation and the tension of living and working in a war zone, the clip brought a new and perhaps unlikely (though still comic) weight to the expansive but otherwise light assemblage.

I use the concept of the assemblage in the spirit of Gilles Deleuze and Felix Guattari's rhizomatic approach to understanding social activity.[13] In brief, the assemblage is a fluid way of describing social and cultural relations, and consequently it nicely describes the flow of a media text like "Lazy Sunday" through various transmedial channels. Rather than place and bracket off such a text into a discrete category like "*SNL* sketch," an assemblage approach emphasizes the diversity of connections it has with other media texts and cultural practices. Essentially, no single way of categorizing a text should be considered finite or complete but instead should be seen as only conditional and partial. Thus, while we could call "Lazy Sunday" a late-night television hip-hop video parody, that's not all it is (or can be). It is obviously connected to a long line of musical parodies and, even more specifically, to hip-hop parodies like Weird Al Yankovic's "Amish Paradise" or Jim Carrey's take on Vanilla Ice's "Ice Ice Baby" from *In Living Color* (1990–1994). However, it also finds relationships with other strains of cultural activity (i.e., other assemblages), including video sketches by regional comedy troupes, media presentations made for class projects, and videos by soldiers overseas capturing their versions of the experience of war.

This last video is noteworthy in that it is both something culturally specific and something culturally dispersed. A prominent cultural manifestation of the U.S. wars of the early twenty-first century—the sharing of soldier-made videos through video-hosting sites—has been widely chronicled, and like most online video, acts as an assemblage.[14] One can, and many have, unified them by referring to them as "soldier videos," but imposing genre frameworks on them tends to obscure the wide variety of practices with which they are in conversation, ranging from the somewhat obvious modalities of home video to direct parodies of popular television programs.

Amid this viral activity, where the cultural model of "Lazy Sunday" came to be recombined with other settings and habituses, NBC's actions initially ranged from neutral to encouraging. As the clip gained Internet buzz, NBC posted it on its own website while making a downloadable version available for free through iTunes. However, this course was reversed roughly two months later, when the network chose to capitalize on its digital popularity by locking down the original.[15] Initially, the viewer-uploaded YouTube version of "Lazy Sunday" and several mirror postings had been allowed to coexist alongside the network-sanctioned versions, but in February, NBC asked the site to remove these posts and instead direct any frustrated users to the official NBC website.[16] Aside from the basic inconvenience this caused for those who had linked to the URL for the original posting, the NBC video player was, at that time, virtually inoperable for Mac users. This was a particular point of irony given that the only other way NBC was making the clip available was through Apple's iTunes where the clip, once a free download, now cost $1.99.

Of course, these moves were not unexpected in the sense that NBC wanted to maximize its opportunity to profit from owned content, but the moves were unfortunate in that they were punishing the users and platform that had helped to keep the sketch relevant long after the night of its initial broadcast. Perhaps it is unfair to expect that during this early, explosive moment in the growth of online video sharing an established mass media corporation would put primary focus on the value of publicity and increased brand recognition, especially within a younger demographic. However, even the typical argument made by the likes of the Recording Industry Association of America and the Motion Picture Association of America—that unauthorized postings of copyrighted content take away from the revenues that would otherwise flow to the content owners—has little direct applicability here. As a television broadcast, the revenue stream for content like "Lazy Sunday" historically would have come in the form of advertising during the initial airing and any subsequent broadcasts through reruns or syndication, not through direct sales.[17] If the concern was that people watching the clip online would have reduced interest in the reruns or syndicated broadcasts, that seems counterintuitive given the logic that has underpinned the "regimes of repetition" that Derek Kompare locates across the mass media industries of the twentieth century.[18] One would expect that repeat viewers are a mix of those who want to experience the episode again after having already seen it broadcast and those who have heard positive things about the broadcast from others who already watched it.

Perhaps the best explanation for NBC's YouTube takedown request was that it wanted to control the flow of its content across this "new" medium, turning it into a direct revenue generator via a digital store like iTunes. However, attempting to impose a new twist in the company's business model upon an object that had already been put into circulation and widely touted as an exemplary participatory phenomenon obviously chafed some fans in ways that may have harmed *SNL*'s, if not the network's, brand. Having already offered the content for free via the television broadcast, YouTube, NBC's website, and even the iTunes store, trying to recapture the object and lock it down to charge for it, with little discernible value added, mostly stifled this early instance of public enchantment with the operation of a more visible cultural virality. Especially for a program with a long track record of ebb and flow in audience interest and critical esteem, the viral second life of "Lazy Sunday" was helping *SNL* to gain traction with the potential of broadening and extending audience engagement in a way that might make the show's reruns gain interest and might highlight subsequent live telecasts as appointment viewing. Of course, contending with the uncertainty of an evolving field of new technology, the takedown was likely an attempt by NBC to assert control over its content in a manner that could be viewed as an important, even if incidentally painful, precedent. Still, in hindsight, this early strategy mostly served to momentarily sour some of the potential new audiences that this bit of *SNL* content was finding, especially given the way that the network has become less diligent (or at least more diverse) in its policing since.

ENGAGING MEMES, CREATING MEMES

Amid the activity following "Lazy Sunday," the Lonely Island, in collaboration with other cast members, writers, and guests, created nine more digital shorts that aired over the course of the remaining ten episodes of the thirty-first season. Among those were more song parodies, including "Natalie's Rap," which treads very similar territory to that of "Lazy Sunday," juxtaposing the trappings of more hard-hitting hip-hop production with the star persona of the waifish, typically soft-spoken, and unmistakably white Natalie Portman.[19] Joined by Parnell, the short is clearly an extension of the same basic logic underpinning "Lazy Sunday." It does heighten the incongruity of the first song by including Portman, in effect expanding an assemblage the shorts had already entered. Incorporating

Figure 13.2. Andy Samberg as Young Chuck Norris alongside *SNL* cast mate
Jason Sudeikis.

Portman's celebrity status into this assemblage only helped to increase
the group's profile, as well as that of its semi-autonomous series.

The "Digital Shorts" series further expanded to include connections to
other viral assemblages, many of them already apparent in online circles
of exchange. A key instance of this is "Young Chuck Norris," which aired
even before "Natalie's Rap." Using another star persona as the basis for
a song parody, the short masquerades as a video for a soft metal tribute
song by Doug Brogar (Jason Sudeikis), fictionally recounting the early
exploits of action star Chuck Norris (Andy Samberg) with a pronounced
sheen of hypermasculine deification:

> Fathers let your daughters know,
> Dreams may come and dreams may go,
> But a man like Norris never dies,
> He lives forever in the children's eyes.

Certainly, to many viewers, these lines were almost pure absurdist non
sequiturs. However, to those who were spending time in various Internet
chat forums or in email-forwarding circles, a faux mythological approach
to Chuck Norris was not unfamiliar.[20]

In the immediate aftermath of the 2004 merger of NBC and Vivendi
Universal, *Late Night with Conan O'Brien* (1993–2009) began a recurring
bit where O'Brien would pull a lever to trigger a seemingly random clip of

Norris from his titular role in *Walker, Texas Ranger* (1993–2001); the footage was now royalty-free for the NBCUniversal-produced *Late Night.*[21] Though a clear link is hard to make, this comic appropriation of Norris likely helped touch off something of a viral boost in his celebrity status in the online forums of *Something Awful* during the summer of 2005. A meme of "Chuck Norris Facts" took Norris as a template upon which to hang claims of outrageous strength, power, and general omnipotence, all as great exaggerations of the action hero's hypermasculine film and television roles. A few of the more popular entries included:

> Chuck Norris counted to infinity. Twice.
> Chuck Norris doesn't cheat death. He wins fair and square.
> Chuck Norris once visited the Virgin Islands. They are now The Islands.[22]

Internet users have generated hundreds more of these (and are still generating new ones to some extent). Using this actor, who is more known for his dexterity and strength than for his nuanced delivery of dialogue, as a screen upon which to project images of an untenably idealized masculinity became a means for stealthily critiquing cultural assumptions surrounding gender and power.

"Young Chuck Norris" thus became an elaborate extension of the already extant meme. It was less a fresh take on a new topic than an entry into an ongoing conversation—a conversation that, at least in tone, had even earlier roots. These messy origins for the comic appropriation of Norris underscore just how fluidly codes of popular culture move into and out of Internet culture. They also highlight the participatory ferment of online comedy in which the Lonely Island had found an initial space to create content as amateurs and from which they were drawing material even after having moved into more professional positions. That they were participating in this growing meme at roughly the same time that NBC was preparing to lock down "Lazy Sunday" underscores that complex and somewhat contradictory logics were at play in the network's relationship with participatory culture.

Of course, that *SNL* was borrowing from the mediascape to make a bit of satirical comedy was nothing new. The program had always used the pop culture landscape as a template upon which to base its sketches, but there was something novel about the source here. In this period, Chuck Norris was a cultural figure largely out of the spotlight. His flagship series (*Walker*) had ceased production years before, and he had not fully segued into his later career of using his celebrity persona as a platform for various conservative political candidates and causes. Clearly, the *Late Night* bit helped to position Norris as an object for comic appropriation, and the "Chuck Norris Facts" meme had proven such appropriation to be viable in a more open participatory mode. In this transmedial mix of television and Internet comedy, both professional comedians and fans (ironic or otherwise) could revive Norris in a public manner, ultimately making his persona into a blank canvas upon which to crack wise about masculinity.

As with "Lazy Sunday," there have been remakes, homages, and other user-generated content that play directly on "Young Chuck Norris." Many of the remakes take their music directly from the *SNL* short, while recreating the footage with video-game engines (e.g., "Oblivion: Young Chuck Norris Is Born Music Video"), anime (e.g., "Sailor Moon Young Chuck Norris"), and amateur live-action recordings. Perhaps the most ambitious of the live-action offerings is a five-episode YouTube series, *The Adventures of Young Chuck Norris,* that depicts a younger man playing Norris and performing some of the amazing feats described in various "Chuck Norris Facts." Although this can be seen productively as part of an assemblage inspired by the *SNL* clip, the preexisting popularity of Chuck Norris as a simultaneously revered and mocked public figure makes it and its offshoots seem less a new thing than a part of a media flow already in progress. As seen with "Lazy Sunday," such live-action restagings or reimaginings are common responses, and amateurishness, rather than simply functioning as a marker of inferiority, is a quality which the "Digital Shorts" themselves share and celebrate.

AMATEUR AESTHETICS AND
PARTICIPATORY SERIALITY

Embracing amateur production values is a recurring aesthetic touchstone throughout the "Digital Shorts" series. "Laser Cats," a series within the series, is a clear case of this. First introduced in the thirty-first season, with additional installments in subsequent seasons, "Laser Cats" openly plays with the aesthetic results of the lower budgets associated with user-generated online videos. Consequently, it functions as a loving, and mocking, homage to the amateur quality of much online video culture while maintaining the connection to that assemblage, which already included the Lonely Island's pre-*SNL* work. Such satirical embrace of the amateur is not unprecedented for *SNL,* as it clearly recalls the public access send-up of the "Wayne's World" series of sketches from the late 1980s and early 1990s. In addition, "Laser Cats" is also a satire of the Lonely Island's position within the hierarchy of *SNL's* production system and the status of the "Digital Shorts" as semi-autonomous segments within the program.

Each episode follows the same basic pattern as the first; the short begins in Lorne Michaels's office with Samberg and Hader pitching their idea for a "short film" that they would like included in the show. The initial installment's pitch revolves around lasers and cats being the "two things that everyone loves," and their concept is to combine them. Subsequent episodes have them providing additional rationales, including making the story a musical with Tom Hanks and utilizing 3D technology with the blessing of James Cameron, but all are met with the same disdain from Michaels. The pair and whatever backers they bring along assure him that he will like what they have made and, to further assert the low-budget quality of their production, proceed to insert a cassette into a VCR to show the short to Michaels. These framing moments for the segments satirize the dynamic of the Lonely Island as a production unit within the larger production concerns of *SNL,* casting their efforts as a bothersome thorn in Michaels's side.[23]

In the first episode, a brief *Star Wars*–like (and, thus, *Flash Gordon*–like) scrolling-text introduction lays out the absurd premise that the aftermath of a future nuclear war has resulted in a world where cats shoot lasers from their mouths. It unfolds with the unsubtly named Admiral Spaceship (Samberg) and Nitro (Hader) using the laser cats to defend themselves against evil users of the cats. Their costumes are a cobbled-together hodgepodge of household items, including a football helmet, a headband, and a towel used as a cape. The cats go back and forth between live house cats and stuffed animals with little regard for continuity. The locations, including Central Park, the halls of 30 Rockefeller Center, and the NBC commissary, are used without any attempt to dress them differently, giving the short (within the short) the production (non)design of a home video. Samberg, in particular, seems to be lost at different points throughout, claiming not to understand the gestures that Hader is making and periodically looking directly into the camera. The princess-in-peril character is the unsuspecting guest host, Lindsay Lohan, who meets Hader and Samberg's request for a line of dialogue (affirming that their characters have had sex) with an exclamation of "What? No!," at which point cast member Rachel Dratch is briefly inserted (in a manner very obviously breaking continuity) in order to willingly deliver such a line. The special effects, mostly superimposed laser beams shooting from the stuffed cats, are perhaps the most well done aspect of the shorts, which otherwise revel in a do-it-yourself home video quality.

The "Laser Cats" shorts close with Michaels either pronouncing each entry to be terrible or simply asking the pair to leave his office. In this way, the frame underscores the outsider status that the separate designation of *SNL* "Digital Shorts" confers on the broader series. It serves as an overt performance where Michaels, a clear signifier of *SNL* as a mass media institution, is the gatekeeper plagued by the amateur silliness of something that would be more at home on YouTube. This framing actually serves to set the playful amateur aesthetics of some *SNL* "Digital Shorts" apart from the similar moves of subsequent late-night television comedy like *Tim and Eric Awesome Show, Great Job!* (2007–2010) and the related *Check It Out! with Dr. Steve Brule* (2010–present). These more recent shows connect more closely to the conceit of *SCTV* (and "Wayne's World" to some extent) with their fictional setting being a public access station. Like the "Digital Shorts" moniker, the framing of "Laser Cats" situates it as an invasive amateur aesthetic, more of the online variety, virally infecting network television's higher standards. In essence, it foregrounds the amateur Internet origins of the Lonely Island's brand of comedy even more overtly than does "Young Chuck Norris."

Although the amateur production values of the shorts within the shorts are certainly a target of the comedy in the "Laser Cats" series, they also serve to make the series an easily replicable and recombinant code for amateur videomakers to embrace. Viewers have created their own installments, without much alteration, of the "Laser Cats" series. Many of these user-generated versions even retain the framing mechanism of having their "Laser Cats" introduced as a video being pitched to an unimpressed authority figure. One example of this can be found on the YouTube channel for the high school ministry contingent of the Dallas, Texas, megachurch Watermark Community Church (username watermarkstudents). Their "Laser Cats" is a close remake that retains the narrative framing by having two members of the high school ministry pitching their video to the program's coordinator.[24] Having attained over a half million views, the clip is the most popular of the direct "Laser Cats" responses. The makers did nothing to imprint a Christian message on the piece; however, the message in the video's description does provide insight as to how the video was intended to function as a fortifier within their faith community: "We re-did the *SNL* skit for a large group of students at our church who (mostly) hadn't seen the original. Some of them thought it was more funny seeing people that they know play the roles. We can understand how it would be less funny and even annoying to someone who doesn't know us personally."[25]

Given the view count, it is nearly certain that a great number of non–church members have enjoyed the remake, but the sentiment gets to the core of what drives much of the participatory comedy that surrounds the *SNL* "Digital Shorts" series. While certain examples like this and "Lazy Ramadi" have broad appeal, many of the videos uploaded in response are more humbly recontextualizing these pieces for specific niche audiences who will appreciate a localized spin on television comedy. Just like water cooler mimics redoing Hans and Franz for their officemates, most online tributes are made not to attain a mammoth viewer count, but to offer something close to home for friendly viewers.

One other prominent recurring subseries within the "Digital Shorts" warrants mention for its heavy fan participation and general viral popularity. Samberg and guest host Justin Timberlake play a musical duo with a sound reminiscent of smooth R&B acts of the 1990s, perhaps most clearly the group Color Me Badd. The first installment, "Dick in a Box," aired during the Christmas episode of the thirty-second season, approximately one year after "Lazy Sunday" made its appearance. With an ostensible holiday theme, the music video finds the duo describing their technique for inserting their penises in wrapped boxes to be given as gifts to their girlfriends. A wholly ridiculous premise that loses its comic bite when synopsized, the short excels in how heartily it embraces the subject. The music is a convincing simulation with squealing synthesizer and a slow-jam drum-machine beat, and Timberlake's tenor carries the lead vocal deftly. Subject matter aside, it could have been a Top 40 radio staple from 1991. However, Samberg's forced bass performance brings a bit of silliness into the mix, which is only amplified by the duo's clothing and the video in general. With both men and their love interests (Wiig and Maya Rudolph) dressed in styles of that era, the visuals underscore the humor. Yet, despite the music and style being anachronistic, the overt sexuality of the lyrics match well the song that first put their clearest parodic target on the map, Color Me Badd's "I Wanna Sex You Up."

Of course, when it was aired during the *SNL* broadcast, the lyrics were censored, bleeping out the offending "dicks," but the postings on the NBC website and later on Hulu and YouTube offered both censored and uncensored versions. Certainly, fewer church groups responded with their own versions of this song, but it was met with at least one very popular female rejoinder in the form of Leah Kauffman's "My Box in a Box," which appeared less than two weeks later. For Kauffman, who would later go on to even greater viral success co-founding the website *Barely Political* and writing its most popular early song parody, "I Got a Crush on Obama," this was only the first successful step into Internet comedy. Another popular female take came in the form of "How to Get a Guy in Silicon Valley" (aka "Mac in My Top") in which YouTubers RandiandJen satirically explain how to woo a technology nerd with Apple products stuffed into their shirts.

The online popularity of the video also evidenced a distinct (if fleeting) attitude change on the part of NBC and their lawyers in that the numerous unsanctioned online postings were ignored.[26] In fact, in the time between the network's cease-and-desist actions against YouTube just a few months prior and the "Dick in a Box" airing, NBC had inked a deal with YouTube to use the video-sharing site as a venue for authorized promotional videos of the network's programming.[27] Though details of the arrangement were not shared publicly, it seemed likely that this was an indication that NBC was reassessing the value of the Internet as a facilitator of viral popularity. However, this arrangement did not last; less than one year later, the network announced its partnership (alongside companies like News Corporation) with Hulu, a more locked-down online video-streaming venture that would keep control of copyrighted content in the hands of its backers.[28] All this played out against the backdrop of Viacom's more overt (and largely unsuccessful) legal actions against YouTube.[29]

Yet, the arrival of Hulu did not spell the end for *SNL* or the "Digital Shorts" as a presence in online culture. *SNL* continued to include regular installments in the series into its thirty-seventh season, and the videos regularly enjoy healthy fan circulation and participation online, including on YouTube. Many of the postings of the original (i.e., not fan-remade) shorts are made through the Lonely Island's official director's account on YouTube. This account clearly has ties with NBC sister company Universal Republic, the recording label that releases music albums collecting many of the trio's song parodies, and this relationship is indicative of the balance being maintained between the economic concerns of mass media as an industry and the open culture of video-sharing websites. The Universal Republic albums have been one way that the Lonely Island has found professional success beyond *SNL,* along with producing many additional non-*SNL* shorts for their website and making feature films (*Hot Rod* [2007] and *MacGruber* [2010]). Taccone chose to quit the show after the thirty-fifth season, though he continued to work on several shorts for the show well after his official departure.[30] However, the exit of Samberg following the conclusion of the thirty-seventh season likely signals that the *SNL* "Digital Shorts" boutique has come to an end.[31] While *SNL* has seen other boosts in popularity in this period, particularly with Tina Fey's repeated appearances as Sarah Palin in the thirty-fourth season, the close affiliation of the "Digital Shorts" with cultures of viral comedy has certainly worked to bring another renewal of cultural relevance to the mix. Given its track record, one would not be foolhardy to believe that another such renewal will likely follow the Lonely Island's full departure, though now it seems certain that the participatory comedy that has always surrounded the program will continue to be increasingly visible.

Notes

1. "The 'Bu"; "Home Page."
2. Colbourne, "How a Rap Rode the Web-Craze Wave"; Itzkoff, "Nerds in the Hood."
3. Gurney, "Give Me That Old Time Virality."
4. While the term "meme" is now a colloquialism used to describe nearly any popular Internet trend, it does have a broader point of genesis rooted in evolutionary science. Richard Dawkins coined the term to describe how certain cultural fragments (and he was intentionally vague in this terminology) were particularly catchy and thus displayed characteristics like those genetic mutations that seem to be naturally selected. See Dawkins, *The Selfish Gene,* 189–201.
5. "Transcripts: The Situation Room 2–8–07."
6. Ratings for almost all broadcast television have steadily dropped since their peaks in the 1980s. See Gorman, "Primetime Network Nielsen TV Ratings Trends."

7. The Sarducci character actually has even earlier televisual roots with prior appearances on both *Rowan & Martin's Laugh-In* and *The Smothers Brothers Comedy Hour.*

8. This moment of increasing accessibility of media making and distribution via digital tools and networks is described in Jenkins, *Convergence Culture.*

9. Williams, "Base and Superstructure in Marxist Cultural Theory."

10. Lessig, *Remix.*

11. Gurney, "Recombinant Comedy, Transmedial Mobility, and Viral Video."

12. "*Chronic-WHAT-cles of Narnia*"; Levin, "The Chronicles of Narnia Rap."

13. Deleuze and Guattari, *A Thousand Plateaus.* Manuel DeLanda's more recent elaboration of this concept of the assemblage is what guides my own usage. DeLanda, *A New Philosophy of Society.*

14. Christensen, "Hey Man, Nice Shot."

15. Kerwin, "NBC Doesn't Believe in Viral"; Jardin, "NBC Nastygrams YouTube over 'Lazy Sunday.'"

16. "Lazy Sunday."

17. Of course, *SNL* has increasingly been repackaged for direct sale in best-of DVD compilations and in box sets of each season's broadcasts.

18. Kompare, *Rerun Nation.*

19. The song is a close parody of Eazy-E's "No More ?'s."

20. Captain Blubber, "Chuck Norris Facts."

21. It should be noted that Universal did not own the rights to *Walker, Texas Ranger,* though its USA network did show reruns of the program at the time.

22. "Top 100 Facts for Chuck Norris."

23. This same dynamic was earlier used as comic material by Robert Smigel's *Saturday TV Funhouse* segments, which had a cartoon version of Michaels saying, "Come back here with my show," while chasing after a small white cartoon dog that appears to be ripping into an *SNL* bumper to reveal each *Funhouse* installment.

24. In an even more recursive mode of recombinant framing, the frame is framed by an introduction mimicking television's *24* (2001–2010). It seems included to further heighten the absurdity of the clip.

25. watermarkstudents, "Laser Cats."

26. Teinowitz, "Skit's Web Popularity."

27. Sandoval, "NBC Strikes Deal."

28. Sandoval, "NBCUniversal Confirms."

29. Fabrikant and Hansell, "Viacom Tells YouTube."

30. Heisler, "The Lonely Island."

31. Elber, "Andy Samberg Leaving *SNL.*"

Works Cited

Captain Blubber. "Chuck Norris Facts." *Know Your Meme,* http://knowyourmeme.com /memes/chuck-norris-facts#.TmAIw5gwnWw (accessed August 14, 2012).

Christensen, Christian. "'Hey Man, Nice Shot': Setting the Iraq War to Music on YouTube." In *The YouTube Reader,* edited by Pelle Snickars and Patrick Vonderau, 204–217. Stockholm: National Library of Sweden, 2009.

"*Chronic-WHAT-cles of Narnia* Spreads Like Frosting." *Boing Boing,* December 30, 2005, http://boingboing.net/2005/12/30/chronicwhatcles_of_n.html.

Colbourne, Scott. "How a Rap Rode the Web-Craze Wave." *Globe and Mail*, December 23, 2005, http://www.lexisnexis.com.turing.library.northwestern.edu/hottopics /lnacademic.

Dawkins, Richard. *The Selfish Gene*. Oxford: Oxford University Press, 1989.

DeLanda, Manuel. *A New Philosophy of Society: Assemblage Theory and Social Complexity*. London: Continuum, 2006.

Deleuze, Gilles, and Felix Guattari. *A Thousand Plateaus: Capitalism and Schizophrenia*, translated by Brian Massumi. Minneapolis: University of Minnesota Press, 1987.

Elber, Lynn. "Andy Samberg Leaving *SNL*." *SFGate*, June 24, 2012, http://www.sfgate .com/news/article/Andy-Samberg-leaving-SNL-3606083.php.

Fabrikant, Geraldine, and Saul Hansell. "Viacom Tells YouTube: Hands Off." *New York Times*, February 3, 2007, https://www.nytimes.com/2007/02/03/technology/03tube .html.

Gorman, Bill. "Primetime Network Nielsen TV Ratings Trends 1954–2008." *TV by the Numbers*, October 1, 2008, http://tvbythenumbers.zap2it.com/2008/10/01/primetime -network-tv-trends-1954–2008/5500.

Gurney, David. "Give Me That Old Time Virality." *FlowTV*, March 21, 2009, http:// flowtv.org/2009/03/give-me-that-old-time-viralitydavid-gurney-northwestern -university.

———. "Recombinant Comedy, Transmedial Mobility, and Viral Video." *Velvet Light Trap* 68 (Fall 2011):3–13.

Heisler, Steve. "The Lonely Island." *A.V. Club*, May 24, 2011, http://www.avclub.com /articles/the-lonely-island,56484.

"Home Page." *The Lonely Island*. http://www.thelonelyisland.com (accessed August 14, 2012).

Itzkoff, Dave. "Nerds in the Hood, Stars on the Web." *New York Times*, December 27, 2005, http://www.nytimes.com/2005/12/27/arts/television/27samb.html.

Jardin, Xeni. "NBC Nastygrams YouTube over 'Lazy Sunday.'" *Boing Boing*, February 17, 2006, http://boingboing.net/2006/02/17/nbc_nastygrams_youtu.html.

Jenkins, Henry. *Convergence Culture*. New York: New York University Press, 2006.

Kerwin, Ann Marie. "NBC Doesn't Believe in Viral." *Advertising Age* 77(9) (February 27, 2006):51.

Kompare, Derek. *Rerun Nation: How Repeats Invented American Television*. New York: Routledge, 2005.

"Lazy Sunday." *YouTube Blog*, February 16, 2006, http://youtube-global.blogspot.com /2006/02/lazy-sunday.html.

Lessig, Lawrence. *Remix: Making Art and Commerce Thrive in the Hybrid Economy*. New York: Penguin, 2008.

Levin, Josh. "The Chronicles of Narnia Rap: It Won't Save *Saturday Night Live*, but It Could Save Hip Hop." *Slate*, December 23, 2005, http://www.slate.com/id/2133316.

Sandoval, Greg. "NBC Strikes Deal with YouTube." *CNET News*, June 27, 2006, http:// news.cnet.com/NBC-strikes-deal-with-YouTube/2100-1025_3-6088617.html.

———. "NBCUniversal Confirms End of YouTube Deal." *CNET News*, October 22, 2007, http://news.cnet.com/8301-10784_3-9802188-7.html.

Teinowitz, Ira. "Skit's Web Popularity: That's Rich." *Television Week* 26(1) (January 1, 2007):1A.

"The 'Bu." *Channel 101*. http://www.channel101.com/show/123 (accessed August 14, 2012).

"Top 100 Facts for Chuck Norris." *The Original Chuck Norris Fact Generator.* http://4q
.cc/index.php?pid=top100&person=chuck (accessed August 14, 2012).

"Transcripts: The Situation Room 2-8-07." *CNN.* http://transcripts.cnn.com
/TRANSCRIPTS/0702/08/sitroom.03.html (accessed August 14, 2012).

watermarkstudents. "Laser Cats." *YouTube,* February 13, 2007, http://www.youtube
.com/watch?v=GRBNkMnG4uY.

Williams, Raymond. "Base and Superstructure in Marxist Cultural Theory." In *Rethinking Popular Culture: Contemporary Perspectives in Cultural Studies,* edited by Chandra
Mukerji and Michael Schudson, 407–423. Berkeley: University of California Press,
1991.

CONTRIBUTORS

Ron Becker is Associate Professor of Media and Culture at Miami University (Ohio), where he is also an affiliate of the Programs in American Studies; Film; and Women, Gender, and Sexuality. He is author of *Gay TV and Straight America* (2006), and his work has also appeared in *The Television Studies Reader*; *Queer TV: Theories, Histories, Politics*; *The Great American Makeover: Television, History and Nation*; and *Television and New Media*.

Mary Beltrán is Associate Professor of Radio, Television, and Film at the University of Texas at Austin. She is author of *Latina/o Stars in U.S. Eyes: The Making and Meanings of Film and TV Stardom* (2009) and co-editor (with Camilla Fojas) of *Mixed Race Hollywood* (2008).

Evan Elkins is a PhD candidate in the Department of Communication Arts at the University of Wisconsin, Madison. His primary research interests are global media distribution, digital media technologies, and the practice of regional lockout. Additional research interests include post-network television, niche branding, and transgressive comedy.

Racquel Gates is Assistant Professor in the Department of Media Culture at the College of Staten Island. Her research focuses on representations of race in popular culture, with specific attention to the importance of disreputable media in discourses of race, gender, and class. Her work has appeared in *Antenna, In Media Res, Velvet Light Trap,* and elsewhere.

David Gurney is Assistant Professor in the Department of Communication and Media at Texas A&M University, Corpus Christi. His research interests include critical approaches to digital media, the role of comedy in transmediality, and contemporary media-branding strategies. His work has appeared in *Velvet Light Trap, FlowTV,* and several anthologies.

Michele Hilmes is Professor of Media and Cultural Studies and Chair of the Department of Communication Arts at the University of Wisconsin, Madison. She is author of *Only Connect: A Cultural History of American Broadcasting* and *Network Nations: A Transnational History of British and American Broadcasting.* She is co-editor (with Jason Loviglio) of *Radio's New Wave: Global Sound in the Digital Era.*

Derek Johnson is Assistant Professor of Media and Cultural Studies at the University of Wisconsin, Madison, where his research focuses on production in the media industries. He is author of *Media Franchising: Creative License and Collaboration in the Culture Industries* (2013) and editor (with Jonathan Gray) of *A Companion to Media Authorship* (2013).

Jeffrey P. Jones is Lambdin Kay Chair and Director of the George Foster Peabody Awards at the University of Georgia. He is author of *Entertaining Politics: Satiric Television and Political Engagement,* 2nd ed. (2010), and editor (with Geoffrey Baym) of *News Parody and Political Satire across the Globe* (2012) and (with Jonathan Gray and Ethan Thompson) of *Satire TV: Politics and Comedy in the Post-Network Era* (2009).

Nick Marx is Assistant Professor in the Department of Communication Studies at Colorado State University. His research on television comedy and digital media culture has appeared in *Journal of e-Media Studies, Velvet Light Trap,* and *Journal of Film and Video* and in the anthologies *Deconstructing South Park: Critical Examinations of Animated Transgression* (2011) and *How to Watch Television* (2013).

Caryn Murphy is Assistant Professor of Communication at the University of Wisconsin, Oshkosh. Her research on television has appeared in the *Historical Journal of Film, Radio and Television* and in the anthologies

The Business of Entertainment (2008) and *Dear Angela: Remembering My So-Called Life* (2007).

Susan Murray is Associate Professor of Media, Culture, and Communication at New York University. She is author of *Hitch Your Antenna to the Stars: Early Television and Broadcast Stardom* (2005) and co-editor (with Laurie Ouellette) of *Reality TV: Remaking Television Culture* (2nd ed., 2009). Her work has appeared in journals such as *Journal of Visual Culture, Cinema Journal,* and *Television and New Media* and in numerous anthologies.

Matt Sienkiewicz is Assistant Professor of Communication and International Studies at Boston College. His research focuses on Western interactions with Middle Eastern media, and on representation in American screen comedy. His publications include articles in *Popular Communication, Middle East Journal of Culture and Communication, International Journal of Cultural Studies,* and *Columbia Journalism Review.*

Ethan Thompson is Associate Professor of Communication at Texas A&M University, Corpus Christi. He is author of *Parody and Taste in Postwar American Television Culture* and editor (with Jason Mittell) of *How to Watch Television* and (with Jeffrey P. Jones and Jonathan Gray) of *Satire TV: Politics and Comedy in the Post-Network Era.*

Ethan Tussey is Assistant Professor of Communication at Georgia State University. His work explores the production and reception of online videos in the workplace; he has authored or co-authored several research reports on media industries; and he has conducted and archived interviews for UCSB's Media Industries Project.

Alyxandra Vesey is a PhD student in the Media and Cultural Studies Program at the University of Wisconsin, Madison. She is a feminist media scholar who studies the relationship(s) between gender, labor, music culture, and convergence. Her work has appeared in *Antenna, FlowTV,* and *In Media Res.* She runs the blog *Feminist Music Geek,* is a frequent contributor to *Bitch* magazine, and volunteers for Girls Rock Camp Madison.

INDEX

Page references in italics refer to figures.

Alternative comedy, 3, 8, 135, 238, 247
Anchorman, 213–214, 221, 226
Animal House, 215, 218
Armisen, Fred, 16; and cross-racial performance, 192, 194, 197–204, *203;* and indie
   aesthetics, 116–117; and political satire,
   53, 84; and race, 191–196, *195,* 205 (*see
   also* Honeyface)
Aykroyd, Dan, 10, 62–63, 84, 175, 219,
   255–256

Baldwin, Alec, 144
Baumgartner, Judy, 5
Belushi, John, 2, 7, 10, 51, 113–114, 256; and
   comedian comedy, 213–215; and Experi-
   mental Comedy, 62–63; and sexism, 175,
   177, 218. See also *Blues Brothers, The*
Benny, Jack, 28
Bergen, Candice, 219
Best of Saturday Night Live specials, 6, 10,
   13, 59–60, 87–88, 132, 242
Biden, Joe, 1, 2
bin Laden, Osama, 103
Blackface, 16, 27, 192–193, 195–198, 204
Blues Brothers, The, 10, 132, 214, 256–257
Bridesmaids, 173, 186
Brooks, Albert, 69, 243
Burns and Allen Show, The, 29–30, *30*
Bush, George H. W., 1, 82–84
Bush, George W, 1, 12, 80–84, 193, 221

Cable television, 77, 113–114; and media
   history, 9–11, 13, 19–20, 26, 37, 134–135,
   237; and representation, 154–155
Caldwell, John, 58, 61, 235
Campaigns: political, 12, 77–78, 80–81,
   86–89, 191; marketing, 43, 50, 52, 130,
   228, 249
Carlin, George, 48
Carrey, Jim, 84, 260
Carson, Johnny, 7, 32–33, 48
Carter, Jimmy, 83–84
Carvey, Dana, 10, 82–84
Channel 101, 238, 248, 254
Chappelle's Show, 134
Chase, Chevy, 2, 10, 49, 226; and catch-
   phrases, 217, 255; and comedian
   comedy, 213–214, 216, 218; and experi-
   mental comedy, 62–63; and political
   satire, 77, 79–80, 84; and sexism, 175–
   176; and TV-to-film trajectory, 218–220
*Chronicles of Narnia: The Lion, the Witch,
   and the Wardrobe, The,* 240, 254
Classic Network Era, 2, 6, 9, 37
Clinton, Bill, 1, 83–84, 88, 98, 108, 134
Clinton, Hillary, 80, 101, 191
Colbert Report, The, 77, 88, 94, 101, 134
Comedy Central, 11, 108, 134, 236, 239
Comedy Clubs, 7, 37, 157, 182, 245; and Internet, 18, 233, 235, 237, 247–250; and
   nightclubs, 40, 48–49

279

CPSIA information can be obtained at www.ICGtesting.com
Printed in the USA
LVOW03s1945240714

395875LV00029B/178/P

9 780253 010827